BROKEN
CONTRACT

BROKEN CONTRACT

A Memoir of Harvard Law School

RICHARD D. KAHLENBERG

*With a foreword by Robert Coles
and a new afterword by the author*

University of Massachusetts Press
Amherst

The author is grateful to the following for permission to reprint from previously published material: *New York* magazine, for "Gotcha! Nancy Collins Cross-examines Crime-Buster Rudolph Giuliani," copyright © 1991 by K-III Magazine. All rights reserved. Farrar, Straus and Giroux, for an excerpt from *The Bonfire of the Vanities* by Tom Wolfe, copyright © 1987 by Tom Wolfe. All rights reserved. Duncan Kennedy, for an excerpt from *Legal Education and the Reproduction of Hierarchy*, copyright © 1983 by Duncan Kennedy. Permission granted without warranties of any kind.

Library of Congress Cataloging-in-Publication Data

Kahlenberg, Richard D.
  Broken contract : a memoir of Harvard Law School / Richard D. Kahlenberg ; with a foreword by Robert Coles and a new afterword by the author.
    p. cm.
  ISBN 1-55849-234-8 (paper : alk. paper)
    1. Kahlenberg, Richard D. 2. Law students — Massachusetts — Biography. 3. Harvard Law School. I. Title.
  KF373.K34A3 1999
  340'.071'17444 — dc21   99-36502
                                                                      CIP

British Library Cataloguing in Publication data are available.

To Rebecca, Cindy, and Jessica

Contents

Foreword

ROBERT COLES

This book's title is, of course, weighted with irony, and also bears a considerable emotional message to the reader. Law school students spend a lot of time learning about "contracts" and "torts," but I doubt many of those young men and women stop and take stock of their legal education in the manner chosen by this book's author. He lets us know, right off, that he writes with disenchantment, even a sense of anger—a touch of the moral indignation, really, that the Hebrew prophets Isaiah and Jeremiah and Micah and Amos unstintingly offered their readers, as well as Jesus of Nazareth at certain moments. Not that Richard Kahlenberg is tempted by the hazards of righteousness—a deterioration into self-righteousness. He is a bemused, careful observer, able to be wry and mildly disillusioned one minute, thoroughly annoyed the next—but overall, I think, melancholy about what he saw and experienced, rather than full of scorn and rage.

Very important, this is a book that depends heavily on a novelist's or short-story writer's angle of vision. That is to say, the author gives us instance after instance, detail upon detail—a participant, a witness, become, finally, a skilled and persuasive narrator. The moralist's energy has to reckon with the documentary tradition—a requirement that tethers mood, opinion, and sentiment to factuality, to the particulars of various situations and scenes. One classroom after another is brought before the reader, as if the author knows we are a jury of sorts and evidence will be required.

That evidence grows with each page, and I fear many readers will want to consent to the author's judgment: a school readily dubbed "great" and "leading" can fail mightily in certain respects. Indeed, the central assertion of this book might be put this way: all too many distinguished legal theorists have consistently lacked the qualities any good teacher needs—a plain old interest in students; and the result can be a galling coldness, an arrogance and smugness, a psychological insularity on the part of such law school professors, no matter their brilliance.

I suppose a skeptic might want to confront the author with that old rhetorical question: What did you expect, anyway? For several years I taught a course at Harvard Law School, "Dickens and the Law" (which Mr. Kahlenberg took, as he mentions in this memoir), and I remember well some strongly worded complaints about the school not unlike those made directly or by implication in the pages that follow. Almost inevitably, it seemed, classmates expressed their cynicism, if not their scorn with respect to those complaints by asking that question—as if only a fool would be looking for a faculty of humble, compassionate, self-critical professors, who are utterly taken with their students, thoroughly willing to attend the intellectual and personal needs of those students as they make their way toward a complex, demanding profession. Moreover, a good number of my students went further, became articulate, even ardent defenders of the very people and practices this book's author so vigorously and persistently takes to task. In that regard, I can still remember the sarcasm mobilized during one spring afternoon classroom discussion of Harvard Law School: "What did you folks think you'd find when you came here—a nursery? These people [the professors] are busy, and they assume we're grown up by now." When a disputant challenged that assertion, by asking about the meaning of the words "grown up," he received the following interpretation: "Look, a grownup is someone who knows what is reasonable and what is unreasonable. It's unreasonable to ask [from the professors] for more than they can give."

Maybe so, one thinks—yet that is our nature, to hope every once in a while for thoughtfulness and considerateness and civility, even compassionate concern from our fellow human beings. Such a line of reasoning (such an undimmed, unashamed hope) is no doubt what prompted Richard Kahlenberg (a very bright and able undergraduate and law student, a lucid, fluent writer, a keenly attentive listener, a lively, perceptive classroom participant, as I well remember) to look back with regret at an important part of his education in this strong-minded psychological and moral brief, of sorts, with its vivid, unsparing academic portraits. I salute him warmly for his courage, for his ethical resolve, for his willingness to take on sharply, even astringently, a place and a time—when an easy nostalgia might have enabled him to put aside all too much frustration and pain, all too many unfulfilled hopes, and thereby keep from the readers of this book certain important, instructive truths.

Author's Note

This is a work of nonfiction; all the events described did occur. I have used the actual names of my teachers, because Harvard Law professors are highly successful public individuals capable of and accustomed to receiving evaluation and criticism. The names of many of the attorneys I met in my search for employment are also real, since virtually all of them were put on notice that I was writing a book. I have, in contrast, altered the names of my classmates, because they are all private citizens, the vast majority of whom did not know about this project.

Throughout the text, I routinely employ the feminine personal pronoun to stand for both sexes in the hope that the more people become accustomed to it, the less need there will be for explanatory notes such as this one.

Although this book is highly personal, it is truly the product of a number of people's efforts. At the outset, I should thank Arthur Samuelson, who first suggested in August of 1987 that I write a book about my law school experience. Thanks to Arthur Rosenthal and Sally Singer of Hill & Wang, who took me on and then made extremely important suggestions about the manuscript, always in a most pleasant manner. Thanks to Nick McConnell, Judy Rabinowitz, and Steven Bonorris, who, over dinner one night, helped me come up with the book's title. Steve also read the manuscript and offered good suggestions, as did Chris Landau and Kerry Walsh Skelly. I owe a special thanks to my family—my parents, Richard and Jeannette Kahlenberg; my sisters, Joy Fallon and Trudi Picciano, and their husbands, Bob and Joe—both for putting up with an invasion of their privacy and for offering helpful advice on the manuscript. Thanks also to my mother-in-law, Dinah Moché, and to attorney Richard Dannay for helping to guide me through the publishing world. Most of all, I want to thank my best friend and wife, Rebecca. This book began about the same time as our marriage did and she has sustained, encouraged, supported, and tolerated me throughout, even as she had, in the end, our two daughters to care for. It is to my three girls—Rebecca, Cindy, and Jessica— that I dedicate this book.

R. D. K.
Bethesda, Maryland

BROKEN CONTRACT

Prologue

Press Secretary Martin Steadman introduced me: "Governor, this is Richard Kahlenberg, whom I've told you about."

Looking up from his papers, over the top of his glasses, Mario Cuomo was the feisty, combative New York lawyer—outwardly obnoxious in an oddly endearing way.

"Who are you, Kahlenberg?" he barked.

I said I was a law student.

"Where?"

"Harvard."

"Why?"

Why? Why law school? And why Harvard?

I was caught off guard. It wasn't the sort of question anyone ever asked. When you told them you were at Harvard Law, they were supposed to be impressed, to accept you as someone smart, someone going places, a possible asset to them. The Harvard Law student is not often asked to justify himself, and the thought that he might be better off spending his time elsewhere never enters his mind.

So, why law school? And why Harvard?

Well, in my application to Harvard I had talked about public service, about wanting to work within the law to make life a little more fair for people. I'd written about Robert Kennedy and said, "Five years from now, I'd like to be pressing civil rights or liberties questions before the courts."

But there was within me another voice, one from my adolescence, which somehow never found its way into my application essay. As a kid, I had wanted to be a lawyer primarily because my grandfather was one. Grandpa was distinguished, respected, esteemed, and successful—which is to say loaded. In applying to law school, I was not unaware that a Harvard Law degree could be parlayed into a great deal of wealth.

Now, standing before the Governor of New York, that rare politician who would not dismiss talk of moral obligation and duty as falsely pious, I was paralyzed. I wanted to say that I was at HLS for only the noble reasons, that I wanted to follow the path of Ralph Nader or Robert Kennedy (or, for that matter, Mario Cuomo). I wanted to affirm that Harvard Law would put me in a better position to help shape humane public policy.

But after one year at HLS, I wasn't sure I bought my own line anymore. All the application rhetoric sounded silly and self-promoting and pompous. I was no longer convinced that I would defy the statistics and pursue the public interest. The money was a large part of it, of course, but the clincher was that the public-interest jobs just didn't *distinguish* you the way the high-salaried firms did. That's what really hurt. I had come to believe that the right career move, whatever your ultimate goal, was to work for a powerful corporate law firm.

Mid-June after my first year, I was still on track. I was working in United States Attorney Rudolph Giuliani's office in Manhattan for no pay. But I was already looking forward to the prospect of working at a firm the following summer for $1,200 a week. My theory was why not just try working for a firm? I'd see how horrible it was and get it out of my system once and for all. At the same time, going to a law firm would "keep my options open." Contradiction aside, I found both these arguments extremely compelling. I would not be selling out, after all, just renting myself for a summer.

I felt like telling Cuomo, "Governor, I am struggling, on a smaller scale, with the same sorts of questions you wrestle with in your published diaries. In our pursuit of careers that promise power and prestige, are we really trying to 'improve the lives of others' or are our ambitions more complicated than that?"

Instead, I mumbled something about not having wanted to go to school in New Haven.

Cuomo shot back: "What happened? Couldn't get into St. Johns?"

From 1986 to 1989, I was a student at the Harvard Law School. I entered committed to public-interest law, but after three years I came within one day of joining the vast majority of my classmates in practicing law at a large corporate firm, a career which I, along with most of them, would find lucrative, prestigious, challenging, and ultimately unsatisfying.

For a century and a half, Harvard has turned out lawyers to represent the most powerful and wealthy institutions in the country. But many of us in the class of '89 came to law school with higher aspirations. The media characterized us as Reagan-era yuppies, but the true picture was much more complicated than that. A 1986 poll of first-year Harvard Law students indicated that 70 percent would like to practice public-interest law. To be sure, few of us followed through, but we *entered* law school wanting our jobs to be more than a way to make a living.

We enrolled in the decade following the publication of two books describing the Harvard Law School as a harrowing place. We had all read John Jay Osborne, Jr.'s *The Paper Chase* and Scott Turow's *One L*, and gone to HLS despite their warnings of lunacy and cutthroat competition. But neither book prepared us for a much more insidious pressure felt in the second and third years, a pressure to compromise and practice a very different kind of law from the sort we had first envisioned.

That is what this book, at its core, is about. If nothing else, it is a warning to prospective law students that Osborne and Turow may have missed the more profound story. *The Paper Chase* and *One L* both end before the second year and thereby ignore the essential paradox of Harvard Law School: how is it that so many students can enter law school determined to use law to promote liberal ideals and leave three years later to counsel the least socially progressive elements of our society? *That* is the remarkable thing about HLS —not the rigor of its first year, but the transformation that takes place in the second and third. We came to law school talking about using the law as a vehicle for social change, but when it was time to decide what we would do with our lives, we fell over each other to work for those law firms most resistant to change.

The old story about the Harvard Law School dean telling students on the first day of class, "Look to your left, look to your right, because one of you won't be here by the end of the year," has been replaced in recent years by Professor Alan Dershowitz's adage: "Look to your left and look to your right, because by the time you graduate, there'll be no Left left." The tale of fierce academic competition has become a much more telling and damning tale of greed. To try to understand why students change, and how they are able to reconcile liberal politics and the pursuit of careers in corporate law is the central purpose of this book.

As we will see, the short but incomplete answer is money. Starting salaries for first-year associates in New York topped $80,000 the year I graduated, a figure especially appealing to those burdened with substantial debt from college and law school. But while the big firms paid very well, they left you precious little time to spend. Besides, since you'd have to work seventy and eighty hours a week, the equivalent salary for a regular work week was actually more like $40,000. And at Harvard, a program had been established to forgive student loans for those who chose to pursue low-paying public-interest jobs.

There was a psychological explanation for this ideological shift that argued that law students were caught between rebelling from their parents and conforming; thus their liberal, even radical politics, and their decision to work for a large corporate law firm. This suggestion I found wrong, insulting, and condescending. The theory assumed that liberalism was a "stage" through which youth passes before settling on the mature, seasoned, adult vision that is conservatism. The movement from left to right might be the more familiar pattern, but some of our most thoughtful leaders—people like Robert Kennedy and Mario Cuomo, in fact—were those who moved in the opposite direction, from right to left, as they grew older.

Another explanation was that the student body was not really all that liberal, that the "silent majority" was actually moderate and conservative. It was the liberals who ranted and raved and sent around petitions, while the conservative students quietly sat back and dominated. But the poll results showing 70 percent wanted to do public-interest work suggested otherwise, and it was obvious to even the most casual observer that the HLS culture was overwhelmingly liberal; you saw it in the causes championed by the journals and extracurricular organizations, and most clearly in class discussions.

In the end, I found that the most important reasons that liberal law students went into corporate law had to do with power, prestige, and convention. After years of savoring other people's reactions when you said you were at Princeton College or Harvard Law School, it was tough to contemplate the reaction to your declaration "I'm a legal-services lawyer." It was flattering when Cuomo said, "Couldn't get into St. John's?" To hear someone say, "That's great, I admire you for doing legal services," was more patronizing than flattering. I came to learn that in the legal profession it was infinitely more important to be *respectable* than to be *admirable*, and that salary replaced grades as the badge of merit and achievement. Moreover, for many of us, the Cocktail Party Factor was reinforced by the hard reality that even Democrats, when in power, bought into the firm mystique. When Jimmy Carter picked a legal counselor, he looked not to Ralph Nader but to Lloyd Cutler of Wilmer, Cutler & Pickering; he chose as Attorney General Griffin Bell, a judge from a prominent Atlanta firm, not Jack Greenberg, who headed the NAACP Legal Defense Fund (LDF).

The fact that so many liberal Harvard Law students went on to become corporate lawyers was, I think, directly linked to the second interesting thing about HLS not found in *One L* or *The Paper Chase*: the number of radical faculty members associated with the Critical Legal Studies (CLS) movement. The roots of radicalism among Harvard professors were many, but some of the most potent had to be the effect of watching one's idealistic students, year after year, join the ranks of the nation's corporate law firms.

CLS began in 1977, when a group of left-wing law professors met in Madison, Wisconsin, to discuss and critique the role of the legal system in securing the wealth and power of the American elite. Building on the Legal Realism of the early twentieth century, CLS proponents argued that current legal doctrine was not neutral, that it was thoroughly political and biased in favor of the rich and powerful. They maintained that law was indeterminate and could yield diametrically opposed results in similarly situated cases. During my three years at Harvard Law, the faculty waged a continuous war over CLS, fought mainly over tenure appointments. In the late 1980s, CLS proponents held about eight tenured positions at the law school, making Harvard, as the faculty's leading "crit," Duncan Kennedy, told Calvin Trillin in *The New Yorker*, "the Rome of Critical Legal Studies." An equal number of conservative professors countered that crits were dangerous Marxists whose "nihilism" had no place in the law. In between was the majority of the Harvard Law faculty—some fifty professors and then-Dean James Vorenberg—whose sympathies alternated between one side and the other, depending on the issue. This book attempts to provide a substantive yet intelligible look at CLS, to simplify the debate without being simplistic.

This book, though, is a memoir not an analysis. It is a story about growing up: about becoming a fiancé, then a husband, then a father; about losing self-confidence and slowly rebuilding it; about arriving with idealism, having it chipped away, and then trying to piece it back together again; about making choices, very difficult ones, between doing well and doing good, between doing what everyone else was doing and trying to break out. And, as I look back, the story is as much about getting a job as about going to classes.

In the end, I think that Harvard Law School had, and has, the potential to be a wonderful place. It brought together exciting, thoughtful professors and extremely intelligent students. It challenged the intellect, but not at the profound level of moral inquiry. It produced students who were smart, but not intellectual; people who could solve the puzzle, parse the cases, and construct the arguments, but who could not or would not put problems in larger perspective. It is the enormous potential of the Harvard Law School that makes its failure to cultivate the best in its students a failure of enormous proportions.

PART I

One L

CHAPTER

1

The Experimental Section

Something was clearly wrong when I arrived for my first Civil Procedure class in Pound Hall. I looked around the classroom, a bit confused, and realized it was the carpeting underfoot. I had firmly in my mind an image of Harvard Law School as austere and competitive and hard-wood. Carpeting wasn't part of the picture, but sure enough, there it was—not luxurious, but there just the same. I found my seat in the back of the room and introduced myself to Jackson Shelby, who was drinking from a Princeton coffee mug. We exchanged pleasantries and turned toward the front of the class, where a diminutive young woman—our professor—was looking over her notes. Her name was Martha Minow, and she was known as a champion of "the Experiment" at Harvard—a new interdisciplinary way of teaching law students in a more humane manner. Hey, I thought, maybe this wasn't going to be so bad after all.

When the hour of nine arrived, Minow made some introductory remarks and then said that she, like most professors at Harvard Law, would use the Socratic method, a dialogue between professor and student in which learning is supposedly enhanced for all. (HLS professor Duncan Kennedy had another description of the Socratic method: "Pseudo-participation in which you struggle desperately, in front of a large audience, to read a mind determined to elude you.") A buzz went around the room. Everyone had seen *The Paper*

Chase; they knew what the Socratic method was and were anxiously waiting to see the process in action.

Professor Minow looked down at the class seating chart and asked, "Is Mr. Kahlenberg here?" The other 138 students sighed with relief; I was panic-stricken.

"Yes," I said. People laughed. The terror I was feeling must have been obvious in my voice.

"Yes, Mr. Kahlenberg. I am going to be calling on you in about five minutes. I just wanted to let you prepare yourself."

Didn't she know I was prepared? If there is one day every HLS student is prepared for, it is the first day of class. Minow was trying to be kind, but giving me five minutes to ponder my predicament only made matters worse. The road to hell, I thought to myself, was paved by the Experiment's condescending liberals. I sat flipping through my notes on *United States v. Hall*, the case Minow had assigned.

Hall raises the question of whether a court has the power to throw an individual in jail for disobeying a prior court order even when the individual is not a party to the original case. Was a court order just like a law? I didn't know it at the time, but *Hall* is not exactly a classic. A traditional Civil Procedure course would begin with a major "subject matter" jurisdiction case, but Minow, teaching in an Experimental section, wanted to try a fresh approach.

After a few minutes, Minow came back to me. "Mr. Kahlenberg, you're still there?" (Laughter.) "Where are you from?"

"New Jersey," I said.

"Let's hear some applause for New Jersey," she said. And the class applauded on cue. But Minow's attempts to relax me weren't working.

"Who was the appellant in this case?"

"Hall," I said.

"Right."

So far, so good.

"And who brought the suit?"

Which suit? Hall was the one bringing the appeal. The U.S. District Court had in a sense brought the charges against Hall. The original suit was brought by Mims, but she wasn't asking that, was she? Was this a trick question?

My mind started racing, and I started blurting out answers without really thinking. Disapproving murmurs circulated around the room. Hands shot up—vicious hands trying to capitalize on my mistake. The Experiment's spirit had clearly not yet been instilled in the students. The correct answer, someone proclaimed, was Mims. Right.

I was mortified. Minow's question was not meant to be thought-provoking; it was a simple one of fact, a warm-up question, really. And I'd blown it. In front of all my new classmates. In the first ten minutes of law school. Minow knew I would be crushed if she didn't call on me again, so she compassionately persevered. I answered a few questions correctly, and then she moved on to Jackson. She continued down the row, some people making mistakes, some not. I didn't really hear them.

My girlfriend, Rebecca, told me not to worry, that people would forget. But they remembered. When I told a group of 2L friends of mine about my fate my first day, they reminisced in minute detail about the first individual to be called on in their section a year earlier. Two and a half months after my fiasco, I saw an old college friend at the Harvard-Yale football game. Next to him sat a man whose face I vaguely recognized. My friend introduced us and the man said, "Sure, Mr. Kahlenberg. You're famous. The first person called on in our section."

Mine was not the only humiliation that first day. Harvard's first-year class of 560 was divided into four sections (two experimental, two traditional), and the story of what happened in Professor Arthur Miller's traditional section was even more legendary. Miller, who combines the tactics of an old-line professor with a show-manly egoism, is reputedly the inspiration for the tyrannical Professor Perini of *One L*. For years, Miller had opened his Civil Procedure class by calling on a student from Iowa because the first case his section studies is set in that state. In my year, the only Iowan was Lillian King. Miller began the class by confirming that his tradition was to call on someone from Iowa. Looking directly at Ms. King, Miller said, "I am sure Ms. King is fully prepared." She was. "So," Miller continued, "I think I shall call on. . ." and as he was completing his sentence, Miller whirled around and pointed to "Ms. Barr." Everyone gasped. Ms. Barr was speechless.

My failure with Minow was, of course, much more shameful

than failure at the hands of Miller. To crumble under Miller's intense pressure was understandable; to blunder in the carpeted confines of Minow's Experimental classroom was truly ignominious. It was the worst of all worlds—having to deal with the Socratic method with its invitation for public humiliation without the comforting excuse that you could blame any failure on a despotic professor.

My head hung low, I trooped over to our Criminal Law class in Langdell Hall with the rest of the section. I found my seat and started pouring my heart out to the two women on either side of me, complete strangers, all of us now bound together by a common fear.

My professor for Criminal Law was Phil Heymann, a 1950s-style liberal—white, clean-cut, Establishment, a high achiever who had his heart in the right place: Yale '54, HLS '60, a clerk to Justice John Marshall Harlan, a protégé of J.F.K.'s Solicitor General Archibald Cox, an Assistant Attorney General under Jimmy Carter, and now a senior counsel to Common Cause. Heymann was not interested in using the law to make himself rich; he simply wanted to help promote some justice.

Heymann was precisely the kind of liberal I had been brought up to be—an upper-middle-class, educated, good-government liberal: for civil rights and civil liberties; for ethics in government and a clean environment; for the consumer movement and the women's movement; pro-choice and anti-Nixon. Mixed in was a good dose of liberal guilt, which recognized that life wasn't fair and the lucky had a duty to help out the less fortunate. At the same time, there was a conservative and traditional side to the liberalism of Phil Heymann and my parents. You were supposed to work hard and achieve success. Believe in meritocracy and in Harvard.

When I began college, I was the perfect reflection of my parents' blend of liberal and conservative. In my freshman year, as I marched in front of the Harvard Faculty Club in opposition to the university's investment in companies that did business with South Africa, I was ribbed by my friends for "protesting in penny loafers." But as I wrote my senior thesis on Robert Kennedy's 1968 presidential campaign, I began questioning some of my liberal assumptions and to find pockets of hypocrisy built into upper-middle-class liberalism. On crime, for example, I saw that a liberal commitment to civil liberties came at a cost, which was born disproportionately by poor and working people in high crime areas. I became interested in R.F.K.'s form of "populism," which was more enlightened and inclusive than the nineteenth-century agrarian populism of William Jennings Bryan. R.F.K. took the core of the old populism—which sought to make life fairer for the average person by more evenly distributing wealth and power—and discarded the negative aspects traditionally associated with populism: racism, anti-Semitism, and anti-intellectualism. R.F.K.'s new populism was at once more radical than liberalism on basic economic issues and more conservative on issues like crime and welfare. As I wrote my thesis, I became convinced that Robert Kennedy was onto something very exciting. Somehow he was able to reach ghetto blacks and George Wallace whites in a way that no politician has since. By the time I arrived in law school, my liberal political views were tempered by populism. I still wanted to do something about poverty and social injustice, but I also put working-class whites in the category of those who'd been dealt a raw deal. Instead of seeing Archie Bunker as a bigoted reactionary, I saw him as an underdog whose anxieties needed to be addressed.

In class, Heymann explained that he'd just returned from Guatemala, where, he said rather dramatically, the lawyers and judges were being killed; the lawyers pose the greatest threat to scoundrels, he said—to make them follow the law. Heymann spoke at length about the lack of regard for civil liberties in Guatemala. It was unclear from his comments whether he meant to say, "We've got it good in this country, let's not bitch about police behavior" or "We better protect civil liberties to the hilt to avoid the slippery slope to Guatemala." Maybe he meant both.

The next morning, we had Torts with David Rosenberg, who was everything Heymann was not. Where Heymann waxed philosophical about the role of lawyers in society, Rosenberg apparently felt his job was to expose such pretensions. His background was the rough-and-tumble courtroom, not the ivy-covered classroom, and he delighted in telling this first class how a plaintiff's attorney decides whether to take on a case: she calculates the amount the suit will bring ("damages"), discounts the chance of losing the case, and subtracts expenses. Period. A student suggested that moral considerations—had the plaintiff been wronged?—may enter in.

Rosenberg scoffed. "Perhaps, but even then: how much will it cost?" Rosenberg went further. When an individual dies in a car accident and the decedent's family sues, you must determine exactly how much his life was worth, the professor said. It was not a grand philosophical question but an actuarial matter of the decedent's future earning potential—based on age, educational level, and skills. Rosenberg smiled at the horror on our faces. Litigation was a form of war, he continued, describing a lawyer's "artillery" with the amoral enthusiasm of a true mercenary, a legal "soldier of fortune." "It's never just winning or losing," he said, "it's the cost of winning or losing." Rosenberg argued that a lawyer representing a woman who used DES and subsequently contracted cancer may get a big damage award, but it may not be worth it (to the lawyer, that is) if the expense of expert witnesses and scientific research mounts too high. He seemed to relish the distinction between law and morality, a distinction epitomized by the appalling tort rule that if an individual comes across a newborn infant face down in a puddle of water, the law does not oblige him to turn the baby on its back.

It was quite fitting that just as we began getting used to Rosenberg, in the second week of classes, the premiere episode of *L.A. Law* aired. As we watched it, we had no idea that the show would become something of a social phenomenon, but it was clear that the program would portray law in a new light. Law was no longer about justice and nobility; audiences apparently just wouldn't find that credible. Perry Mason had become Douglas Brackman. The show's appeal was so powerful that it would later be said to substantially boost the number of law school applications, which, if true, is surely a triumph of Dave Rosenberg over Phil Heymann.

The reality of law school was, of course, much different from the glitz of *L.A. Law*. During the first month, I found myself having lunch in Harkness Commons (known as "the Hark") with Debbie Houston, a bleached-blond New Yorker who stood out among her classmates mostly because she chose to wear makeup. Over lunch, Debbie and I complained about the workload, which was significantly heavier than it had been in college. The amount of assigned reading was so extensive that one could never feel fully prepared for class. You had to study during the day, stay up late to finish your reading, and then go to class and hope to stay awake. As the weeks wore on, I had begun turning in early, leaving large hunks of reading unread, on the theory that being alert in class was more important. Amazingly, some people were able to do the reading and volunteer to participate in class. More amazing still, Debbie was among those who still did all the reading. "I go straight from class to the library to study," she said. Under all that makeup, even Debbie was a grind.

The vast, silent majority of us were, on one level, eternally grateful for the ones who did the reading and actively participated—after all, they kept the rest of us from being called on. At the same time, the voices of these brown-nosers quickly began to grate. Little things became annoying. Lois Engel would begin each of her frequent comments with the disingenuous disclaimer "It seems to me . . ." while a middle-aged man invariably intoned, "Well, I've had some experience with this." Certain students ceased to use standard English and adopted the vocabulary of our professors. They didn't make an argument, they "posited"; they labeled arguments as "policy," as opposed to "doctrine"; and they began, in answering simple questions, to formulate elaborate hypotheticals. Lois Engel's continual need to speak started a betting pool among classmates estimating the number of her utterances per week, with most bets over twenty-five. Students organized Turkey Bingo games, in which pictures of the big talkers took the place of numbers on the bingo card. There was an element of cruelty in it, of course, but those targeted could be the cruelest of all. Time and again, when one of the silent majority was called on by a professor and choked, the vultures sitting directly next to her would raise their hands; or worse, when she was in the middle of a thought, and failure was anticipated, the next student might raise her hand midsentence. Too often, I felt as though I were in a Woody Allen movie, or a Dickens novel, so filled was my class with caricatures.

Many of us tried to laugh at the vultures and at those who ran up after class and chatted with the professors. But we were also utterly intimidated by the fact that they seemed to love the material and could discuss it with facility. Over time, I caught on to the important distinction between being truly intelligent and merely articulate. But to be articulate wasn't bad, and many were both.

The one thing that actually drew the student body together was a widespread disenchantment with our teachers. Many of my friendships with other students were based almost entirely on griping about our professors. I was especially disappointed in my faculty advisor, Heymann, who I thought might be someone who'd help guide me, but instead repeatedly canceled our scheduled appointments. Professional inaccessibility was only one of the complaints. Students disliked the fact that professors insisted on using the Socratic method, which seemed to produce more anxiety than learning. Many of us worried that our Experiment professors, so intent on promoting certain ideas, were not really teaching us the law. Worst of all, some of us realized that we did not find the law, with all its intricacy and detail, particularly interesting. So wide was the despair that Harvard employed a psychiatrist in the basement of Pound Hall. One student wrote his third-year paper on why so many students at Harvard Law School were so unhappy.

The paper's advisor, ironically, was Martha Minow, whom many of us saw as a primary source of alienation. To be fair, Minow had the close to impossible task of making Civil Procedure interesting. "Civ Pro" is about the rules of federal litigation—when, how, and where to file motions—the knowledge of which underlies the principal distinction between lawyers and nonlawyers. Minow had been trying to make Civil Procedure interesting by drawing the cases we studied from fascinating areas of substantive law. But the civil rights and sex discrimination cases she taught simply served to highlight the contrast between the inherently interesting nature of the substance and the tedious nature of procedure. Moreover, Minow rarely got to the basics of procedure law. My roommate, Arthur Le Palm, would talk about fundamental, classic Civ Pro cases like *Pennoyer v. Neff*, which most people in my section didn't know existed. Other professors of Civil Procedure realized long ago that you could not teach Civ Pro in an interesting manner; you either taught it or attempted to be interesting. Minow had chosen the latter to the exclusion of the former.

The one bright spot among our professors was Rosenberg. I didn't fully appreciate his appeal until one dark cold day in late November when I found myself walking toward Langdell Library at 6:15 a.m. As I approached the library, I saw my friend Seth Rubenstein, and we grinned sheepishly at each other. Inside were dozens of other students from our section, slurping coffee to stay awake. And in the center was Dave Rosenberg—known as "the maniac" because he worked so hard—grinning at the turnout. All during the week, he had been giving 6:30 a.m. library tours. The tours were optional, but 90 to 95 percent of the section went, higher than the rate of attendance for regular class sessions. Arthur was in another section and couldn't understand why I trudged to the library in the pre-dawn darkness—and all I could say was that one had to know Rosenberg.

Part of Rosenberg's appeal was that his motto—You've got to work "twenty-four hours a day"—filled a void for those of us who felt cheated by the Experiment. Rosenberg's 6:30 a.m. library tour typified the rigors for which Harvard Law is known. It is what we had come to expect as the authentic law school experience from *The Paper Chase* and *One L.* Sure, we had far too much work to do, but we lacked a Kingsfield. (If we'd wanted soft, we would have gone to Yale, where people are said to like law school.) Other sections were being primed for Wall Street, bragging about how many hours they work a week as a form of intellectual machismo. As bad as it was, we craved a bit more of the first-year boot-camp experience. Once, when our Contracts professor Todd Rakoff told a student that he'd "lapsed into incoherence," you could almost see people light up with excitement.

But more important, in an environment which I came to see as rife with hypocrisy, Dave Rosenberg's actions coincided with what he proclaimed. Despite his annoying penchant to ridicule idealism, his actions demonstrated an endearing sincerity, in spite of himself. Even those like me who disagreed with his motto, "twenty-four hours a day," had to admit he lived by it. In addition to the 6:30 a.m. library tours, Rosenberg taught a series of six extra classes on Litigation in early November. It was a compressed version of his spring-term Federal Litigation course, in which he discussed fascinating cases: the prosecution of a prominent black doctor in Boston charged with manslaughter for conducting an abortion; a case contesting the constitutionality of the Hawaii Housing Authority's decision to take and buy land from a small group of wealthy landowners and then redistribute it. He went into detail about Professor Larry Tribe's strategy for arguing cases before the Supreme Court. Throughout, Rosenberg stressed that hot-shot lawyers at prestigious firms had made mistakes and that we, as first-year students, could do better. The sessions were always well attended, even though none of the material would appear on any exam. In addition,

Rosenberg seemed genuinely interested in students. He was the only professor I ever saw working in the student library, and he attracted a group of self-proclaimed "disciples" who religiously attended the weekly lunches he presided over to discuss various issues of law.

Finally, people liked Rosenberg's irreverence. He was a rebel, very critical of Harvard's teaching method and grading system. During the early months, when we came to class with clenched stomachs, Rosenberg parodied the Socratic method by dramatically stabbing his seating chart with large pushpins, to determine who might be called on that day. If the victim wasn't prepared, Rosenberg would graciously move to the volunteers. If those volunteers were too arrogant, he'd shoot them down by citing obscure works and cases. "You want to be great? You gotta do it, you gotta read it all," he'd exclaim. Rosenberg was cut from a different mold from most other professors. He had gone to law school at New York University, not Harvard or Yale, and rumor had it that he hadn't made Law Review. He was a street fighter and an extremely successful litigator known for his aggressive courtroom tactics. He was the anti-hero, which made him a hero to us.

Rosenberg notwithstanding, anxiety about not being taught the law reached a climax among some of my classmates in section in November, when regular classes were suspended for a "bridge" on the history of legal realism. Bridge weeks were key to the Experiment's notion that our regular classes are artificially segmented, that in fact there is a great deal of overlap between Contracts and Torts and Civil Procedure and Property.

Arthur and others in the "traditional" sections didn't do bridges. They just kept learning the regular legal curriculum, as we fell farther and farther behind. Our first bridge covered Legal Realism, a movement begun in the 1920s, which, building on the writings of Oliver Wendell Holmes, Jr., criticized the classical notion that law was apolitical and scientific, capable of producing easily discernible "correct" answers. Guest professor Terry Fisher argued that now everyone's a realist because no one believes that answers can be easily deduced from neutral abstract principles. Everyone knows that, like statistics, you can line up precedents to say pretty much anything.

The most interesting aspect of Legal Realism is the post-1960s outgrowth, Critical Legal Studies (CLS), of which everyone was decidedly not an adherent. To introduce us to CLS the second day of the bridge was crit professor Jerry Frug. This was exciting. CLS, whose central tenet was that law is indeterminate, incoherent, and used by the wealthy to oppress the masses, had, since its inception a decade earlier, caused a firestorm in the legal community, and particularly at Harvard University, which one professor had likened to Beirut. I had first heard about CLS when I was in my junior year of college. I was taking a tutorial on Alexis de Tocqueville with Edward Banfield, a crusty old conservative professor who loved nothing better than to engage a liberal student in discussion. I had written a paper about Tocqueville's view of human nature, and somehow the topic turned to my future plans. I told Banfield that I wanted to go to Harvard Law School to become a public-interest attorney, which unleashed from Banfield an extensive discussion of a former student, Duncan Kennedy, and CLS, which was tearing up the Harvard Law School faculty.

This was 1984, the year Calvin Trillin told readers of *The New Yorker* what was already well known in Cambridge: that there was "a deep and at times bitter division in the faculty" which pitted CLS adherents against more traditional-minded professors. In the early 1970s, Kennedy and two other professors—Morton Horwitz and Roberto Unger—arrived at Harvard Law School and began attacking what they called "illegitimate hierarchy," which much of the faculty saw as perfectly legitimate hierarchy. Academic faculties have always had their share of left-wingers. The difference at Harvard was that the Kennedy-Horwitz-Unger triumvirate weren't armchair Marxists; they applied their radicalism to everyday life in the law school. Kennedy told Trillin, "Resist at the bourgeois dinner party as well as on the assembly line." (Later, the wife of a prominent editor, upon learning that I was at Harvard Law School, told me that Duncan Kennedy had, indeed, at a recent Cambridge dinner party, said over and over again, "No. You don't understand. I'm a radical.")

The crits unsuccessfully advocated making the Law Review an "open forum," not a merit badge, and grading more classes pass/fail. By 1982, however, they successfully defeated the tenure bid of a professor they opposed. In March of 1982, Professor Charles Nesson, a liberal, wrote an internal memo pleading for peace among the faculty. "What is involved," Nesson wrote, "is recognition by the right that the left is not a lethal threat to the future of the school—that, to the contrary, they have helped to revitalize it— and that the statements and actions which the right finds so provocative do not justify ignoring or disparaging the accomplishments of the left. The left, for its part, must be more open and generous to others, personally and intellectually."

Nesson's memo didn't bring peace. There were demonstrations against a proposal to grade student participation in class, and a black professor's appointment was blocked by the right, which escalated the tensions by making race an element in the debate. The battle culminated in the departure of conservative law professor Paul Bator, who, after twenty-six years at HLS, left what he called the "guerrilla warfare" of Harvard in January 1986 for the more congenial atmosphere of the University of Chicago. Duke's law school dean, Paul Carrington, wrote that if the crits really believed that law was evil, they had "an ethical duty to depart the law school."

What had much of HLS's faculty up in arms was the fact that CLS attacked the very process by which law students were taught. In this class, Frug paced madly around the room, decrying the way law school teachers conducted class. All student arguments are treated as equal, he said, as if the particular merits of any position don't matter. All are treated, that is, as equally wrong, creating an air of uneasiness, until the end of class, when the professor provides the Answer and there is closure. (Hadn't I already seen that dozens of times?) Then, with equal fury, Frug tore into our Contracts textbook, citing his wife's Law Review article cataloguing evidence of the volume's sexism. This was just too much for the conservatives in our class. Go ahead and attack our professors, the law school classes for which we were spending tens of thousands of dollars, but why pick on the poor Dawson, Harvey and Henderson text? One student was particularly livid, with a degree of anger one expects more from an attacker of sexism than a defender. "You're looking for witches," he kept saying, adding a new spiritual dimension to the debate.

Mary Joe Frug's article did seem to stretch its case, but the other CLS readings assigned for class were perceptive, lucid, and thought-provoking. Stanford professor Robert Gordon's article asked the basic question about "whether it is or is not a contradiction in terms to be a 'radical lawyer.' " His answer—and the crits'—was, basically, yes. They had believed that they could employ legal techniques to further justice but soon discovered that "the system was not a set of neutral techniques available to anyone who could seize control of its levers and pulleys but a game heavily loaded in favor of the wealthy and powerful." Duncan Kennedy said that he had once thought of being a "bright young staffer" to a liberal congressman or senator but soon realized that endeavor was fruitless. This was powerful stuff for me to encounter, especially now that I was growing increasingly alienated with legal education, if not with the law itself.

Frug seemed to recognize the problem and started to pull back from the full nihilistic nature of the pure critique. With all the wealth and perks traditional legal practice offers, the only thing the left (and the far left) has in its arsenal is idealism. But Frug didn't seem to have it in him to inspire, so he plunged ahead, debunking traditional private law practice on the theory, I guess, that the best defense is a good offense. For one thing, he exposed the fraudulent axiom "Keep options open." The phrase resonates with law students, most of whom are at law school precisely to do just that. Once at law school, the slogan is used to justify taking a corporate law job; it is said that if one goes into public-interest law, one cannot later go corporate, but that the reverse is eminently possible. Frug argued that the law firm route can effectively close options, too. One becomes accustomed to a certain lifestyle as a mortgage is taken on and lower-paying options are silently squeezed shut. "The tombstone of many a Wall Street lawyer," said Frug, "is carved with the epitaph 'I kept my options open.' "

The next morning, we heard from representatives of the Law and Economics movement, a young right-wing school which rebels against both Legal Realism and Critical Legal Studies. Steve Shavell, a bespectacled economist, gave an abstract, conservative, and, at times, nasty lecture. In the specific case we were studying, Shavell argued that a judge should not order a landlord to improve living conditions, because it would be more "efficient" for government to aid in the redistribution of wealth and let the tenants decide for themselves whether they wanted to use the money to move to better housing or for something else. The argument, of course, completely ignored the political reality that a direct cash payment to the poor lacks a powerful constituency; programs need corporate beneficiaries, farmers in the case of food stamps, developers in the case of housing. Or worse, maybe Shavell was fully aware of the political reality. When my friend Ed Murphy began making an argument against Law and Economics, Shavell cut him short with a dismissive "I know what you're going to say." Students grumbled. Strategically, the L&E folks were as bad as the crits in recruitment.

By the end of the bridge week, I was disillusioned with both the left and the right. Phil Heymann, perhaps by design, spoke last, for the middle ground. He rejected both Law and Economics and Critical Legal Studies and showed a tape of his mentor, Archibald Cox, responding to the country after the Saturday Night Massacre, in which Nixon fired Cox as special Watergate prosecutor. At that moment of constitutional crisis, Cox spoke calmly and deliberately about a commitment to the rule of law not men, about working within the system, about respecting the office of the Presidency.

I was moved, in a way one doesn't expect to be moved by a centrist. After the unsatisfying diet of the left and the right, Cox filled a void, reassuringly. Cox symbolized part of why I'd come to law school. He was the White Knight who slew Richard Nixon and the generous old professor who said the right things to students. My freshman year of college, I had taken Cox's Constitutional Law course for undergraduates on the recommendation that I take Cox before he retired. In those uninhibited days, a friend and I asked Cox out for lunch at the Atrium. Over an omelet, the former Watergate prosecutor told us about Justice Black's view of the First Amendment, about civil rights, and said things that old professors tell freshmen, like "Those battles are for your generation."

On the skewed political spectrum at HLS, however, Cox and Heymann were seen as nothing more than closet conservatives— and I, too, found myself in the uncomfortable new position of being a moderate, the liberal, moral high ground having been seized by those to the left of me. On one occasion, Heymann explored the tricky question which arises in rape cases of whether or not the woman consented to sexual relations. One line of cases held that to be guilty the man must have actual (subjective) knowl- edge that the woman was resisting. Another standard—akin to "negligence"—argued that if a "reasonably objective man" would know that she was not consenting, then he was guilty of rape. But most of the class argued for a third position, akin to "strict liability" in torts. Whether or not the defendant knew or should have known, if the alleged victim later says she did not consent, he's a rapist. The "reasonable man" test does not provide the woman enough protection, a number of students argued, because a jury may find that it's "reasonable" for a man to think a woman means yes when she says no. This argument may be right or wrong, but it was astounding coming from a group which on every other issue was willing to give the defendant every benefit. I realized the full political pressure on the rape question a week later, when Alan Dershowitz, the quintessential civil libertarian, gave a speech in which he said he didn't have trouble helping guilty people get off, but he would have trouble exploring an alleged rape victim's prior sexual history.

The same ideological bias guided the Criminal Law class discussion a few weeks later, when race, rather than gender, was at issue. Two black men in our section, Martin Francis and Tom Holmes, had been stopped by the Cambridge police while walking down Massachusetts Avenue and accused of "casing" a store. It was a horrifying incident. Martin said he had had trouble concentrating ever since. Interestingly, some of the black students were less affected than many of the whites. One black student said privately that it happens every day to innocent black males who don't happen to have the power of Harvard Law School to throw behind their complaint. A white student from Berkeley expressed the outrage we all shared, but added that until the economic lot of blacks is improved, the police are naturally going to be more suspicious of black males. The comment unleashed a torrent of anger from the left, most bitterly from my Civ Pro seatmate from Princeton, Jackson Shelby.

Earlier that morning, the racial sparks had flown in Civil Procedure. Minow had us read a number of decisions on busing as a remedy for desegregation, but inevitably the discussion turned to the merits. The discussion focused on the lamentable fact that by breaking up the local black neighborhood school, busing had destroyed the focal point for many black communities. A black student from Alabama went further. The idea behind *Brown v. Board of Education*, she said, was not that blacks sought integration to be with whites, but that the only way to get money for black education was to mix the students. Forget about that Martin Luther King, Jr., "brotherhood" stuff.

The sources of my disenchantment with law school were varied—rooted in my annoyance with intolerant ideologues, the cynicism of both the left and the right, the indifference of liberal professors and insecurity about my own capabilities dating from the first day of classes. But, in large part, law school diminished in importance to me as my personal life off campus blossomed.

On Thanksgiving Day, my girlfriend of five years, Rebecca Rozen, and I announced our engagement. Rebecca was my first and only real love; she lived upstairs from me in Weld Hall my freshman year of college and was now working at Oxfam America while applying to graduate school. We had never dreamed we'd marry: she was raised a Conservative Jew, attending Yeshiva through junior high school, while my father had been a Presbyterian minister before becoming a schoolteacher. But after five years of trying, unsuccessfully, to break up, we decided to stop fighting a good thing. Having someone say to you that, yes, they want to share the rest of their life with you is a most wonderful thing and stood in sharp contrast to all that was happening at law school. The moment we began discussing marriage, I had felt elevated and removed from the law school, not only from the social scene, but from its games and obsessions. Class discussions about promissory estoppel and summary judgment couldn't excite me, as they seemed so petty in light of the step Rebecca and I were planning to take together.

Still, as the semester wore on, I began to notice I had begun to think like a (Harvard) lawyer, which was a not altogether welcome development. In Legal Methods, a noncredit course taught by third-year students, they drilled home the point that a lawyer needs to be able to know both sides of an issue. We were to argue a landlord-tenant case against another student, and then, ten days later, switch sides. I was paired with Lisa Chen, a small and fiercely radical Asian woman from Berkeley, who was actually even more alienated from HLS than I. We both personally sympathized with the tenant.

As is often the case in landlord-tenant disputes, the lease was pro-landlord, but "fairness" considerations cut in favor of the tenant. The first round, I argued for the tenant and she for the landlord. I was impressed that she could marshal arguments with such agility for the side which she thought to be wrong. In the second round, representing the landlord, I made the twisted argument "to disregard the lease because the plaintiff appeared 'poor' and 'sympathetic' or because he didn't 'understand' the lease would have grave consequences." My brief continued: "Once leases lose their sanctity, landlords will feel free to break them at will. Worse, landlords whose tenants are 'poor' and 'sympathetic' will move into other businesses where contracts remain binding." But I had more trouble making the case in oral argument. When my advisor, playing the judge, asked, "So the plaintiffs will be better off if they lose?" I said, "Yes," but couldn't keep a straight face. We all broke into laughter.

For most students, however, litigation was not a joking matter, and when it came time to choose one elective for the second semester, almost every 1L chose Federal Litigation ("Fed Lit"), even though the course required writing lots of briefs and pulling many all-nighters—perhaps because of it. I declined, in favor of Administrative Law ("Ad Law"), the body of law developed by administrative agency rulings. I signed up for the course in large part because my sister Joy, who had graduated from Harvard Law School in 1982, recommended the professor, Chris Edley, a Democratic activist who had worked as a domestic policy advisor in the Carter Administration. Taking Ad Law was like *choosing* the Experimental section: it would be humane and low-key, and frowned upon by the fast trackers.

Just as I was opting for the slow track, in early December, exam hysteria swept the first-year class, a full month and a half before the first exam. One afternoon, Heymann played a videotape of Professor Charles Nesson's lecture on how to take a law school exam. Nesson explained that law school finals, unlike college tests, present concrete problems to solve. You couldn't simply regurgitate material, you had to have "active knowledge" which you could apply to a specific case. That is why study groups are so helpful in law school, he said. (Thanks for telling us now! I thought.) Nesson also said that because time is short, a student should attempt only to describe the problem, "spot the issues," rather than attempt to resolve them. The people who came out of exams thinking they did well often did the worst, Nesson said, because they failed to spot the gaps and ambiguities in the law.

These two- to three-hour exams, time-pressured and requiring "active knowledge," would be the sole basis for our grades. All my professors assured us that grades were not important, even though all of them owed their jobs to them. Duncan Kennedy reportedly told his students that professors average five minutes of grading time per exam and joked that he threw the blue books down a set of stairs and whichever landed on top did best. Rakoff told us that he hoped, in all seriousness, to still be friends with us after he gave out our grades.

But grades were extremely important in the first year: they were important for getting on Law Review, for getting summer jobs after the second year, and for getting judicial clerkships. And, of course, good grades were going to be harder to get than ever before, as we were all accustomed to being at the top of the class.

As we broke for Christmas vacation, the pressure became unbearable. I looked forward to going home and being with my family, especially my father, who was in New York's Lenox Hill Hospital recovering from a serious operation. Just before I left, I noticed a sign-up sheet going around the class for those living in New York City who wanted to get together to study over the break. I declined. My family celebrated Christmas at Lenox Hill, hoping against hope that Dad would be okay.

When I returned to Cambridge, Arthur said he had studied in his dad's office every day over Christmas break. Word had it that the New York group—James Parks, Sarah Stern, and Alfred King—had come up with an amazing Contracts outline, complete with an elaborate flowchart. I began studying harder than I ever had, with commercial outlines, hornbooks, my notes. When motivation ran low, Arthur and I read *One L* to get ourselves pumped. (Turow claimed to hate the competition and elitism at Harvard, but the book's subtext celebrated it.) Increasingly, I felt the need for aspirin and Pepto-Bismol. As the pressure grew, Arthur— who'd been valedictorian at Groton and Harvard College—began questioning whether all this anxiety was worth it.

Exams brought out the ugliest side of people. One woman supposedly began calling her fellow students with the express purpose of making them nervous. She called me to report, incredulously, that a particular classmate hadn't even read a particular case—one which I, too, had neglected to read. When Heymann scheduled a review session to go over criminal procedure, the class voted not to put Heymann's lecture notes on library reserve, presumably so those who attended class could maintain their advantage over those who had missed it. The pace was too much for me. I considered myself a reasonably hard worker, but this was absurd. One could not say, "If only I studied harder, I would do better." At this level of intensity, the ability to study just a bit more than others, the rigid discipline, was itself a skill. I started studying at the Graduate School of Design to avoid law students.

Five days before the first exam, I met with an ad hoc study group formed in large part on Nesson's exam-taking advice about active knowledge. Ours was a sorry crew compared to Arthur's power group, which had been going since the first weeks of the semester. (Arthur's group would later become legendary—even at other law schools—for putting three of its five members on Law Review.) Our casual group met twice, but even the other members intimidated me with their advanced knowledge. With the countdown at three days, I met with my squash buddy, Paul Mazzoli, to discuss criminal law. We were supposed to work with Sarah Stern, too, but she disposed of us in favor of another group. Sarah was suddenly a hot commodity with bargaining power. She was an active class participant and her brother was on Law Review, so everyone was hoping some of her brilliance and insider knowledge might rub off.

On January 12, we took our first law school exam: Contracts. Before the final, James Parks whipped out his camera and began taking snapshots; he was confident, his flowchart in hand. The exam didn't seem that difficult to me, which, according to Professor Nesson's advice, was bad news. Two days later, I took Heymann's Criminal Law exam in cavernous Memorial Hall. The exam was closed book and read like the Bar—technical, procedural questions about whether you can search a car trunk but not a briefcase in the trunk. But the Torts exam two days later was a disaster. For the first time since high school, I panicked badly and ran out of time. Stunned, I went out afterward with some people from class to celebrate. "We can't talk about exams or law school," someone said. The group fell silent. There was nothing else to talk about.

2

The Loony Left

Of course, the first semester of first year we didn't spend all our time reading cases and preparing for exams. We also obsessed about getting jobs. Those who continued to entertain the illusion that Harvard Law was more than a trade school joined cultlike radical reading groups to divert themselves from the classroom competition and the careerism. But even the radicals had to get a job, and a surprising number eventually ended up in corporate law. This struck me as, well, anomalous, but the tone had been set back on orientation day that, in the legal world, "inconsistency" was acceptable, even expected.

The orientation proceedings the first week of school had culminated with Dean Vorenberg's address at noon in the Ropes-Gray room, a large hall in the corner of the Pound building. Ropes-Gray isn't a former dean or Supreme Court Justice; it's a corporate law firm in Boston. Most law firms would start competing for Harvard students during the second year of law school by holding fancy functions with an open bar and hors d'oeuvres at the Harvard Faculty Club, the Charles Hotel, or Upstairs at the Pudding. But Ropes & Gray was more sophisticated; it had circulated its name among young virgin law students even before classes began.

Dean Vorenberg, who had begun his career at Ropes & Gray (as had Archibald Cox and the dean-to-be, Robert Clark), earnestly advised us to consider public-interest law as an alternative to a corporate-law career; heads nodded. He said public interest could be more rewarding than private practice. Yes, that made a great deal of sense. But wait. Here was the dean, in the room named after the law firm where he once worked, singing the virtues of public interest. Didn't he sense the irony?

The odd thing about it was that Dean Vorenberg really *was* a committed liberal who wanted law students to do public interest. Not too many, of course; there were bills to pay, new wings to be added, and alumni who were legal-services lawyers would be a poor source of funds for the law school. But Vorenberg did hope that at least a few of us would try public service or public interest, and had, in fact, established a public-interest placement office at HLS. The part-time public-interest advisor, Ron Fox, held a series of eight career meetings for 1Ls in the early fall, which is when he had his best shot at influencing students. The first meeting was in a crowded room on the second floor of Pound Hall. Fox, a middle-aged Boston attorney (HLS '63), seemed to be a reassuring mixture of right and left. He played Harry Chapin music at the beginning of each session, but he also wore a suit. A liberal, but not a loony. The room continued to fill with students, as more than 130 of us —nearly a quarter of the entire class—streamed in. Fox, looking pleased, turned off the music and began his pitch. He would help us in the tough task of getting public-interest summer jobs, help us keep from becoming part of the 90 percent of American lawyers who represent 10 percent of the population. The pressure to sell out would be immense, he said, but if we worked together— networked—we could survive with our ideals intact.

Fox then asked each of us to announce her name and background in public interest. My Section 4 was well represented. Lucy Anderson had worked for the public defender in Greenville, South Carolina, Fred Pynchon had been at Neighborhood Legal Services in Pittsburgh, Ellen Pearson at the Monroe County public defender, Barbara Chandler had worked at the Lawyers Committee for Civil Rights under Law, Lisa Chen at a Nader group in California, and Ed Murphy had been with Nader in Washington, D.C.

I looked around the room, elated. These were the people who would become my friends, I thought, the people who had come to Harvard with the same goals I had. Fox asked us to check off our legal interests on a card, which he said we should keep as we progressed through our three years—as if predicting our failure,

from too much experience. Mine were civil rights, consumer, and
federal government.

That evening, I attended the law school Student Activities Fair,
which gave me even more reason to believe that my fellow students
were not just another bunch of would-be yuppies. As I looked
around the room, there were several organizations dedicated to
providing legal services for the poor: Harvard Defenders, Harvard
Legal Aid Bureau, Prison Legal Assistance Project, and Students
for Public Interest Law. Between five hundred and six hundred
students participated. Many did not do so out of unalloyed altruism
(practically speaking, poverty law is the only kind of law that students can practice before passing the Bar), but most of those involved seemed very much committed to careers in public-interest
law. The liberal law journals clearly outnumbered the conservative
ones. On the left were the *Civil Rights–Civil Liberties Law Review*,
the *Environmental Law Review*, the *Human Rights Yearbook*, and the
Women's Law Journal, balanced only by the *Journal of Law and Public
Policy* on the right. There were recruiters for the Alliance for Public
Interest Alternatives, Amnesty International, the Anti-Apartheid
Committee, the Civil Rights Action Committee, the Committee on
Gay & Lesbian Legal Issues, the Environmental Law Society, the
Fellowship in Public Interest Law, the Human Rights Group, the
Labor Law Project (which organized boycotts against union-busting
firms), and Student Funded Fellowships. The left-leaning Lawyers
Guild was more active than the Student Bar Association, and the
Democratic Club membership outnumbered the Republican Club's
several times over. There was even a group which sponsored an
Anarchist Film Festival. So desperate were the conservatives on
campus that, in order to get students to volunteer for Congressman
Jack Kemp's presidential campaign, they had to appeal to something
other than ideology. "Wary of stuffing envelopes and licking stamps
for candidate X?" a Kemp advertisement asked. "The Kemp campaign has substantive opportunities available at state headquarters
involving surrogate speaking, research, and strategic planning." So
what if you disagreed with all that Kemp stood for: your high-level
title would look good on your résumé!

Various ethnic and minority groups historically excluded from
Harvard Law were now represented by support groups at the student fair: Alianza (for Latinos), the American Indian Law Students

Association, the Asian-American Law Students Association, the Black Law Students Association, and the Women's Law Association. Even the one social club on campus, the Lincoln's Inn Society, was egalitarian. Unlike the elite all-male final clubs at Harvard College, whose admission is based on social standing, the Lincoln's Inn Society chose its members by lot.

Two groups were conspicuously absent from the activities fair: the Board of Student Advisors (BSA) and the *Harvard Law Review*. The BSA, which ran the Ames Moot Court competition and other activities, and the *Harvard Law Review*, the venerable student-edited journal, were not open to first-year students. Although both organizations were ostensibly nonpolitical, their affirmative-action programs reflected the progressive character of the student body. The BSA nondiscrimination admissions policy went on endlessly to include every conceivable group, and the Law Review's affirmative-action program was criticized by none other than *The New York Times* when first instituted in the early 1980s. For all their democratic rhetoric, however, the absence of BSA and the Review from the fair only added to their aura of mystery and exclusivity.

As I was surveying the scene, I bumped into Elizabeth Whitman, a friend from college now in her third year. She encouraged me to get involved in legal aid. I said that, yes, I would like that very much, but that I would wait a while until my workload became manageable.

Most of Whitman's colleagues in the second- and third-year classes had their mind on something other than legal aid that fall. A few weeks after they arrived, we 1Ls witnessed a sudden, dramatic change in the appearance of upperclassmen. Beards were shaved, hair was combed, suits were donned, and, among the women, makeup was applied! It was recruitment time for the nation's top law firms, a truly astounding time of year to be at Harvard Law School. Jonathan Rosen, a 2L whom I knew as an unkempt radical undergraduate who would periodically emerge from the stacks of Widener Library with his hair in every direction, was now to be found walking through Harkness Commons in pinstripes, his political stance shed as easily as his jeans. The halls buzzed with talk of astronomical salaries, fancy hotels, expensive lunches, and "fly outs" to warm-weather firms in Miami and Los Angeles. What was astonishing to us in the first-year class was the pervasiveness of it all. It quickly became obvious that all but a small handful of upperclassmen were interviewing with firms. There was no shame in it; a sense of inevitability hung in the air.

Ron Fox's second public-interest meeting drew a much smaller crowd than the first one two weeks earlier, although Fox looked happy to have as many students show up as did. He spent most of the hour outlining the different types of public-interest and government jobs available. Sensing he was losing the crowd, Fox offered a new twist on who constituted the "underrepresented." Citing attorney Lloyd Cutler, Fox said that 95 percent of legal time is spent on the wealthiest 10 percent, 5 percent on the poor through legal services, and close to o percent on the 160 million Americans in the middle. I almost raised my hand to ask why Lloyd Cutler's Washington law firm spends thousands of dollars every year recruiting law students to represent the wealthiest clients if Cutler was really so disturbed. But I thought it might be impolite.

Later that evening, I attended the kickoff meeting of the Alliance for Public Interest Alternatives. I came to hear Professor Abe Chayes, who had won fame for taking on President Reagan's Nicaragua policy in the World Court. Chayes, dressed in a foppish sweater, told us to consider public-interest law. "Don't go to the big firms for training," he said; they no longer offer the apprenticeships they did fifteen years ago. In the days when young Abe Chayes graduated from Harvard Law School, it was different, it seems. Then it made sense to go, as Chayes did, and practice at the great Washington law firm of Covington & Burling for an "apprenticeship," doubtlessly the same sort of schooling Dean Vorenberg received at Ropes & Gray. In the great tradition of St. Augustine, Chayes and Vorenberg counseled abstinence, after their own feast.

All of this was beginning to make a bit of a cynic out of me. Everyone seemed to go to corporate law firms, not least of which were those who argued most vociferously against them. Did the 2Ls, 3Ls, and professors know something that we 1Ls didn't?

One afternoon in early October, I joined a group of 1Ls to visit a federal district court in Boston. As we filed into the courtroom, I felt sorry for the poor defendant being used as a learning experience for young Harvard students. During a recess, the judge, a

Harvard alumnus, called us up to talk about the case and asked each of us what type of law we planned to practice. Most of us said we wanted to do public-interest or government work. The judge brightened, saying he was surprised and pleased. I felt the sudden desire to set him straight. "Remember, we're still first-year students," I blurted.

Session three of Ron Fox's dwindling support group met in mid-October. The topic: "The Survival of Pre-HLS Values While at HLS." Fox had given us an article by Harvard Law School career counselor Mark Byers, in which Byers warned against going with the pack to private law firms if that career path conflicted with your individual identity. He exposed the fallacy of seeking success—the blue-chip law firm—for its own sake. Students "may even find law intrinsically boring," he wrote. Above all, he warned, be introspective. "It is this kind of talk that goes on a good deal in college, and it should not cease in law school." Fox then brought in three upperclassmen to talk to us about maintaining our values. One had spent a summer at the Children's Defense Fund and planned to stick with public interest. She said that she came from a working-class background where "no one you know makes $65,000," much less at age twenty-five. It was ridiculous to think of anything less as a colossal sacrifice.

In late October, the placement office held a general meeting for first-year students on interview and résumé strategies. I felt a little embarrassed about going, but when I arrived I found the hall was packed with more than two hundred students. The official material we had been getting from the placement office downplayed first-year recruitment, saying that 1Ls should concentrate on their studies and not worry about summer jobs. Firms who flew recruiters to Cambridge to woo 2Ls and 3Ls were, in fact, forbidden to make contact with 1Ls in the Boston area until March. For years, law schools did not even offer any recruiting services to first-year students on the theory that it was healthier for students to have a summer away from the law. But here, at the front of the room, was the recruitment coordinator, Dr. Mark Byers, explaining that it was not too early to start "cranking out" cover letters and résumés. Even if the firms couldn't contact us, we could contact them. "How many letters?" someone asked. "One hundred is probably excessive," Byers said.

Could this be the same Mark Byers who had written so movingly about not following the pack if doing so suppressed your individual identity? The man who had dared to say that private law practice might be "intrinsically boring"? This was the professional Mark Byers, just doing his job as Harvard Law School career counselor. If revving up the pack was necessary to success, so be it. After a brief pitch, Byers began fielding questions from the now-enthusiastic crowd.

"How can we network?"

"How can we best capitalize on college connections?"

I was embarrassed by the hungry pack's lack of restraint. Capitalizing on connections? Networking? This was classic Harvard Law School—the crude side of the fact that most HLS students have never dreamed of making 65 grand. Ambition and drive were more unabashed, more overt in law school than at Harvard College. The law students were more openly and unashamedly on the make, more aggressive about making "contacts" with professors by pursuing them after class and in the hallways. This made life a little more raw and less pleasant than in the college, where people adopted a certain "Ivy League sophistication," which, if disingenuous, at least gave the appearance of civility.

But in a very limited sense there was something positive about this opportunistic competition. While the student body at Harvard Law School was less diverse in its interests, it appeared more economically diverse than that of Harvard College. "The Harvard Law School is," as Kennedy Administration aide Richard Goodwin (HLS '58) has said, "one of the great agents of upward mobility in this country. You come in there and you do well and suddenly you're put on a different track in life."

Exactly one week after the Byers meeting, the placement office released the *1L Employer Directory*, and the wolves dove in with a vengeance. Many firms did not hire 1Ls, but those who did paid top dollar, up to $1,200 a week. Names, addresses, and salaries of participating firms were all there, organized by city, and within a week the letters were being cranked out.

Arthur wrote to a small number of the top New York firms that hired 1Ls. Most such firms base their decision almost entirely on an applicant's undergraduate record, so Arthur was ideally positioned. Other people were sending out reams of letters. In our Harkness mailboxes, we began to receive ads for cover letters that promised "50 firms only $30; 100 firms only $60." Another entrepreneur, cruelly feeding on paranoia, was offering "250 firms only $99" and provided a list of 464 firms to choose from. All you had to do was circle the firm's name and write a check, an option especially attractive to those still trying to do all the assigned classroom reading. To make students look good for interviews, local tailors began advertising competing rates for custom-made wool suits and cotton shirts. Our mailboxes soon represented the cacophony of inconsistent voices at HLS. Along with the ads for suits and cover letters came invitations to join the Legal Services Center, to attend meetings of the Alliance for Public Interest Alternatives, and to help out with the Women's Law Association drive to collect socks for the poor.

The day after Thanksgiving, I sent out fifty-three letters to public-interest groups in New York, Washington, and Boston: the ACLU, NAACP Legal Defense Fund (LDF), Ralph Nader's Public Citizen Litigation Group, the Department of Justice, the Senate Judiciary Committee, as well as a number of private firms involved in public interest.

I called my sister's friend and law school classmate Ann Kennedy, an attorney at the well-known Washington firm of Williams & Connolly, to find out which public-interest jobs were the most desirable. She said the "résumé builders" were the LDF, Children's Defense Fund (CDF), Public Citizen, and the U.S. Attorney's Office for the Southern District of New York (Manhattan). Yes, even in the egalitarian world of public-interest law, there were widely acknowledged pecking orders. I had lunch with a 3L who had worked for CDF, and attended a "brown bag lunch" with Professor Elizabeth Bartholet, who had worked for the LDF. I followed up my letters with calls on the public-interest phone, provided by the law school for long-distance calls.

But nearly a month after sending out résumés, I became depressed. Most places didn't respond at all. Of those that did, some said they hired only 2Ls and 3Ls; some said they wouldn't hire until March; others, that they would take only volunteers. When I called the U.S. Commission on Civil Rights to follow up on my letter to them, a disheartened attorney apologized that the organization was being severely cut back and he was not sure if they could hire anyone. But a few groups did respond, and when I went home to New York for Christmas break, I was able to schedule three interviews there.

The first was with the NAACP Legal Defense Fund. When I arrived at the LDF office, the receptionist was busy buzzing people in and out of a secured door. I wondered whether the high security was necessary to protect against loony white supremacists. Maybe it was just New York. On the wall there was a framed front-page clipping from *The New York Times* the day after *Brown v. Board of Education* was handed down—clearly the most important case LDF had ever argued and one of the most important cases of the century. I flipped through the organization's brochure, including the picture of the nine attorneys who argued *Brown* standing on the steps of the Supreme Court. Next to Thurgood Marshall, then director-counsel of LDF, stood Jack Greenberg, a white man who later succeeded Marshall. A few years back, a group of HLS blacks had protested the decision to allow Greenberg to teach a course on civil rights. They wanted a black professor; a lifelong dedication to the cause of civil rights was not enough. But the LDF was clearly more in the tradition of Martin Luther King, Jr., than Malcolm X; it sought integration, not black separatism.

In fact, my LDF interviewers were mostly white liberals—a Yale woman who'd clerked for Justice Blackmun, a man who concentrated on death penalty cases, and an adjunct professor from Stanford who was focusing on the black underclass. My final interview was with a black HLS graduate. She quizzed me on civil rights cases and then talked about an incident that had occurred two days earlier in which a black youth had been killed after being chased by a gang of whites in Queens. The Howard Beach episode represented an unambiguous case of right vs. wrong—and reminded me of why it was still so important to support groups like LDF. I left the interview knowing that if it was offered, I'd accept the job in a second.

The next day I had an interview with Fred Simpson at the U.S. Attorney's Office in Manhattan (known in legal circles as "the Southern District"). When I arrived, the receptionist made it clear that Mr. Simpson was not, in fact, expecting me. When he emerged from his office twenty minutes later, he sat down next to me in the reception area and announced that he didn't have my résumé but was glad I had stopped by. I handed him a spare copy I had brought and he looked it over. It turned out he had relatives who were auto dealers in my hometown of Ridgewood. He told me it made sense to try the U.S. Attorney's Office for a summer. "Then you can go work for a law firm for $1,200 a week and make your wife happy." Wink, wink. After five minutes of this, Simpson thanked me for coming by. I left convinced I'd blown it. The LDF interview had lasted more than two hours and here I hadn't even made it into Simpson's office. One week later, Simpson sent me a letter offering me a job. I later learned it was a "snot and drool" test. If you didn't have either on your face, you had the job.

The day after Christmas, I interviewed with the Southern District's poor sister, the U.S. Attorney for New Jersey. The office was in an enormous ugly government building in Newark, a symbol of white justice in a black city. The assistant U.S. attorney in charge of hiring for the summer was very friendly, perhaps because he had been a classmate of Joy's and a good friend of Ann Kennedy's from the Law Review. Or it might have been because his office didn't have the glamour of the Southern District and he had to sell as much as buy. When I asked him whether the position paid anything, he said the 2Ls got paid but not the 1Ls.

Yes, money. There was always the looming question of money. In early December, Ron Fox had devoted an entire public-interest meeting to getting public-interest money—fellowships, loans, work-study. The Alliance for Public Interest Alternatives put together something known as the "Money Book," which outlined a number of programs: Student Funded Fellowships, the Human Rights Fellowship, and the Summer Employment Loan Program. For graduates, the Low Income Protection Plan (LIPP) forgave part, and in some cases all, of a student's law school loans if she chose a low-paying law-related job. By 1988, a student taking a $20,000 job would have her law school loans entirely forgiven for each year her income stayed at that level. For salaries above $20,000, the law school paid back a portion of the loan on a sliding scale, up to the $35,000 salary level. The program had proved quite successful, and according to Dean Vorenberg's March 1989 report, LIPP was "the fastest-growing item in the operative budget for the last two years." The money was there, Fox said, but for the summer grants you had to work to get it. Money should not be an excuse. Fox quoted Joan Didion in *Slouching Towards Bethlehem*: "Character—the willingness to accept responsibility for one's own life—is the source from which self-respect springs." Dealing with the money problem was supposed to build character.

As I churned out a series of essays for the Law Students Civil Rights Research Council (LSCRRC) grant, due December 31, the process seemed more a pain in the ass than an exercise in character building. To make matters worse, my LSCRRC interview was scheduled for the night before my first exam. A small group of 2L and 3L public-interest types sat around questioning my commitment to public-interest law. The fact that I had applied to the U.S. Attorney's Office seemed to raise some suspicion. After all, the government was the Establishment, and the U.S. Attorneys' Offices were run by Republicans. I explained that after writing my undergraduate thesis on Robert Kennedy, I realized that being tough on crime should be a "liberal" position in that most victims of crime are the downtrodden. This idea was met with blank stares.

Sensing that I was not winning their hearts, I told them that I chose law because it seemed that judges could do things that democratically elected legislatures would never do. I cited a Massachusetts judge who had recently ordered the state to increase its welfare payments. I realized how shockingly elitist my statement was, and I was about to start backpedaling furiously when I noticed that their heads were nodding. I'd finally said something with which they could agree. I began to wonder why I was putting my financial security in the hands of these people.

After the horror of exams, I fled Cambridge to see my father, who was still in the hospital, and to continue interviewing in New York. In Boston's South Station, as I waited for the train to New York, I ran into James Parks and Vicki Jefferson from my section. James, the student who'd taken photos of the class before our Contracts exam, was a vocal black Republican, fond of free-market thinking. Vicki was a black radical who spoke earnestly and often about the legacy of slavery. I knew James and disagreed with him, and I found Vicki a bit strident, though I didn't know her personally. I even began resenting her when I found out she was Washington-bound to interview with the Children's Defense Fund, which had, a week earlier, sent me a rejection letter. But as the hours passed, our seat compartment was filled with laughter and good humor. Vicki joked about having to change her hair, losing her dreadlocks, so as not to appear too radical for CDF.

I encountered the opposite problem the next day when I went for my interview with the National Employment Law Project in a gray suit and clipped hair and drew stares from the bearded attorneys in casual attire. I immediately dismissed them as a fringe group, my defenses on overdrive. Their tiny office, located near Riverside Church and Columbia University, was removed from the spheres of power, I rationalized. Interviews with the ACLU and the New York Attorney General's Office followed on subsequent days, but my heart wasn't in them. If only I could get some funding, I had the U.S. Attorney's Office offer sewn up, and was still waiting for LDF's response.

The first week back at classes, our section held another "bridge," this one on "the legal profession." The cynics in our section said it was a good way to ease us back into the routine of daily classes, but I thought the topic was incredibly important, given the summer job search we were all going through. The bridge tried to address various ethical questions lawyers face: whether a legal-services attorney should get involved in the personal affairs of her clients; what a corporate lawyer should do when her client suggests skirting the law because he doesn't think he will get caught. But the grandest ethical question involved what type of law we wanted to practice. Our liberal professors assigned a wonderful account of the "Geography of the Legal Profession," written by Peter Kochenburger, an HLS researcher. The paper documented the familiar but undeniable argument that lawyers, for the most point, toil for the wealthy. According to the study, Harvard wasn't helping matters. In 1986, of 508 graduates surveyed, eight (1.5 percent) were going into government, nine (2 percent) into public-interest jobs, five (1 percent) into academics, and seven (1.4 percent) into legal services. The rest went to law firms, private industry or banking, or clerked for a judge—with clerking, in most instances, merely postponing the decision to practice at a large firm. The median income for Harvard private corporate and commercial lawyers from the class of '69 was $150,000. Sixty-seven percent of them believed they were contributing to the public good.

In the meantime, I continued with my plan to serve noncorporate, yet important, interests. I called upperclassmen—Judith Goldberg, who'd worked at the LDF, and Miriam Simon, who'd worked at the U.S. Attorney's Office for the Southern District of New York—to find out how they'd liked their summer jobs. Judith raved, but Miriam was more cautious, saying only that while people had very different experiences, the Southern District had "a great rep." Shortly thereafter, the LDF informed me that I was on a waiting list. Two Ls received priority, I was told. I quickly shot off a letter to Fred Simpson accepting a position with the Southern District.

The U.S. Attorney's Office was not going to pay anything, so I hastened my search for public-interest funds. In mid-February, I sat down and pounded out a lengthy essay for Student Funded Fellowships, a program in which students earning enormous summer salaries working at large corporate law firms donate one day's pay to help students who want to do public interest. It sounded like a good cause to me, especially since I was a potential beneficiary. So I spent the evening of February 22 on the telephone hitting my classmates up for money. A week later, I had my SFF interview with Susan Sorensen and Luke Houghton, and it quickly became obvious that my phone calls weren't going to give me much mileage. Houghton was tall and blond and already becoming well known on campus as an outspoken radical. Conservatives had labeled him a "limousine liberal," pointing to his degrees from Andover and Stanford. I told him and Susan that I was going to work for the U.S. Attorney's Office on the theory that fighting crime benefits society, and the poor especially (strike 1). Then I said that, although my family was paying for law school, my wife and I would need some money to live on (strike 2). Finally, when Luke and Susan mentioned that they were in Section 3, I brightened and told them Arthur Le Palm was my roommate. Arthur was an unabashed conservative and had told me he was ideologically opposed to donating part of his corporate salary to SFF (strike 3). Five days later, when I was checking my Harkness mailbox, Houghton slipped me my rejection letter. Rumor had it that some of those who received funding got as little as $30 a week.

I relentlessly plunged ahead and applied for the newly established Emmanuel Kurland Fellowship, which provided a $1,200 summer stipend. I was, by this time, somewhat desperate for funds, so I spent hours looking up information on Kurland. I combed his essays published in various Harvard class-reunion books for quotes to include in my essay. All of this work, to earn in an entire summer what my roommate would earn in a week.

I began to feel, well, a little put-upon. Public-interest organi-

zations didn't wine, dine, flatter, and pursue you the way the corporate firms did. You pursued them. And, in the end, they didn't
pay you. I was ultimately rejected by Kurland, as I had been by
SFF and LSCRRC, but Ron Fox felt so sorry for me that he was
able to rustle up a $1,000 donation from some recent alumni.

Despite all the hassles with getting a summer job and summer
funding, March of 1987 was a very good time to be a liberal student
at the Harvard Law School. In mid-month, one of our own, Michael
Dukakis (HLS '60), declared his intention to run for the presidency
of the United States. Although my sister Joy worked in the governor's Office of Legal Counsel, I didn't know much about the
Massachusetts governor and wasn't entirely sold on him. But when
Dukakis came to speak in the Ames courtroom on March 19, with
a host of lights and TV cameras, the atmosphere was electric, and
he seemed almost, well, charismatic. Dukakis, who often made
somewhat forced parallels between his candidacy and J.F.K.'s, now
harked back to the days when he was a Harvard Law student and
John Kennedy was beginning *his* presidential campaign with a
speech at the law school. Dukakis was stacking his campaign with
Harvard lawyers like Paul Brountas, Susan Estrich, and Chris Edley, and the idea that we might all be part of an effort to restore
the Cambridge-Washington axis was genuinely exhilarating.

A week after Dukakis spoke, another Harvard Law alumnus
returned to address the student body. On March 25, Ralph Nader
(HLS '58) delivered a speech he'd given a thousand times—and
which I'd heard on a dozen occasions—containing the familiar old-
time liberalism I'd been brought up on. My father had first told
me about Nader in the early 1970s. During one summer vacation,
he read aloud endless excerpts from Charles McCarry's biography,
Citizen Nader. A few years later, when I was in grade school, my
father dragged the family to hear Nader speak. We saw Nader again
when I was in high school, this time at my urging, and I heard
Nader lecture a few more times in college. He was a near-mythic
figure to me, and in truth, Ralph Nader had a lot to do with my
decision to become a lawyer.

On this night, he was classic Nader: speaking, hands in pocket,
for too long, until only the diehard supporters were left, the people

he was really speaking to anyway. He railed against corporate law, but in a different way from the crits. He held out law as a possible instrument to reform and improve society, not something that is hopelessly and inevitably a tool for the rich and powerful. And, as always, Nader got the audience to think about and question the little things we take for granted. Why, for example, do we let advertisers get away with making older women deeply distraught about having natural brown spots on their hands, in order that they might feel compelled to buy spot-remover ointment? When it came time for questions, Houghton, the man who'd denied me my SFF fellowship, stood up. "Ralph," he asked to my horror, "what can we do about the law school?" Nader said that more time should be spent studying white-collar crime and there should be greater emphasis on serving the poor. He said that the best and brightest students, at Harvard and elsewhere, should tackle the toughest problems and not demean themselves by serving as drones to wealthy clients. As we left, Rebecca began signing the inevitable petitions that pop up wherever Nader speaks. I declined. I had just filled out my clearance forms to work for the United States Attorney's Office in the summer, and I had heard of people getting rejected in Ronald Reagan's Justice Department for lesser offenses. Rebecca was furious. Nader had given a stirring speech, and here I was worried about clearance. Was I changing?

If I needed reminding of what was wrong with the conservatives, it came the next day. As part of a bridge on *caveat lessee* Professor Louis Kaplow gave the right-wing perspective on housing law. Kaplow wasn't a crusty, old-guard conservative; he was a young Law and Economics nerd, whose charts and graphs convinced him that society's problems were better solved (as Steven Shavell had argued) by increased efficiency (i.e., giving direct cash transfers to the poor). A hyperrational school of thought, Law and Economics attempts to quantify the worth of everything, from the importance of clean air to the value of human life. Standing before the class, Kaplow reminded me of so many high-school debaters, smart kids who knew all the arguments but didn't have strong convictions about any of them. Kaplow appeared to be "spreading"—a debate strategy that involves spewing out arguments, a mile a minute, without much reference to which ones really make sense, to overwhelm the opposition. Kaplow had a debater's cadence and the characteristic lack of appreciation for the broader picture. As Kaplow chattered on, I looked around the classroom and realized that I could have been at a high-school debating tournament; my classmates were just as nerdy, only older, and would very soon be much richer. Such an audience was a receptive one for Kaplow and the Law and Economics movement he represented, for his highly intellectual message could make wealthy people think their position in society was indeed preordained and inevitable.

As I grew disenchanted with my classes, I considered getting involved in extracurricular activities. In the spring, I attended a meeting of the *Harvard Civil Rights–Civil Liberties Law Review*, commonly known as "*CR-CL*." The group was in the process of planning its upcoming issue: a minority critique of CLS. It was the left attacking the left, as always, with the attacker taking the furthermost left position. *CR-CL*'s point was that the Critical Legal Studies movement, for all its egalitarian pretensions, was primarily a movement of white males citing each other's articles for support. There was some truth to the charge, but I wondered whether it didn't make more sense to funnel this moral anger in the direction of the conservatives, who posed the real threat to civil rights and civil liberties.

I attended the *CR-CL* meeting, in part because I was interested in civil rights and civil liberties, and in part because I wanted very badly to avoid being a Law Review reject who wrote for *CR-CL*. At least half the 1Ls at the meeting were there to learn how to "subcite," a skill which our 2L friends told us was crucial to making Law Review.

Subciting is quintessential lawyering—it's the drone work of checking facts, case citations, and punctuation in articles written by someone else (usually law professors). Subciting requires the use of something called the "Blue Book," a manual put out, not incidentally, by the *Harvard Law Review*, which sets out the rules of citation for scholarly articles, legal briefs, and other legal writing. The editors of *CR-CL* were aware, of course, that many of us volunteered only to learn subciting, but no matter. We were the army who would do the drudgery of fact and citation checking for free.

I hated subciting and realized that unless I got all the glory of being an editor of the Law Review, I didn't want to "write" (subcite) for a journal. Besides, *CR-CL* was a little too radical for my tastes. I decided to try the Harvard Law School Democratic Club in search of some mainstream progressives who wanted to use the law for constructive purposes. In late April, I walked into a Democratic Club meeting and heard Jackson Shelby speaking. "For black people, the difference between the Democratic Party and the Republican," he declared, "is the difference between indentured servitude and slavery." I shook my head. I usually liked to listen to radicals because they made me look at problems from a new angle, but hearing Shelby talk this way was just too much. Jackson would be taking his Princeton coffee mug in the summer to Kirkpatrick & Lockhart, a Pittsburgh law firm which had no black partners and only one black associate among its 118 lawyers. Was this radical rhetoric a way of atoning for his embrace of the Establishment?

In the late spring, my displeasure with the left at Harvard increased as I watched it react to Clare Dalton's tenure battle. Dalton was my second-semester Contracts professor, a crit, and the worst teacher I had ever had. In class, she would move from case to case, failing to tie them together or distill any broader meaning from them. She tried to employ deconstructionist analysis and critical legal theory, but her methods were never convincing. The level of noise in our classroom was embarrassing evidence of how little respect she commanded.

On May 14, there was an uneasy tension in Contracts. Someone whispered to me that the faculty had voted the previous day to deny Dalton tenure. I felt sorry for her. There she stood in front of the class, still trying to teach, when everyone knew that she had been rejected by her peers. But to my mind, she seemed almost defiant, confident that students would rally around her and call her denial sexist, political, and a blow to academic freedom.

Even she could not have known how her case, over the next weeks, would become the *cause célèbre* among the liberal community in Cambridge. Favorable pieces appeared in the media, petitions circulated, and rallies were held. At graduation, students wore yellow armbands, and one group of graduates raised letters spelling

TENURE DALTON. Professor Derrick Bell staged a four-day sit-in to protest the denial of tenure. During exam period, I came across a crowd being addressed by Morton Horwitz, who calmly argued that Dalton's scholarship was strong: she had, after all, been published by the Oxford University Press and the *Yale Law Journal*. Then Luke Houghton took the microphone and started chanting about diversity among the faculty. Students turned away. My friend Joel Lewis shook his head and said simply, "Luke."

I followed Joel into the Hark, where two of my classmates were collecting signatures for a petition opposing Dalton's rejection. I tried to slip past them, but one called out to me, "Could you sign this petition, Rick?" I said something about having to think hard about it.

I was torn. There was some serious evidence that conservatives on the faculty were simply trying to stomp out the crits. A year earlier, CLS adherent Daniel K. Tarullo was denied tenure by the faculty, the first time a junior professor had lost a faculty vote in seventeen years. And David Trubek, a crit who had won faculty approval 30–8, was denied tenure in May when Derek Bok stepped in and vetoed the offer upon appeal from traditionalist Robert Clark and others. Now, after Dalton's rejection, Larry Tribe told the *Boston Globe* that anyone who believed the three cases were "a coincidence has more faith in the neutrality of the tenure process than I can muster." And it was truly appalling that Harvard Law School had but a handful of women professors out of a faculty of more than sixty. Harvard Law's track record on women was abysmal: the school, in fact, had not even admitted women until 1950. Arthur E. Sutherland's official history of Harvard Law, written on the occasion of the school's 150th anniversary, was aptly entitled *The Law at Harvard: A History of Ideas and Men, 1817–1967*.

The Dalton question was a hard one, pitting the progressive notion that teaching should matter as much as scholarship against the possibility that Dalton was denied for illegitimate ideological reasons. The great liberal dilemma should have been how to come out on the Clare Dalton tenure question—there were good, progressive arguments on both sides—but the left saw the case as closed.

Dalton's eight-hour take-home Contracts exam was an outrage. It contained two questions, one of which involved a hypothetical professor, Joe Levin, who was suing the "Nameless School of Law" for denial of tenure. His case was based on "ideological discrimination" and "denial of academic freedom," since he was affiliated with the Conference on Incompatible Legal Studies, a "diverse collection of unconventional legal schools." He had begun a "reading group" which was met with "grumblings of the conservative element within the faculty." We were supposed to apply, not surprisingly, Massachusetts law, to analyze the merits of his case. The case was clearly not his but hers, which was disturbing and distracting for a few reasons. First, you felt that if your exam made powerful arguments on the university's behalf, Dalton, having so close and emotional a bond to the facts, would have trouble grading objectively; and second, there was a sense, perhaps unjustified, that you were being used as a source of theories and ideas upon which Dalton could base her own case. I have no evidence that Dalton used any of the ideas in her subsequent battles with Harvard, but as a crit, she should have been sensitive to the perception that she was exploiting us just as surely as the worst capitalist exploits his workers. Illegitimate hierarchy, indeed.

CHAPTER

3

Dropping Out

If it seems that I spent the entire second semester looking for a summer job (and a salary) and trying out various extracurricular activities, it's because during this period of my first year I "dropped out," at least spiritually. I was still on the rolls, attended most of my classes, and took my exams. But like a large portion of my class, I was already defeated, with five-sixths of my law school career ahead of me. I was defeated by the Socratic method, the large classes, and the mundane quality of much of the law I was taught. But the biggest contributor to my anomie—and the single most important event of the year—was the announcement of first-semester grades on February 26.

The pressure that built up to that day was not unlike the hype that accompanies the Super Bowl. The tension was palpable when we returned from break and it grew daily for a month. Rumors swept the school that students who had failed an exam would receive a dreaded blue (some said it was pink) slip in their Harkness Commons mailbox. Students who had received nothing but straight As their entire life approached their mailboxes each day with fear and dread. Everyone was "lowballing"; even Arthur was convinced he'd blown his exams. He continued to say so up to the day grades were released, even though a week earlier, Arthur had received a hand-written note from his Criminal Law professor, Lloyd Weinreb, praising him for writing an A+ exam.

On February 25, signs surprisingly were posted throughout the law school announcing that 1L grades would be released later in the day. A shock wave was sent through the class. It was our collective moment of truth. Minow made the obligatory speech about how unimportant grades were, which was as convincing as a rich man telling a group of beggars that money wasn't important. I stopped by my Hark mailbox between classes and found a small pink flyer that read:

WE ARE PROUD

How did you get into HLS?
How did you get / not get housing?
How was your Ames case chosen?
How about your 1L elective?

See the newest results of
THE LOTTERY
9–10:30 (or did you miss it?)
Get your GRADES in:
P200 (A–K) or Ames (L–Z)

We're not upset BY RANDOM GRADES:

AT LEAST THEY'RE FAIR—WE ALL HAVE
AN EQUAL CHANCE

The note was signed and put out by a left-wing group known as the Counter Hegemonic Front.

The next day, though, was the real thing. My heart pounding, I entered Langdell South, where students with initials E–N were to receive their grades. We filed through like sheep, showing our ID cards and receiving a folded computer printout on which, it seemed at the time, our careers depended. Harvard didn't have to do it this way. Grades could have been mailed or stuck in our mailboxes. But this was a ritual vestige straight out of *The Paper Chase*.

I looked down at my grades. Bs and B+s. Better than my worst fears, of course, but disappointing and far worse than my college and high-school grades. They were mediocre and put me smack in the middle of the class. They meant I would never clerk for the

Supreme Court and that it would be very tough to make Law Review.

I tried to be philosophical: they were just grades. But there was something deeper going on, which went not only to my future but to my very identity. The thing that made us special, that got us into one of the top law schools in the country, was our grades. And now Harvard Law's Darwinian system had taken that away from most of us. Harvard Law gathered together all the people who'd gotten As in college, the top 1 percent, and spread them over a bell curve, so that most of us, by definition, could not do nearly as well as we had in the past. The effect was devastating; students who came to law school believing they could do anything they wanted would, for a time, feel as though they were capable of nothing.

Arthur, of course, did extremely well. I told myself that I was lucky to be liberated—that Arthur would not be happy until he made Law Review, was elected an officer of the Review, was appointed a Supreme Court clerk,.and so on. But the truth was, I didn't get off the fast track voluntarily. I was thrown off.

Immediately after the release of grades, student behavior changed dramatically. Most of those who had never received Bs before in their lives became withdrawn and alienated, a process I had begun months earlier with my first-day humiliation. Those who did well took their grades as a license to talk in class more frequently than ever. One A student began to consider himself the class spokesman, beginning every statement with the pompous phrase "The reason we think that . . ." The arrogance of those who did well got so intolerable that professors began to publicly cut them down to size, which always won points with the silent majority in the section who delighted in those moments of comeuppance.

The second-semester classes brought new subjects and some new professors—Frank Michelman for Property, Chris Edley for Administrative Law, and of course Clare Dalton for the second semester of Contracts. To my horror, the only continuity was a second helping of Civil Procedure with Martha Minow.

Michelman was fairly popular among students, only in part because he was especially good at shooting down hot-shot students. For one thing, Michelman had little use for pretense. He announced on the first day of class that since everyone used study aids for courses, he'd assign the Gilbert *Law Summary on Property*. Students also found his modesty endearing. Michelman didn't take a great deal of interest in his appearance and could be seen wearing what looked like the same set of clothes for weeks. The class preceding ours had all pitched in to buy him a new sweater, to replace one with holes in the elbows.

Michelman's problem, and it wasn't a small one, was that he was incomprehensible most of the time, which made people think he had to be brilliant. Michelman was said to be cited more frequently in Supreme Court decisions than any other law professor, a fact which some students attributed to the desire of Supreme Court clerks to demonstrate that they understood him. It didn't help matters that Michelman spent several weeks on Hohfeldian terminology and followed this with the dreaded Rule Against Perpetuities, the formulation which limits the conditions people can place on transfers of property.

But what made Michelman lovable was his unabashed passion for fairness. Many of his articles were about using the words in the Constitution to help poor people. In Property class, he would go through a long discussion of estate law — in which the question was whether the will of the decendent as expressed in a particular section should count more than an attempt to reconstruct the general spirit of the will — and then pause and note, "It's very interesting that we don't even consider which heir needs the property."

Martha Minow shared many of Michelman's ideological principles, but she rarely seemed to get around to the law, even in the second semester. It wasn't until April that we got to the famous case of *Pennoyer v. Neff*, which Arthur had been talking about since the first day. Instead, throughout the semester, Minow labored mightily to be hip. She would read poetry, make references to Freud, and begin many classes by asking if anyone had seen a good movie. She generally acted as if she was our friend, even though she was one of the few professors never to learn our names. By the end of the year, many of us felt that her father, Newton Minow's, description of television programming as "a vast wasteland" was an apt description of his daughter's course, too. A number of us studied Professor Arthur Miller's taped lectures because we quite simply had not learned the course material from Minow.

Professor Dalton's teaching was even worse, if this was possible. At the beginning of the semester, I wanted to give her the benefit of the doubt. I thought the school would be enriched by her approach. I agreed with her that the traditional pedagogy—whereby the professor holds back until the end of class, when the heavens open up and the light shines down as the professor provides the Right Answer—was silly. But in an attempt not to end classes with a false sense of closure, Dalton would leave absolutely everything hanging.

My fourth professor, Chris Edley, was refreshingly good. As an elective, Edley's Ad Law course had new faces and a "small" class size (40 students as compared to 140). Edley, one of the few black professors at HLS, was very involved in Democratic politics, so it was natural that he should teach Ad Law, which is about public policy as much as law. Because the course involves the law argued before administrative agencies rather than "real" courts, other professors disdain it. But I found the range of topics interesting: price controls, worker safety regulations, and auto safety standards. Edley seemed to enjoy teaching 1Ls (he was used to teaching upperclassmen) and was taken aback when, at the end of the semester, we asked him to schedule an extra review session. I planned to experiment in this class. I decided I would read all the material and see how well I could do.

The other bright spot second semester was the set of Section 4 bridges, which I now saw as enriching rather than wasteful. One bridge session focused on consumer law, another on *U.S. Steel vs. Steelworkers*, in which the union sued management for refusing to sell a defunct Youngstown, Ohio, plant to the unemployed steelworkers. The final bridge was on the celebrated Baby M case, in which the surrogate mother, Mary Beth Whitehead, decided she wanted to keep the baby she was to deliver for William and Elizabeth Stern, an upper-middle-class couple who said they could not have children on their own. Here, the women professors—Minow and Dalton—shone, displaying what was to me an enlightening female, though not necessarily feminist, perspective. (There was not really a clear "feminist" position on the issue.) Minow made a powerful case for Mary Beth Whitehead. She said the term "surrogate mother" is itself loaded, because it implies the bearer of the infant is not the real mother. And Minow ripped into the class bias in the New Jersey judge's decision to award the Sterns custody. The decision painted the Whiteheads as "white trash" (unemployed and on public assistance) and the Sterns as respectable (upper-middle-class, highly educated, and the type of people with whom the judge might socialize). Minow was concerned about the class implications of upholding a contract which says rich women can rent poor women's bodies to bear children. Dalton pointed out two other problems with enforcing a surrogate contract: What if the Sterns decided they didn't want the baby? Did the Sterns really have a right to abort the fetus, as the contract provided?

But Elizabeth Bartholet, the professor who had worked at the LDF, was the most insightful. She said she had been pro-surrogacy, but what had changed her mind was her decision to adopt a child. She said she came to realize how wonderful adoption could be and, also, the strength of her maternal bond. She said that Mary Beth Whitehead simply couldn't have known in advance how hard it would be to give up her baby. A tear welled in her eye—an involuntary but convincing denunciation of everything we had been taught all year about the primacy of logic over emotion in legal thinking.

The bridges were for me a hopeful sign that law school after the first year might be more interesting, once the required courses were out of the way. At Harvard, second- and third-year students are generally free to choose their subjects. There are, however, a couple of guidelines: two credits must go toward a course in legal ethics and professional responsibility, and the faculty "recommends" that students take Taxation, Corporations, Constitutional Law, Evidence, and Accounting. I don't know exactly how many students end up taking most or all of these courses but my guess is that it exceeds 95 percent. As the realization set in that second year would be, *de facto*, as structured as first, I grew despondent and then defiant. I would take my stand! I would not be railroaded! I would refuse to take Accounting! I asked a fellow rebel, Wilson Gore, to pledge that neither of us would take Accounting. Wilson refused, which made me wonder, would my legal education be deficient without Accounting?

In the latter part of the first year, Harvard organized a Course

Selection Advice Fair, where students could get tips from practicing lawyers and judges on which courses to choose. One judge told me to take all the basics. I knew that was what the corporate attorneys would tell me. Yearning for support in my rebellion, I set out to the public-interest table. "Do I really need to take Accounting?" I asked.

"Well, it's not a bad idea" was the response, "even for a public-interest lawyer, because you might need to evaluate the financial statements of a corporation you are suing."

For a final reality check, I went to see my academic advisor, Phil Heymann. Heymann looked over my list: Constitutional Law, Evidence, Taxation, Corporations—and, yes—Accounting, plus a few interesting courses, a First Amendment course, a Poverty Law course, and a seminar on Dickens and the Law. Heymann approved of my selections, which he deemed "conservative." It was not the adjective I wanted to hear. But he was right: my courses, and the course offerings as a whole, were overwhelmingly geared toward business or corporate law. And the danger was that, once trained, I would feel comfortable practicing this type, and only this type, of law.

But before I could fully concentrate on second year, I had one major first-year hurdle to jump: the Ames Moot Court competition. The process had begun back in November, when the Board of Student Advisors (BSA) got the whole class together to announce how Ames would work. Students would form groups of four— two teams of two—and would prepare opposite sides of a given case. (There were more than a dozen cases to choose from.) The teams, with the help of a 2L or 3L BSA member, would prepare briefs and oral arguments, culminating in a live argument before a panel of three judges.

There was, for the next several months, a certain degree of uneasiness, not unlike that associated with the senior prom. Who would ask whom to be partners? And what if you asked a friend who'd already paired off with someone else? Luckily, Seth Rubenstein asked me to join him and Fred Pynchon, so I was spared the humiliation of being spurned. But still, we had to find a fourth. I suggested Wilson Gore, to whom I turned more and more often to commiserate about the state of Harvard Law School. Seth disapproved of the idea. Wilson had been called on in class a few times and had proven unable to answer. In the end, we couldn't find a fourth, so a "floater" from another section was assigned to our team. His name was Jonathan Hush, a nice enough fellow who was quiet and, like me, simply didn't care about Ames. Everyone else, it seemed, took Ames very seriously. When the BSA moved up the deadlines for when some argument outlines were due, it provoked a full-scale petition drive. The intensity of Ames got people who normally don't sign petitions to sign this one, including my roommate.

My group chose a torts case. Jonathan and I represented plaintiffs suing a nonprofit fertilizer company for polluting their water with a carcinogenic chemical. I was to argue that, even though the company was not negligent, it should have to pay damages under a theory of "strict liability." The case was tricky, because the fertilizer company had a practice of donating 70 percent of its product to the Third World and thereby saved thousands of starving Africans every year. Applying strict liability would probably drive the company out of business, so the issue was Third World lives vs. our thirty plaintiffs likely to contract leukemia. It was thus a much more philosophically complex case than the real one in Woburn, Massachusetts, upon which our case was modeled. A rights-based Kantian theory would say you can't "use" the local residents in order to save even a large number of lives elsewhere. A utilitarian theory would say that since more lives are saved than sacrificed, the company must continue to produce fertilizer, thus ruling out strict liability. I argued for a middle ground, a mixture of fairness and efficiency, where harmful activity may continue if it benefits, on balance, those who are asked to suffer—i.e., the local residents of Ames.

The case was interesting, then, but not overly so. Seth and Fred thought otherwise. On February 17, the four of us met with our student advisor, Lori Johnson, for our Issues Conference in Austin North. Maybe Seth and Fred really cared deeply about the case. Maybe they had crushes on Lori. Whatever the reason, it was a meeting that would not end. A week later, after we turned in our analyses of the issues, we returned for an even longer session, this time because some male egos couldn't handle Lori's criticism. Jonathan and I looked at each other, eyes rolling. Who really cared? There were two more of these meetings, until finally, on March

13, we turned in our briefs. A BSA member was checking and noting whether briefs were turned in even one minute past the 5:00 p.m. deadline.

Lori suggested that we watch some other students argue our case before the night of our own oral argument. One of the judges was Charles Nesson, who had, in real life, argued the Woburn case. I cringed as he peppered a poor student with questions about facts outside the parameters of the case we were given to argue.

Two nights later, we were up. We didn't argue against Seth and Fred but, instead, against two of the more quiet and passive individuals from my section. I wondered whether this was planned. Put all the shy, quiet shrinking violets together so no one would get hurt. Our judges were a lawyer, a real judge, and a student. I was very nervous and asked Rebecca not to come. Jonathan was ashen and our opponents looked even worse. The defendant's counsel started out, his voice shaking. I went up to the podium, delivered my statement without any gross errors, and even got a laugh when I said that to save Third World lives at the expense of local Ames residents was what Dickens called "telescopic philanthropy." But I, like the student two nights earlier, was a victim of an examiner who didn't know the rules. The lawyer, Mr. Hoar (of Boston's Goodwin, Procter & Hoar), began asking me to discuss cases never cited in either brief. Maybe he was just testing to see how I reacted under pressure. None of the judges seemed to like my brief. They were particularly upset that I had cited Kant. "The court decides cases, not philosophy," the student judge snapped. Jonathan loved it. He said the lawyers he had worked with in New York didn't even know who Kant was. I wasn't trying to impress anyone. I was just much more interested in discussing what the law ought to be than what it is.

After Ames, it became clear to me, for the first time, that I might not ever want to practice law. Ames was all litigation—to me the most interesting aspect of legal practice—but I had not fallen in love with it the way Seth and Fred had. They had grown obsessed with Ames, as had other students. People had missed classes and had cared enough to cheat by consciously distorting cases and exceeding the page limit. You couldn't blame it on grades, for Ames involved no grades. It might be attributed to compulsive competitiveness, but that was not the whole story. I have a hunch that

Seth and Fred, and dozens of other Harvard Law students, dove into Ames because they loved the law. I didn't, and my grades seemed to suggest that the law didn't love me either.

I found myself increasingly interested in other things—like my fiancée. I ceased having lunch in the Hark with my classmates and, instead, ate lunch at home and talked to Rebecca on the telephone at work. As our August wedding date approached, we became more and more excited about the reality of marriage. Arthur agreed to move in with some friends from his study group, and Rebecca and I began planning how we would redecorate the apartment. In May, we met with Anne and Marty Peretz, whom we knew from college, to discuss interfaith marriage. Marty shared with us a wonderful passage from the book of Ruth—"Your people shall be my people"—which we used in our wedding. For spring break, Rebecca and I flew to Tucson to get as far away from HLS as possible. Most of my classmates used the week to pick up the slack from Ames, but I didn't bring a single book.

In mid-spring, I hurt my back playing squash. I was bedridden for some time, and later missed classes to attend physical-therapy sessions. I resigned myself to the pain; both my parents had back trouble and I figured it was preordained. But a 2L friend told me he'd seen it happen in a dozen of his classmates. Part of the problem was that law students carry around lots of very heavy books. I had an enormous hiker's backpack, complete with a waist belt to distribute the weight, filled to the top with Contracts and Torts and Civil Procedure texts. Part of it was sitting and studying all the time, without getting up. But I am convinced that most of it was stress, the tie that binds law students. Later, when I spent a summer at a Boston law firm, I discovered that dozens of the attorneys had bad backs, dating since their law school days and continuing on in the glorious practice of law.

Despite my bad back, I put in a good-faith effort preparing for finals. I studied especially hard for Edley's Ad Law exam with my friend Paul, and felt as though the exam went well. For the other courses, I got back together with my old study group—Seth, Fred, and Ruth—though I wondered why they still wanted to work with me.

Minow's exam in Civ Pro, on May 27, was a nightmare. It involved an enormous, open-ended question for which I was utterly unprepared. I tried answering the question six or seven different ways. I looked around in a panic. I was shaking uncontrollably. The student next to me was calmly writing neat paragraphs. But there were several stricken faces. Minow had included a *New Yorker* cartoon on the back page of the exam. It was supposed to relax us, the way her asking me where I lived was supposed to relax me the first day of class, but again the effort failed. If ever there was an exam I should have flunked, it was this one.

Minow gave me a B. Edley, whose exam I thought I'd aced, whose every case I had read, gave me a B+. The conventional wisdom was right: the difference between killing yourself and blowing off an exam was a half grade.

My Property exam was eminently forgettable, and my Contracts exam with Dalton was, as I have said, disturbing. The exam itself was no more distressing than the feeling I had at 4:30 as I handed it in. I felt the mixed emotions you always feel at the marking of a personal milestone, but my mixed emotions were very different from those I had felt at the end of each college year. My sorrow stemmed not from the fact that the first year was over but from a sense of lost opportunity. I felt more relief at having completed an unpleasant task than any real sense of accomplishment. I felt as though I had grown some intellectually—I had learned how to spot circular reasoning and how to see when an argument proves too much. But I also knew my classes seemed to be dulling my idealism and passion for justice. As an undergraduate, I had always had a certain awe for the law school north of the Yard. And now I had the unpleasant sensation, much what a child experiences when she realizes her parents aren't always right, that the Harvard Law School might not, in fact, leave its first-year students at the end of the year better off than when they came.

4

Summer Fun

For nearly half of the 1L class, the first year did not really end when we handed in our last exams on June 1. After one day of rest, about two hundred of us dove back into the law as we began the week-long competition to make Law Review.

To the layman, the *Harvard Law Review* is a periodical containing scholarly legal articles written generally by law professors and judges. But to the legal community, the *Harvard Law Review* represents the most highly prized of merit badges. A friend of mine who was chosen as an editor the previous year told me that once you make Law Review, suddenly everyone wants you. From then on, law firms clamor, the most prestigious judges compete for you. And if the Johnnie Walker ad is to be believed, Law Review membership attracts the opposite sex. ("She Was Law Review. *And* she drinks Johnnie Walker.") Another friend of mine, not on Law Review, told me that the quality of your second and third years is determined entirely by whether or not you are an "editor" (all members are editors). If you are, professors, who were themselves Review editors, invite you to their dinner parties and you have wonderful intellectual encounters; but if you are among the more than 90 percent of the class not on the Review, you're ignored. Joel Seligman, author of *The High Citadel: The Influence of Harvard Law School*, compared the obsession with getting the grades required for Law Review to "Gatsby's distant dim green lights."

Somehow, it is generally known among the law school population who, in fact, made Law Review. Unlike Phi Beta Kappa, whose members meet once, at the time of graduation, the Review is an all-encompassing extracurricular activity with its own building, Gannett House. Perhaps the greatest tribute to the Law Review's prestige is the way the rejected 2Ls and 3Ls scorn it—with the same envy that students turned down by Harvard Law School say that name schools are overrated. When I toured HLS in college, the 2L guide told us that the only reason Law Review students got offers from the best firms was that Review editors were known as a bunch of drones willing to put in long hours doing scut work. When it came time for 1Ls to decide whether or not to compete for the Review, a number of 2Ls and 3Ls took to wearing T-shirts that read *Make Love, not Law Review*. Moreover, Law Review stays with you throughout your life. When you get married, and when you die, *The New York Times* includes your Law Review membership in its article.

Given my first-semester grades, Law Review should probably have been a distant thought. But with my 1L mentality, my average grades made it even more imperative that I make Law Review. Only this honor could save me from mediocrity. And I wasn't yet ready to count myself out.

In the old days, grades were the sole criterion for making the Review. But by the early 1970s, there was a sense that since the Review was a journal, it might make sense to conduct a writing competition. By my year, the Law Review had developed a complex formula for selection. Half the Review editors got on by their writing alone. The other half got on by virtue of grades and writing, with grades weighted 70 percent and writing 30 percent. The writing competition consists of subciting a professor's article and writing an original case note.

I figured there had to be a trick to doing well on the writing competition, so I went to the basement of Langdell Library and looked up old *Harvard Law Review* articles to see the style in which case comments were written. When the Review set up a program in which the editors were made available to advise 1Ls on the writing competition, I met with Bill Samuelson, a 3L member, in hopes of getting an edge. I asked him a slew of questions about how I should approach the competition. He didn't answer any of them and viewed me with suspicion. He didn't realize that, out of desperation, I was preparing for the competition instead of studying for exams. I was convinced that I could still do great things, even with my average grades, if only I made Law Review. I asked Bill what he liked about the Review, and he said that it brightens your future—and what could be more enjoyable than thinking about one's own bright future.

On June 3, the games began. I joined the long line of two hundred 1Ls to pick up the 650-page packet containing the article to be subcited, the information for the case note, and all the relevant cases. The packet also contained the rules, including an annoying prohibition against the use of computers. This rule might have made sense a few years earlier, when computers would give an unfair advantage to the wealthy, but now that most students owned computers, or had access to them, it was just a stupid, hyper-egalitarian, unenforceable rule. I went out and rented a typewriter.

The packet also included an "affirmative-action personal statement form." The *Harvard Law Review*'s affirmative-action program has been extremely controversial since its implementation in the early 1980s. Even some liberals expressed outrage at an affirmative-action plan which originally included stated quotas. "When an institution that has always defined and upheld merit for an entire profession shrinks from the burden," wrote *The New York Times*, "it sends an unwelcome message through the entire society." William T. Coleman, Jr., one of the first blacks elected to the *Harvard Law Review*, said, "The *Review* is something that must be based entirely on merit, and I would have problems with any program that varies from that." Indeed, Harvard Law School—and its Review—were supposed to symbolize merit in its purest form. Getting in was based on grades and LSATs more than geography or character. Excellence, divorced from class and ethnicity, was the touchstone. The *Harvard Law Review* was the law school's meritocratic answer to Harvard College's aristocratic final clubs. But now the Review said certain ethnic origins would be favored, albeit not the traditional ones.

I was supposed to be for affirmative action—and always had been. In high school and college, I had heard all the arguments about meritocracy and the irrelevance of race, but I ultimately thought that the country had to go through a transition period, to exorcise our nation's history of slavery and segregation, before we could apply the pure meritocratic ideal. But as I stood in line waiting for my Law Review packet, I felt anxious and found myself half resenting the minorities who queued up along with me. For the moment, I forgot that by being white I had benefited from formal, and informal, "affirmative action" over a number of generations. I just felt frustrated.

The piece we were given to subcite involved "wrongful birth actions," suits brought by parents of disabled infants against healthcare providers for failure to notify them that the fetus might be deformed. The article argued that laws prohibiting the action were an unconstitutional infringement on the right to abortion. I took a standard liberal line, in part because that was me and in part because a 2L had told me there was an ideological bias in the grading. The case comment, which we were to write, involved an analysis of *Pennsylvania v. Ritchie*, a case which pits the rights of the defendant to put forward exculpatory evidence against the need for keeping confidential certain state agency child-abuse documents. There was, with this case, no clear "liberal" answer.

Although both cases were interesting, it was June, the weather was beautiful, we had just finished exams, and so I had trouble sticking with the work. I scheduled daily tennis matches with a good friend from college and fellow 1L, George Alexander. We told ourselves that exercise would sharpen our minds for the competition. Arthur moved out of our apartment to one that was air-conditioned, and for several days I didn't see him. (Arthur had toyed with the idea of not trying out for Law Review at all. He was so serious that his father recruited me to talk him out of such nonsense. But now that he had made the plunge, there was no stopping him.)

After several days, George dropped out, saying the process was absurd (which, of course, it was). Here we were, killing ourselves in the week following exams, trying to earn the right to spend the next two years voluntarily fact-checking sloppily written pieces by authors who knew someone else would clean their work up. And we competed for this right with the full knowledge that the chances of success were infinitesimal. Of the two hundred people who tried out, about thirty were really in the running for the twenty GPA slots, while the other 170 were aiming for the twenty slots left over. George said it was especially difficult for a white male to compete for one of the write-on spots. It turned out that he was half right. Contrary to popular wisdom, there was no affirmative action for women. But clearly some of the write-on slots were going to go to minorities who wouldn't have otherwise qualified. Facing that fact squarely clouded my thinking about affirmative action. When I tried to think about it at a theoretical level, I found the moral imperative to remedy certain historical wrongs powerful. But, in practice, I found that affirmative action could breed a certain amount of gut-level resentment, even among those liberals—like George and me—who, on an intellectual level, favored preferential treatment.

Although logic was not on my side, I persevered with the Law Review competition and, on June 11, handed in my subcite and case note. It took some time for the Law Review editors to complete examination of our applications for membership. By mid-July, I heard a rumor that the Review had made its decisions, and I called up Arthur and said, "Well, I assume you made it."

"Yes, did you make it, too?"

I gulped hard. "I haven't heard yet."

"Oh."

The rejection letter, dated July 20, arrived a few days later. It was frustratingly curt. There was, of course, no explanation provided, just this form letter that didn't let you know if you were next on the rung, had just barely missed out, or never had a prayer. More than one hundred identical letters were being opened that day by people who, until then, hadn't experienced much rejection in their lives—but it still seemed as though everyone I knew had gotten on. Arthur's 1L study group became the talk of the law school: of five members, four competed for the Review and three made it.

With the selection of Law Review editors, life changed. We had all come in as equals in September, equally afraid of whether we would do well in the law. The first day, we had heard Justices Blackmun and Brennan speak and there was the shared feeling that any of us might one day be clerking in their chambers, helping draft important Supreme Court opinions. But now we were on entirely different tracks. The Law Review editors would be invited to the dinner parties, have a chance to clerk for the Supreme Court, feel the exhilaration of having the world at their doorsteps. For

most of us, though, our haunting feelings of inadequacy had simply
been validated.

On Monday, June 15, just four days after the Law Review competition, I boarded the 7:20 a.m. Ridgewood, New Jersey, train to
Manhattan for my first day on the job at the U.S. Attorney's Office
for the Southern District of New York. I was commuting to work,
like any other adult, wearing my suit and carrying my briefcase.
Of course, most of them weren't commuting with their mothers
(Mom worked close to my new office), but this didn't lessen the
maturity of it all. Mom and I were going in as equals, workers in
the great professional New York City labor force.

I was going to the greatest prosecutor's office in the country, now
run by a vibrant, energetic, forty-two-year-old U.S. Attorney who,
in a recent *New York* magazine cover story, had sounded more like
a Democrat than a Reagan-appointed Republican. Rudolph Giuliani
had told the reporter that he had thought of becoming a doctor or
a priest before deciding on law. "I wanted to do something that
made me feel like I was helping people. It's important to me to feel
that I'm doing something bigger than just supporting myself. It's
one of the reasons—when I was in private practice—I wanted to
go back into public service." Giuliani had, in fact, been a Democrat,
and an admirer of John and Robert Kennedy, until George
McGovern's candidacy drove him into the Republican Party.

Giuliani talked about insider trading in a way that resonated with
my feelings. I had always agreed with C. S. Lewis's remark that
much of our crime is committed by men in dark suits with clean
fingernails. But Giuliani went further, pointing out that the inside
traders possessed, in a sense, a higher degree of moral culpability
than other criminals.

I understand why—when somebody put $1,000 in a detective's
hand and said, "This is your take from the arrest"—that was
tempting to him, especially when he explained his feelings that
first night. He drove home not knowing whether to give the
money back or bring it home because he and his wife were
trying to figure out how to get two or three thousand dollars
as a down payment on a little house on Long Island. And here

he had the down payment in his hand, plus some dollars for
the kids. I can understand how those things tempt a human
being and he falls. What I do not understand is how a guy
who's already got a million dollars defrauds for another
hundred thousand or trades information so his firm can make
another $3 million instead of $2 million.

These were my feelings exactly, which was why I was especially
excited about the insider-trading prosecutions that he was then
pursuing. Giuliani was responsible for the highly publicized prosecutions of Dennis Levine and Ivan Boesky, and I hoped to get
involved in some of the new cases being brought. For the moment
I had been assigned to the chief of the Civil Rights Unit, Peter
Roth. Fred Simpson had told me it was a "plum position," so I
had decided to give it a chance.

When I arrived that morning at the office, Peter had not yet come
in. I was given some forms to fill out and told that he would arrive
soon. I was somewhat startled that there were yet more forms. I
had already been through "form hell" and could not imagine how
the U.S. Attorney's Office could possibly need any more information. I had spent much of the spring semester filling out Department of Justice materials. I had had my fingerprints taken by
the Harvard police and filled out the notorious Standard Form 86
(Security Investigation Data for Sensitive Position), which required
a listing of all roommates for the past five years (including their
present addresses, telephone numbers, and dates of birth), dates
and places of residence going back to 1937, all employment supervisors since high school, and all foreign countries visited since 1930.

Today's form was much less intimidating and I finished it
quickly. There was still no sign of Peter. I took out my *New York
Times* and began reading. A little later, in walked a bespectacled,
white, slightly balding, slightly overweight, sweating man. Peter
introduced himself, wiping his brow. He said I could share his
corner office and his phone and use a side table as a desk. I hadn't
realized that I would not have an office of my own. But, as it turned
out, I was somewhat lucky. Most interns had to work out of the
library. Peter gave me the secrecy speech and told me what a
sensitive position I was in. Then he asked me to make him some
tea.

Peter told me the first day that I would be his shadow. I would go with him to court, help him prepare indictments, meet with judges, investigate civil rights complaints. But much of the first week I found myself making photocopies and filing and was told by the other interns that I was fortunate not to have been stuck transcribing inaudible electronic surveillance. My one substantive project was to check the footnotes in a document used in the decision not to prosecute the white police officer who shot Eleanor Bumpers, a black grandmother.

And then, after one week, the man I was to shadow was off for a week's vacation. Peter painted this as a great opportunity. I would be manning the office of the chief of the Civil Rights Unit in the greatest prosecutor's office in the country—maybe even on the planet. He gave me an enormous pile of backlogged complaints which needed to be looked through to determine which were important enough to investigate further. These were all low-priority cases which had failed the rather disturbing test of urgency: the complainer hadn't called back. The wisdom was that if they didn't follow up, it couldn't be all that serious. The assignment was tedious, eye-glazing work, and after one day I was going crazy.

One evening that week, I attended a Harvard Law School alumni reception at Sotheby's. I walked down toward Wall Street to pick up Arthur in his office at Fried, Frank. He had a real desk, and a phone, and pleasant secretaries, and a view of the Statue of Liberty. And he was earning $1,200 a week more than I was. At the reception my classmates who were at law firms were not particularly thrilled with their work either, but at least they were being handsomely paid for their boredom.

I took the following day off to interview Mario Cuomo, whom I saw as a politician capable of forging the same coalition of working whites and blacks that Robert Kennedy had succeeded in uniting. I drove up to Albany in the morning and arrived in plenty of time for my 4:00 interview. As Marty Steadman, an advisor to the Governor, guided me past a row of secretaries into Cuomo's chambers, I felt dizzy. I had only a handful of heroes—R.F.K., Nader, Hubert Humphrey—and I was about to meet one in person. Seeing Cuomo was reassuring in the same way that hearing Nader was. They both spoke the old truths on which I was raised—that with privilege comes obligation and that we all need to look beyond our own narrow circumstances. I talked with Cuomo about Kennedy and class in America, and he conceded that affirmative action based on economics might make more sense than on race, although he said the former was politically impossible. At the end of the interview, Cuomo ribbed me about working for Giuliani—another intellectual, Italian, Catholic lawyer—whom he clearly saw as a rival. "Why are you working for Giuliani?" Cuomo asked. "You want to lock people up?" I knew he was kidding. Cuomo had for years been saying that Democrats needed to be tough on crime because our constituents were the chief victims. But Cuomo's words managed to touch something else that had been gnawing away at me. In Rudolph Giuliani's shop, you could try only one case at a time. A prosecutor could try to shape public policy by focusing resources on certain crimes, but in the end he was supposed to enforce the laws drafted by other people.

But if the U.S. Attorney's task was ultimately limited, his impact on individual lives was very real. When Peter returned the following week, things got moving on our case against a Rikers Island prison guard accused of violating the rights of inmates during a prison uprising. On July 2, Peter won a grand jury indictment. At 2:00 p.m., Giuliani and Peter held a press conference announcing the indictment. Giuliani kept mispronouncing the guard's name, Knutsen—emphasizing the silent K. It was a big press event and I felt a little sorry for Knutsen, who had a horrible job and, yes, may have gotten out of hand during the prison riot but had probably been terrified with all those wild prisoners. The next day Knutsen appeared in court for his arraignment with what appeared to be his family, and I realized how very tough the prosecutor's job is, how very sure you have to be that the defendant is guilty.

Most assistant U.S. attorneys seemed to deal with the weighty responsibility of their jobs with bravado. Day after day, I watched otherwise wimpy Ivy League attorneys attempt to appear tough. Peter had gone to Williams College and Yale Law, but when we called in a tough witness it was as if Peter had grown up in a prison—everything was "fucking" and "bullshit." And then they'd leave and Peter would talk about how he wanted to go home and play with his three-year-old daughter. Bruce Baird was a wiry, mild-mannered lawyer, but as he began describing his prosecution of the Colombo family, he was transformed into a table-pounding hard ass.

The afternoon of the Knutsen arraignment our weekly intern lunch featured John Carroll, an assistant U.S. attorney who had prosecuted an international heroin ring operating in the United States dubbed "French Connection II." Carroll passed out a *Newsweek* cover story from April 13, 1987, entitled "The Return of the French Connection." The article, written in dramatic prose, painted Carroll in an extremely favorable light, as part of "the best and the brightest" in Giuliani's office. The trial was described as "Frazier v. Ali in pinstripes." Apparently Carroll had begun to believe all this bloated rhetoric. When an intern asked how the Southern District office got jurisdiction over the case he said the office was the best in the country. "We don't go home at 6:00," he said proudly. (Early on, Peter had told me how tough it was to get a job in Rudolph Giuliani's office: "We have rejected people from Cravath," he said, referring to New York's top private firm.)

And yet, for all the status associated with being an assistant U.S. attorney in the Southern District, you weren't supposed to stay too long. "Otherwise you become a 'government attorney,' " Peter said. God forbid. For most attorneys, public service was a pit stop. Some, like Fred Simpson, said it would launch a litigation career in private practice. ("Work for a law firm for $1,200 a week and make your wife happy.") For others, like Peter, the U.S. Attorney's Office was largely a credential, like his editorship at the *Yale Law Journal* and clerkship in the Second Circuit, which would help him get a professorship at a top university.

There were a few exceptions to the way-station rule. In mid-July, the intern lunch guest was an eight-year veteran, Charles Carberry, who was prosecuting insider traders. *Newsweek* had also done a long piece on this fat, balding powerhouse. He was said to have a brilliant mind, which worked twenty hours a day, and was unique for not having sold out, even though he could easily quadruple his salary as a white-collar defense attorney.

I had never managed to wriggle into his program, and seeing him now reminded me about my disappointments with the summer. That morning, I had had "library duty" and was required to re-shelve all the books. Just because we weren't being paid didn't mean we got more responsibility. Money wasn't supposed to matter, but as the summer didn't match interns' expectations, the issue of re-muneration became a constant topic. When it was learned that the few black summer interns were being paid, all hell broke loose.

The black interns were paid out of a private fund established by those who thought a city with a large black population should have at least a few black assistant U.S. attorneys. A number of white interns were outraged, and argued that any fellowships should be based on class not race, which was precisely my argument to Cuomo: far from being politically impossible, class-based affirmative action might achieve the widespread political support that preferential treatment for blacks never has or will.

One of the highlights of the summer was supposed to be the "Lunch with Rudy" in the eighth-floor library. My group's was on August 6. Giuliani walked in and smiled to the ten of us, said he had already eaten lunch but was glad to entertain any questions we had. The questions flowed out, mostly from a few of the more vocal interns. The discussion was marred by the typical "Student–Big Name lunch problem": heads nodding in sycophantic unison; nervous, forced laughter at jokes that are not particularly funny. I had seen it when I'd interned for Senator William Proxmire and he took the summer interns to lunch and when Harvard president Derek Bok would come to a North House cocktail party in my undergraduate days. But this was the worst. One woman from NYU Law School gushed, "What's your favorite opera?" Someone asked Giuliani about his political ambitions, and he said New York politics were like those in Moscow and gave as his example Mario Cuomo's heavy-handed purging of the hapless Abe Hirschfeld, a candidate for lieutenant governor. The tone in his voice was similar to the tone Cuomo had used when referring to Giuliani. Giuliani ended the period by asking, "Don't you want to know how to become an assistant U.S. attorney?" No one had asked.

As the summer began to wind down, Peter invited Rebecca and me to dinner at his West 67th Street apartment. It was good to see Peter relaxed with his wife and kids, his cynicism set aside. I asked him how he had felt when Giuliani appointed him chief of the Civil Rights Unit. Peter sighed, nodded his head, smiled, and said he was thrilled. "That's, like, why I went to law school."

PART II

Two L

CHAPTER

5

Liberal Chic

I returned to Cambridge in September of 1987 with the renewed confidence of a second-year student—a confidence not in my academic ability but in knowing I had survived the worst: the first year. I was also buoyed by my two-and-a-half-week-old marriage —still astounded at how lucky I was to have found someone with whom I wanted to share a life and who wanted to do so with me! I wore my ring proudly on the first day back, and when I saw my friend Greg Jenkins, who had been engaged the previous spring, I rushed up to him, flashed my ring, and said, "It's a great life, huh?" Greg swallowed hard and mumbled that his fiancée had gotten cold feet. It turned out that the other engaged person in our old orientation group had not gone through with his wedding either. This is not what statisticians would call a "representative sample," but it still gave me reason to pause. *One L* had warned this would happen, that law school would put a severe strain on personal relationships.

To affirm my wedding vows, my first act as a married second-year law student was to resign from the Harvard Legal Aid Bureau, which I'd signed up to work with at the end of first year. The student-run bureau, which provides legal services to indigent clients, required a twenty-hour-a-week commitment. Over the summer, I had grown less enthusiastic about the bureau. I wasn't very good at the public speaking which litigation requires. Nor did I enjoy it. In addition, I had come to realize that poverty law was essentially social work and, as such, couldn't change the world (although it might for particular clients). I had also started to work on this book, which made its own demands on my time. I could juggle family, law school, and the book, but I didn't feel I could do more. I didn't feel particularly good about myself for passing up the bureau, and it made me realize that my drive to do public-service work had as much to do with my *interests* (public policy) as my *values* (wanting to make life more fair). But I remained committed to working on the same side as the poverty lawyers—for the Democrats—even if I didn't have their level of professional dedication.

My semester schedule was a hodgepodge of the exhilarating and the obligatory. I was excited about taking Larry Tribe's Constitutional Law and Anthony Lewis's First Amendment classes, both for the content of those courses and for the professors. More obligatory was Accounting for Lawyers and Evidence, a trial lawyer's course on what can and cannot be admitted in court.

My Evidence class, which met at 8:30 in the morning, was taught by Charles Nesson, someone Joy said I should get to know. Nesson was a mainstream liberal who was involved in civil rights and had defended Daniel Ellsberg, the procurer of the Pentagon Papers. Nesson was decidedly not a radical. When the CLS dispute had peaked earlier in the decade, it was Nesson who had attempted to play peacemaker, urging an end to open warfare. And no one would call him a bohemian. In the semester's first issue of the student newsletter, *The Advisor*, Nesson placed the following notice:

STUDENT WITH AN AUTOMOBILE: Prof. Nesson's ten-year-old daughter takes riding lessons in Concord three days a week. He would like to find a responsible person to pick her up at school (3:15 p.m.), take her to Concord (a 25–30 minute ride), wait for an hour or so, then return to Cambridge. Expenses plus $25 per trip.

The ad ran for several weeks. I never found out whether he got his daughter's well-educated chauffeur. Nesson's fondness for the good life was unwittingly documented in a *New York Times Magazine* story on how to give dinner parties, which contained a picture of

Nesson's familiar face enjoying what appeared to be an especially lavish evening.

Nesson was rumored (along with others) to have graduated from Harvard Law School with the highest grade-point average since Felix Frankfurter's. This morning, Nesson appeared nimble, especially given the hour. He set out what would be the key theme of his course: the "acceptability" theory, which holds that judges are above all concerned that their judgment be "acceptable" to society. Thus, the judiciary is in fact much more democratic than it at first appears. Nesson used the story of King Solomon's judgment to illustrate his theory. In the legendary dispute between two women, both claiming to be an infant's mother, King Solomon declares the true mother to be the one who urges him not to cut the baby in half. From a logical standpoint, Solomon's test only proved who was the *best caretaker*. The test did nothing to say who was the true *biological mother*. And yet Solomon could not openly say that he was just looking out for the best interests of the child (even though that is precisely what he was doing), because that would open up the competition to any number of people who would claim to be the best caretaker. So Solomon framed his decision in terms that were more acceptable to society—that he had found the true mother. I came away thinking Nesson was kind of neat—he had a new idea.

Next, it was off to Accounting class, which was, well, less cerebral. Professor Donald Trautman, speaking to a class of two hundred or more, said, in a weary, knowing voice, that we should either read the text or come to class. My friend George and I looked at each other. We were out the door, never to return.

At 4:00 p.m., I went to the first meeting of Anthony Lewis's class on Freedom of the Press. When Lewis walked in, I smiled to myself. Lewis was, quite simply, part of the reason I wanted to come to Harvard Law School, and his book *Gideon's Trumpet* was part of the reason I wanted to become a lawyer. The book tells the story surrounding the 1963 Supreme Court case *Gideon v. Wainright*, which established the right of indigent defendants to be represented by an attorney. When I read it in high school I was spellbound by this portrait of law as ennobling and Supreme Court Justices as dispensers of justice. Lewis's columns in *The New York Times* were eloquent, forceful, and compassionate, written with a level of passion impossible for mushy centrist commentators to muster. I was especially intrigued by him because he had successfully combined the world of law and letters in the great tradition of Dickens, Tocqueville, and Kafka.

While Lewis has a legal background—he attended law classes for one year—as he began to speak it became clear that he was different from most law professors. He was more anecdotal and historical, less concerned with hard-line doctrine. A sizable number of the students were not from the law school: many were journalists studying at Harvard as Nieman Fellows, and several others were Kennedy School of Government students. As Lewis opened up for discussion the first case, *New York Times v. Sullivan*, it became easy to spot the law students. A distinct law school style came through in the way questions were posed and issues framed. It was one of sharp, clear thinking. But "thinking like a lawyer" was also, in practice, being impatient with history, or with things not directly on point, or with error. The law students appeared arrogant, even in a room of journalists.

There was an immediacy to Lewis's discussion of *New York Times v. Sullivan*. He said he had covered the case as a reporter, and he talked a great deal about its historical context and, in particular, the importance of the Northern press being able to cover racial events in the South. The case involved a $500,000 libel judgment handed down by a Southern jury not fond of Northern newspapers—a penalty which, along with other similar verdicts, could have literally driven the *Times* out of business. Lewis added that *Times* attorney Herbert Wechsler had to pitch his case carefully to get the votes. Although Justice Black defended the press to the end, he had no love for the *Times*, which, at the time of his confirmation, noted his youthful membership in the KKK and questioned whether his white robe would show through the black one. In all, Lewis presented the case with a journalist's eye to detail that went far beyond the legal standard of libel for which the case stood.

Larry Tribe's Constitutional Law course the next morning had its own electricity. Tribe was an interesting character: a math major and "debate nerd" in college, he had blossomed after law school into the nation's most celebrated liberal professor of constitutional law. He was very tied into politics, public policy, and the press. (During the semester, for example, he was working with Professors

Freund, Cox, and Heymann on an *amicus* brief for Common Cause in favor of the Iran-contra independent counsel.) This morning, he announced that he would deviate from the Socratic method in favor of lecturing. In most of our courses, professors had used the Socratic method as a stick to prod students to do the reading, but Tribe knew that he could rely on the inherently interesting subject matter—and his own enthusiasm for it—as a carrot. I was thrilled: maybe this course would be like the ones in college where you looked forward to class, to an entertaining professor, and to a subject you freely chose on your own—with absolutely no terror in the heart.

Moreover, we were fortunate that, in the fall of 1987, Constitutional Law went public when Ronald Reagan nominated D.C. circuit judge Robert Bork to the Supreme Court. For perhaps the first time in American history, negative ads were run against a Supreme Court nominee. Although Bork's intellectual abilities were acknowledged, his right-wing views on civil rights and civil liberties made many people nervous. Tribe was leading the charge to defeat him and was more than willing to share the inside gossip with us. At the end of the first week of classes, there was Tribe, on ABC's *This Week with David Brinkley*, discussing the Bork nomination with big-time journalists. Three days later, he was back with us, spending the first half hour of class talking about Bork. Bork had defended his opposition to the Supreme Court decision in *Shelley v. Kramer* by saying, "Even Professor Tribe" disagrees with *Shelley*. Tribe told us he had, in fact, criticized the Court's reasoning in *Shelley*, but not the result. The next week, Tribe was in Washington testifying against Bork before the Senate Judiciary Committee; and the next day, he was back, telling us that Wyoming senator Alan Simpson's criticism—that Tribe had supported Ted Kennedy in the past—was "a rather moot point." Tribe said the comparison of Bork and the literal-minded Justice Black was off base, and that two former Black clerks would be testifying to that effect. After Justice Burger testified in favor of Bork, Tribe jibed that the Robert Bork of which the former Chief Justice spoke "may or may not have had points of tangency with the real Robert Bork." It was all wonderful insider stuff that made Constitutional Law come alive for us.

In late September, the student body got into the act and held a

Bork "teach-in." Langdell North Middle was packed with more than five hundred students, even though the recruitment season had just begun. The statistics said that about 475 of us would be working in corporate firms the following summer and that was obvious. The teach-in was orderly, subdued, and responsible. The student speakers wore suits. They calmly argued that Bork's problem was that he saw the world in abstract, intellectual terms, with no grounding in social reality, a criticism that dates back to Oliver Wendell Holmes's famous declaration "The life of the law has not been logic; it has been experience." An anti-Bork petition was organized, a document which would, in the end, garner more than 950 HLS student signatures. The liberals spoke—Richard Parker, Alan Dershowitz, Randall Kennedy, and, from my 1L section, Martha Minow and Frank Michelman. Tribe and Professor Kathleen Sullivan had gone down to Washington to testify. Where, I wondered, were the hard-core crits? Where were Duncan Kennedy, Roberto Unger, Clare Dalton, and Mort Horwitz? While the liberals were out fighting, Duncan Kennedy was busy writing dense pieces for publications like the *Buffalo Law Review*, pages few people read and even fewer understood.

I had to leave the teach-in early to go to class, and as I left I ran into James Parks, the conservative from first year.

"Are you spying here?" I asked.

He grinned.

"They said conservatives were welcome to speak their mind," I said.

"Let's see how strongly they feel about free speech when Calero comes," James said.

A few days later, I read a story in *The New York Times* headlined CONTRA LEADER'S HARVARD APPEARANCE DISRUPTED. The article explained that Adolfo Calero, a leader of the Nicaraguan contras, had been prevented from delivering his speech at HLS when he was attacked by a Tufts University senior shouting, "Death to the contras." As it was announced that Calero would not speak, dozens of students in the audience had clapped. Luke Houghton wrote in the student-run *Harvard Law Record* that the "disruption" of Calero was "merciful" and asked, "What happens when our morals become simple rule-following, so that procedural 'fairness' takes precedence over substantive justice?" When the Harvard Civil Liberties Union organized an open forum in Austin Hall to discuss the incident, Mark Kimball, a leftist 3L, declared that Calero was a murderer and should not be allowed to speak at HLS. "Calero has nothing to do with free speech and exchange of views. He was winning political support for mercenary murderers and it is the moral duty of people who oppose murder to do something about it." He said that the contra side of the debate got plenty of attention. Whenever genocidal figures like Calero came to speak, Kimball asserted, they would be "met with physical responses against them."

The left's negative response in this instance was as shortsighted and unprincipled as its positive response to Clare Dalton had been. In Dalton's case, the left abandoned the idea that teaching was important; and now it was willing to forget the primacy of free speech, a principle which had, throughout American history, been the lifeblood of dissent. Didn't Kimball realize that his statements only pushed liberals like me to the right? That he actually made a figure like Calero look victimized and sympathetic? Not only was the left's position tactically stupid, it was also intellectually arrogant. Who was Kimball to decide for the entire university that Calero was not fit to speak? Who gave him that veto power?

If a free dialogue on Nicaragua was impossible at Harvard, an open discussion of rape law was even harder to achieve. The physical assault on Adolfo Calero was followed in mid-October by a much more devastating verbal attack on Professor Nesson for his opinion on what constituted admissible evidence in rape trials.

Nesson began his class discussion by noting that the number of rape convictions had increased markedly in states with Rape Shield Laws, statutes which prohibit the introduction of evidence concerning the victim's past sexual history. One woman said that Rape Shield Laws were necessary because male judges had been unable to properly balance the "probative" value of the evidence against its "prejudicial" impact. A woman's sexual history is irrelevant, she said, because past promiscuity has nothing to do with the question of whether a woman consented on this particular occasion. Allowing evidence of that sort in merely inhibits women from bringing rapists to trial.

Nesson brought up for discussion a hypothetical case from his textbook inartfully titled "Occupational Hazard," about a woman who charges that an exterminator raped her while making a service call to her home. The defendant admitted having sex with the woman but wanted to offer into evidence testimony that she had initiated sex on a number of occasions with various other delivery-men. As was true of the discussion of rape law first year, I still personally found the issue extremely tough, pitting the right of the victim not to be "raped again" in court against the defendant's right, when facing a long prison sentence, to present facts to support his case that the woman consented. Nesson suggested that admission of the evidence might be constitutionally required—not that the information was dispositive, only that it couldn't be kept out. At that point, there was an outburst from a number of students. One called Nesson's discussion of rape offensive. Another said his argument was obscene. The issue didn't die there.

A month later, all hell broke loose. I walked in one morning, and instead of giving a lecture on evidence, Nesson flipped on an overhead machine with a transparency of Luke Houghton's cartoon from the November 20 issue of the *Harvard Law Record*. It was a lampoon of Nesson called "Travails with Charlie," in which the indelicate point was made that Nesson was a sexist. The cartoon read: "Little Charlie, like most perfessers [sic], / Hasn't yet heard of the word 'hers' . . . / But uses only 'him's' and 'he's,' / Oblivious to the 1980s . . . / Judges and lawyers, guards in the jail / Appear in hypotheticals, invariably male." But then the cartoon turned nasty: "Oh, 'ladies' do show up in class, / For Charlie likes his 'tits and ass'— / Helpless clients, the willing rape victim, / Help him explain the High Court's dictum. / And when students' anger reaches a crescendo, / Charlie's answer is smug innuendo. / Yes, Charlie's quite a guy, / Oh so clever and oh so sly . . ." The cartoon quoted allegedly sexist statements Nesson had made in class and culminated with a caricature of Nesson saying, "But I'm not sexist. My wife tells me so!" Nesson read the cartoon aloud, frame by frame. As he did, Luke Houghton walked in to take his seat; a murmur went around the room. Would they confront one another directly?

"When I saw this last Friday, my initial reaction was not to show it," Nesson said. But he said he wanted to defend himself—to explain why it was important to have a full discussion of the evidence rules pertaining to rape—and to make some amends. He apologized about the class discussion of rape. "I handled it badly," he said. He said that any sexism on his part was unconscious at worst, but that he now realized that the "Occupational Hazard" title might be offensive and he would take it out of his book.

A month earlier, when we had discussed rape and Nesson had been accused of being obscene, there had been no student support. But now the class rallied to Nesson's side. "I found the cartoon to be in incredibly poor taste," one student volunteered. There was sustained applause. But Nesson didn't ride the wave. He was ready to make more concessions to Houghton. He said he thought that saying he or she was "superficial," not at the heart of feminism. But, he continued, "I'm ready to make the change."

Nesson continued his public soul-searching on seemingly unrelated matters. "This course didn't seem real to me until about two weeks ago," he confessed. "For the last year or so, I've dropped out of Harvard Law School." When the faculty denied Clare Dalton tenure, he said, he left the school emotionally. "I was alive somewhere else." It was unclear what all this had to do with Houghton's comic strip, never mind Evidence, but students listened with rapt attention.

Nesson flipped the tape in his recorder, which, for some unknown reason, was recording the entire class. Responding to the last panel of the cartoon, he put his wife Fern's home and work phone numbers on the chalk board and said we should call and talk to her if we really thought he was a sexist. "This is obviously important to me," he said. It was weird but understandable. Here was Nesson, the civil rights attorney, defender of Ellsberg and Woburn, Massachusetts's cancer victims, suddenly told at mid-life he wasn't the great liberal he thought he was. That had to be wrenching.

Nesson spoke for an hour and then said he was finished. We sat in silence, the class, plus two parents from the Midwest who'd come to see their son's Harvard Law School class. There was a smattering of applause, and Nesson apologized to the visitors for not having talked about Evidence.

Arthur was furious that Nesson had devoted an entire class to Houghton's cartoon. I was more disturbed about Nesson's reasoning on the he/she issue. If he had quietly begun saying "she" rather than "he," as my first-year professors had done, he could have sent a subtle message of inclusion to the women in class without looking as though he was caving in to student pressure. Or Nesson could have challenged the criticism, said that "he or she" is too awkward and that "he" was meant to be read "he or she." That would have turned the class against him, since law students, trained in logic, know that if "he" can be read to apply to both sexes, so can "she."

Instead, Nesson chose the one path which would make Houghton look bad and advance the interests of women least. He said that he found the difference between he and she to be "superficial" but would switch to "he or she" anyway. By giving in, he made himself look like the victim of Houghton's heavy-handed tactics. By refusing to recognize the change as more than "superficial," and by adopting the cumbersome "he or she," Nesson belittled the feminist position. I was also upset with Houghton's approach. His he/she point was a good one, but by calling Nesson a sexist interested in "tits and ass," he had clearly gone overboard.

The right countered the next morning. An anonymous plea appeared on the chalk board: "Professor Nesson, please don't cave in to intellectual terrorism." Some sycophants circulated a petition singing Nesson's praises and attacking Houghton's cartoon as indecent and libelous. These actions prompted another half hour of introspection. Nesson rambled on about how we need to go the extra mile with women and minorities to make them feel welcome. He told a story about having invited Charles Ogletree, a black Harvard Law professor, to his health club. Nesson, it seems, was working out when "Tree" appeared at the front desk. The receptionist told him he had to be accompanied by a club member in order to get in. The club sent someone around looking for Nesson but couldn't find him, so Ogletree was asked to leave. The receptionist was just following club rules, Nesson said, but she should have been especially sensitive to the feelings of a black man in a predominantly white club. As Nesson told the story, students became restless. I noticed that only a quarter of the class signed the pro-Nesson petition. Sympathy for Nesson eroded as it became clear he was taking the issue, and himself, far too seriously.

Unbelievably, Nesson returned to the cartoon once again the following week. And once more, he glided into a discussion of the school's divisions over CLS. Having shed his regular suit for a leather jacket and scarf, Nesson seemed liberated. "There is an enormous rift at Harvard Law School," he said. "Some say it does not affect the students, but it does. It comes into the classroom all the time." Students squirmed in their seats. We liked to think CLS didn't affect us, that the shots being fired in the faculty's guerrilla war left us unscathed. But Nesson said CLS mattered, not only because of the important social and legal issues it raised, but because of its effect on faculty morale. He said that his own teaching of Evidence had suffered this semester and that ever since Dalton had been denied tenure he had had trouble even coming to school. By speaking so openly and candidly about the rift in the faculty and his own lack of enthusiasm for the class, Nesson destroyed what is called at Harvard "the cult of the professor," the myth that professors are demigods—always having the right answer, always a little more prepared, a bit more agile than their students—devoid of personal problems or crises.

Nesson's comments on the subject of Evidence, always progressive, took on a rather strident left-wing tone that matched his new clothing. Nesson said that the lawyer-client privilege, which protects as private conversations between attorney and client, was devised more for lawyers than for clients. He claimed it helped consolidate lawyers' power and made them more influential in the United States than in any other country. The proof that the privilege is more for lawyers than clients, Nesson said, was a proposed Federal Rule of Evidence which would release a lawyer from privilege if her client didn't pay. He also cited a pair of Supreme Court cases—*Couch v. United States* and *United States v. Schmidt*—which found that information supplied by an accountant is not privileged but information supplied by an accountant hired by a lawyer is privileged. Likewise, the *Upjohn Company v. United States* case held that an internal investigation ordered by lawyers is privileged, whereas an internal investigation ordered by the media—like the CBS investigation into its own story on General Westmoreland and troop counts in Vietnam—was not. "Does this mean that lawyers can 'sell' secrecy?" Nesson asked.

Nesson was now on a roll, which I found quite exciting. Professors do not usually question basic, well-settled areas of law like lawyer-client privilege. This new, liberated Nesson was upsetting to the conservatives in class. They took their attack on Houghton, and all that he symbolized, outside the classroom and distributed a response comic strip, modeled after *Star Wars*, entitled "Radical Chic Strikes Back." It read: "As the rebel forces reunite after escaping the empire's attack on the ice planet Self-Righteous, young Luke's ship whines through the vacuum of space towards the I-know-you-are-but-what-am-I system." Underneath was pictured a spaceship, *The Silver Spoon* (Daddy's Car). In the next frame: "Luke fantasizes that Gorba, the Red-I Master, speaks to him," with Gorbachev saying, "There is much work to be done: you see, the Chic Side is the weaker side of the force," and Luke Houghton thinking to himself, "But what's in it for me?" In the next frame, Daniel Ortega says he knows how to get attention. "Shout down speakers! Make cheap ad hominem attacks on professors! Then Mummy will see how important you are." And it continued, with Luke, "Andover '82," finding out his father is Darth Reagan and jumping aboard a ship carrying the sign KRAVATH OR BUST.

Something bothered me a great deal about that cartoon, at least as much as Luke's, and I figured it out one afternoon when George and I met to play squash at Hemenway gym. We walked past the observation court and there was Duncan Kennedy, practicing alone, in court 4. He wasn't playing particularly well and looked rather silly in his cut-off jeans. No one had worn them in Hemenway for nearly a decade. George and I laughed: that's Critical Legal Studies—playing squash in cutoffs; teaching at the great prestigious law school and thinking of oneself as the vanguard of the proletariat; trying to be radical but only in the most traditional context.

But then again, I thought to myself, what was he supposed to do? Duncan Kennedy was criticized when his personal life didn't jibe with his ideology; but when his tactics (advocating guerrilla warfare in faculty meetings) did match his ideology, people called him strident. When *The New Republic* did a piece on CLS, they ridiculed Kennedy ("Duncan the Doughnut") and the crits, in large part because of their elite educations. The cover story began: "Duncan Kennedy—Andover, Harvard, and Yale Law School, now a professor at Harvard Law—advises young lawyers to resist oppression by refusing to laugh at the senior partners' jokes." The story had the same unappealing stench as the cartoon about Houghton's silver spoon and Andover '82.

The anger that welled up against the radical chic at Harvard was fundamentally class-based. The real dislike of Houghton and Kennedy within Harvard Law School—and of Harvard itself as seen by the outside world—was a hatred of those who try to have it both ways, those high-minded liberals and radicals who don't suffer the consequences of their rhetoric. The liberal writer who advocates gun control in his column and then shoots an intruder in his pool.

The civil libertarian who preaches about the rights of criminals and then retires at night to his safe, wealthy neighborhood, leaving the poor and middle class to deal with the consequences. A friend of mine went so far as to say that he preferred the conservative Texan who made no bones about coming to Harvard for big bucks to the liberal hypocrite. Given those choices, I couldn't agree. As a college professor once told my history class, he'd rather have the radical chic of Leonard Bernstein than the indifference of Eisenhower on a golf course. If hypocrisy is the homage vice pays to virtue, then the Duncan Kennedys and Luke Houghtons at least keep our sights high. In the end, that is part of why the two were so widely hated. You could attack them for their wealth, which was, of course, easier than attacking the merits of their ideas. But the truth was, their ideas were often scary: maybe we didn't really deserve to be at Harvard Law; maybe it wasn't that respectable to work for a law firm. Kennedy and Houghton, in their own strident, unpersuasive ways, were speaking some truth; if they had been completely wrong, they would not have touched the nerves they did.

Nesson ended the semester with a "plea for civil dialogue." He said people should listen to each other, not just for the weaknesses in the opposing case, but for the strengths. At Harvard Law School, Nesson said, people were "afraid to listen and be persuaded." A fair enough point, but a number of people feared that Nesson, so shaken by Houghton's cartoon, had gone overboard and was conceding points just for the sake of being "open." The fear was realized when, following exams, Nesson held a dinner party at his house for a small number of students whose essays he had found interesting. (Nesson's exam had included a wide-open essay asking us to write about what we learned from the course, an open invitation to write about "the Incident.")

A friend of mine was among those selected. He told me when he arrived in coat and tie at the Nessons' posh home off Brattle Street, he was greeted by Nesson, dressed in flannel shirt, jeans, and tennis shoes. Nesson said he didn't recognize my friend and asked him where he had sat during the semester.

On the left side of class was the reply.

"Oh, that's where Fern sat when she was a student of mine."

Nesson introduced my friend to his wife, the famous Fern, who had figured prominently in the discussion of sexism and the Incident.

Luke was invited to the party, of course, and showed up wearing a T-shirt that read, *Fuck the law, let's dance.* After dinner, Nesson had everyone read their essays out loud and then played an hour-long tape containing his views on Dalton's denial of tenure, a copy of which he was planning to send to every member of the faculty. The gist was that she should have gotten tenure—which was plausible. What was weird was the texture—instrumental music played in the background as if to soften Nesson's use of profanity—and the references to how "Luke" had taught him so much.

If Nesson seemed tentative and vulnerable, my other professors that semester—Tribe and Lewis—were self-confident and assured and genuinely seemed to have answers to extremely important questions. Tribe fortunately skimmed over the dry constitutional topics and spent three-quarters of the semester on civil rights and civil liberties. (Tribe joked that, when he took Con Law, "the class centered on the Commerce Clause, much to my chagrin.") He frequently shed new light on old constitutional quandaries. As an undergraduate, I had found Justice Black's literal interpretation of the First Amendment—" 'No law' means 'no law' "—tempting but not entirely satisfying. Black said speech was protected, not conduct; but that interpretation seemed to give too little protection to expressive conduct, like flag burning. Tribe had a new angle on the question: the First Amendment, he said, protects "functional" speech. Speech is supposed to communicate an idea—so yelling boo to a cardiac patient is unprotected, but symbolic communicative speech like flag burning is protected.

Tribe supplemented these flashes of insight with a memory for detail (as in, "Footnote 12 of such and such case makes that precise point") that often drew laughter. On top of this, Tribe shared with us his insider's view of constitutional law, which made us feel a part of constitutional adjudication. Tribe had argued a number of landmark Supreme Court cases—*Hawaii Housing v. Midkiff*, which upheld the constitutionality of land redistribution; *Larkin v. Grendel's Den, Inc.*, which struck down a church's veto over liquor licensing; and *Richmond Newspapers v. Virginia*, which upheld the right of the press to attend public trials—and he loved to tell anecdotes about the Court. He had clerked for Justice Potter Stewart, who was famous for his comment on obscenity: "I can't define it, but I know it when I see it." Tribe said he once asked Stewart whether he'd ever seen "it." Stewart replied, "Once, off the coast of Algiers." When arguing a case before the Supreme Court on the right of the Hare Krishnas to approach visitors to the Minnesota State Fair rather than being stuck in a booth, Tribe said he had made the point that while a rule which says no one can wander and distribute leaflets might appear neutral, it would in fact be especially harmful to the Krishnas, since people might be embarrassed to go up to their booth. Justice White told Tribe that his argument "is interesting, but lacks force." Tribe grinned sheepishly as he recounted the story.

But best of all, Tribe cared about constitutional law and the people affected by it. He spoke movingly about *Lynch v. Donnelly*, the Christmas crèche case, saying the Court should look through the eyes of the outsider to know the feelings of those not included. When the LDF lost *McCleskey v. Kemp*, which cited studies showing the racially discriminatory impact of the death penalty, Tribe agreed to help the LDF draft a bill to prohibit capital punishment in instances when it furthered a racially discriminatory pattern.

Tribe cared about what he taught, and I found his boyish enthusiasm contagious. The class met three days a week: for two hours on Thursdays and Fridays and for one hour and fifteen minutes on Wednesdays. One Wednesday, Tribe got confused and when the class was supposed to end he said, "Let's break for ten minutes, and afterward we'll discuss [such-and-such]." The class made noises and Tribe, realizing his mistake, turned bright red. It was an error that most law professors, eyes on clock, would not have made, a fact which made Tribe's sincerity even more winning.

And, in contrast to Nesson, Tribe was able to stand up and face the radicals with confidence and self-assurance. The enthusiasm for civil liberties at Harvard Law School diminishes as quickly when the issue involves pornography as when it involves rape, but Tribe held firm. When Houghton rushed to defend an unconstitutional Indianapolis anti-pornography statute, Tribe didn't yield. And when an African student said Tribe's discussion of immigration law legitimized it, Tribe responded that he did not mean to justify the current state of law, only to explain it. A central CLS tenet holds that even describing the law gives it the air of legitimacy, but Tribe saw that the logic of that argument meant law professors could never teach "black letter" law.

Anthony Lewis's class was also a joy. Lewis, like Tribe, had been involved in many of the famous Supreme Court decisions we discussed in his First Amendment course. When we studied the Pentagon Papers case, for example, Lewis gave us the journalist's inside scoop. He told us that when the Pentagon Papers started to run in the *Times* and Attorney General John Mitchell sought a preliminary injunction, Lewis was having dinner in London with *Times* publisher "Punch" Sulzberger. Sulzberger had to continually interrupt dinner to take phone calls from New York. His wife told Lewis, "I certainly hope Punch doesn't go to prison." When the *Times* began to waver about publishing the articles, Scotty Reston took the hard line, Lewis continued, and said that if the *Times* refused to print the story, he'd put it into his Martha's Vineyard paper. Lord, Day & Lord, the *Times*'s law firm, couldn't be trusted with the case, Lewis said; the worry was they'd sell out to Mitchell. This was all wonderful stuff for law students used to dry textual analyses of major cases. We ate it up and were willing to forgive Lewis's imperious manner. (He would always interrupt students mid-sentence, to the point where it became a class joke.)

Lewis even scheduled a field trip to Washington, to hear the oral argument before the Supreme Court in the case of *Hustler v. Falwell*—the preacher's lawsuit against *Hustler* magazine for publication of a parody allegedly intended to inflict emotional harm. I didn't go, because the flight seemed extravagant, but those who did enjoyed the meeting he had arranged with the attorneys and appreciated Lewis's awareness that the trip was qualitatively different from reading about the case in the paper.

For me personally, the class also provided a rebirth of sorts. One afternoon in early October, we were scheduled to discuss *Gertz v. Robert Welch, Inc.* I walked in late and my seat was taken, so I took a spot near the front. Mr. Lewis looked around at the empty seats, noted some absences, then called on me.

"Your name?"

"Mr. Kahlenberg."

"Yes, Mr. Kahlenberg, please give us the facts of *Gertz* . . ."

It was the first time I'd been called on since the very first day of the first year and I felt my face turn red. I had only glanced at the case right before class. I started to recite the facts. I felt as though I were in a movie, looking at myself from the outside, just as I had in Minow's class. I feared panic would set in. But this time it didn't, maybe because I was speaking before 50 not 150, maybe because I now realized Harvard Law School professors weren't so imposing. I did a credible job for my fifteen minutes of celebrity and left knowing I was up to the task.

Exams were somehow much more manageable this time around. For my two Constitutional Law courses, this was because I liked the material and enjoyed studying it. I prepared a massive Constitutional Law outline, running 114 single-spaced pages, because I wanted to understand and master the course. For Evidence, Arthur had given me a copy of the Law Review course outline, so I had the confidence of the Review behind me and hoped that some of its mythical power would rub off.

But most of all, my mediocre performance first year had, ironically, taken all the pressure off exams. During the semester, in Evidence, Arthur and I joked about the fact that he did all the reading while I rarely opened the book. At mid-term, when our pass/fail Accounting exam was scheduled, George and I went to New York for the weekend; Arthur stayed behind to study—even though he was the only one of us to actually attend class. It was really quite simple: Arthur had the Supreme Court clerkship and the Sears Prize for top honors riding on his performance; I was out of the running. When Justice Scalia came to judge the Moot Court finals in November, he represented to Arthur a potential employer; to me, he was just a famous jurist. The pressure for Law Review editors to do well was, if anything, more intense than in the first year. One Law Review editor refused to lend George his corporation notes covering Mergers & Acquisitions, which turned out to be the key to the exam. For a brief moment, I was very, very happy to be among the mortals.

For winter term, I managed to arrange to do a long, independent research paper under Lewis's direction. I was really quite excited about it. I hadn't had a chance to get to know Lewis in his class, and I looked forward to working with him more closely. In late October, I approached him in his office in Langdell Library. He was on the phone but motioned for me to come in. Lewis glanced at my topic proposal—an analysis of a bill to reform American libel law—and said it was fine. I had expected rejection, and now my spirits soared. I went to the library and looked up the best student research papers. This was an extraordinary opportunity and I wanted to do well.

When winter term arrived, I scoured the library for all relevant articles on libel law, and began my analysis of Congressman Charles Schumer's bill to create a new cause of action for defamation. The measure would allow public officials and public figures to bring an action in federal court for declaratory judgment (no money) against media defendants and to win by merely showing that the defendant's statement was false and defamatory. The bill offered a trade: public figures and officials would not be required to show the presence of the defendant's "actual malice" and media defendants would not have to pay large damage awards, or the expensive discovery costs, involved in adjudication under the "malice" standard.

After a week and a half, the solitary research began getting a bit monotonous. I began to crave more contact with the outside world, more structure. At one point, I ran into Seth Rubenstein in the bowels of Langdell and he made me feel better by saying that his winter-term course in Ad Law with recently rejected Supreme Court nominee Douglas H. Ginsburg was terrible. Ginsburg, he said, gave wooden lectures, an especially bitter disappointment for those who were expecting "a hip, pot-smoking dude."

Two weeks into the project, I finally got up the nerve to call Lewis to get some advice, direction, and inspiration. I opened the morning *Times* and there was Lewis's column, written from Jerusalem! The last line of his piece read, "But at the beginning of a visit here . . ." I called Lewis's secretary, and she said he would not be back until January 26. I forged ahead on my own.

At 8:30 a.m. on January 25 Lewis called. Rebecca and I were still asleep and didn't hear the telephone, but when we got up his message was on our machine. I called him back and asked him if we could meet. "I'm a bit tied up," he said, so we planned for me to drop off a rough draft at his home on the twenty-eighth and we would discuss the paper later.

I didn't finish my draft until 11:00 p.m. on the twenty-eighth, and wasn't certain whether or not I should drop it at that late hour.

But I wanted to hand it in and forget it, so Rebecca and I drove over to his large home on Lowell Street. I dropped the piece off on his doorstep and scampered away quickly.

Three days later, Gideon's Trumpet sounded at 5:30 p.m.

"Mr. Kahlenberg?"

"Yes." I thought it was a friend, joking by speaking so formally.

It wasn't. It was Lewis. He didn't identify himself. He just said, "I'd like to discuss your paper with you."

"Great," I said.

There was a silence, after which Lewis said, "I'd like to do it over the phone if possible—I'm a bit tied up—unless you have some overwhelming need to meet in person."

What can you say to that? You can't go into the *Gideon's Trumpet* story, so I said, "No, of course not."

"I think it's fine," he began.

Ugh.

If he had said he liked it, I would have been ecstatic. If he'd said he didn't like it, at least I would have had opportunity to engage in discussion and learn something. But it was "fine," which probably meant he'd heard it all before.

He mentioned a few criticisms, points which I might emphasize more, footnotes which seemed a bit off. We spoke for a total of maybe three minutes. Then he disposed of me. "Well, I wish you luck. Enjoy the game." The Super Bowl would begin in half an hour. I didn't watch it.

A lump developed in my throat. I felt another opportunity slipping away, another chance like clerking for the Supreme Court. I had hoped Lewis would take me under his wing, would tell me stories about his friend Robert Kennedy, about reporting on the Supreme Court, about where his values came from, what he thought might be a worthy career combining law and journalism.

To be fair, Lewis had many demands on his time. But so did a lot of other hot-shot professors who were more willing to show an interest in their students. Rebecca happened to be working at the time on a Kennedy School term paper with Middle East expert Nadav Safran. He had given her endless comments, had met with her, and invited us over to his house in Brookline. In college I had been lucky enough to have teachers who wanted to be friends with their students. Richard Neustadt had taken me canoeing with him at his house on the Cape and Marty Peretz, who had taught my junior-year seminar, had had Rebecca and me over to his house a half-dozen times and had attended our wedding. The rap on Harvard College was that the faculty was distant, but my experience was that if you showed a little initiative, the faculty welcomed student contact. Harvard Law School was different. My initiative was forever running up against a stone wall. I couldn't even get my paper advisor to meet with me face to face.

Over time, I realized that Lewis was not an unusually distant person. Indeed, his story is included precisely because it is typical of the faculty at Harvard Law. My failure to know Lewis was particularly poignant because I admired him more than the other teachers. But he probably thought nothing of it, as the relationship we had was of the detached formality typical of the entire law school. Indeed, on the surface Lewis did all that I had asked: he agreed to advise my paper and later wrote me a letter of recommendation for judicial clerkships. But I wish people like Lewis who've written stirring books like *Gideon's Trumpet* would realize that small words of encouragement, gestures of interest, can mean the world to a student. In the cold environs of Harvard Law School, students look to a small group of teachers who have the capacity to inspire as a source of strength, and when the students are let down, their disappointment is quite bitter.

6

Everyone Does It

If I felt ignored by certain professors the first half of my second year, I basked in the warm, loving arms of the nation's best placement office. It was September 14, not a week into the second year, when I found myself at the placement office in Pound Hall to pick up *The Employer Directory*. The massive volume was the size of a telephone book, double the size of the 1L Directory. The book listed job openings with 1,000 firms and 100 public-interest and government organizations. I flipped past the public-interest section, which had been my sole interest the previous year, and went straight to the firms. I had seen public interest, and though I still had qualms, I now wanted to taste life on the other side.

Rebecca and I were interested in New York, Washington, and Boston for the summer, so I greedily flipped through those cities' listings, looking for firms I had heard of, the "name" firms where powerful lawyers preside: Cravath, Swaine & Moore, Sullivan & Cromwell, Davis Polk & Wardwell, and Paul, Weiss in New York. Arnold & Porter, Covington & Burling, and Wilmer, Cutler & Pickering in D.C. Ropes & Gray and Hale and Dorr in Boston. The salaries were astounding! Weekly salaries of $900, $1,000, $1,250. With bonuses, the weekly salaries reached up to $1,600! I could earn more in one week than I received in a public-interest grant for all of last summer. Examining these salaries, I felt like a naughty boy looking at pornography. It seemed vaguely wrong and forbidden, and this only strengthened the allure. I began to lose all perspective: "Why settle for $900 a week?"

The firms' profiles all read alike, as if, someone quipped, they were written by the same person in a basement in Iowa: "Our firm is divided into departments of corporate law, litigation, tax, and estates." They all promised an informal, congenial atmosphere, top-notch legal work, exciting cases, and a lot of responsibility early on. But Harvard also requires the firms to list certain objective data; for example, what the chances are for making partner after several years as an associate. This figure was often 10 percent or less. At Cravath, for example, the chart showed that, in a recent year, only three of forty-five associates made partner. At Davis Polk, in the previous year, one in thirty-nine made partner.

Still, that was eight years down the road. For the summer, these guys were going to pay big bucks, and the recruitment process would be a cakewalk. There would be no need to send out cover letters, no need to get funding, no need to call and plead for interviews. Second-year students seeking law firm jobs submit a résumé and computer form indicating firms of interest, and the placement office sets up the interviews at a local hotel. There was a danger to making it so easy: application inflation. The average student applied for seventeen jobs. I signed up for thirty-four. Being in the middle of the class academically, I wanted to have plenty of safeties.

The twenty-minute, first-round Cambridge interviews occasionally yield a summer job offer from a law firm, but usually an interested employer will fly the student out to the firm's city for intensive interviews with more lawyers. The firms reimburse students for travel expenses—flights, taxis, meals, hotel accommodations. The entire process is made as hassle-free as possible. These firms are keenly aware that making the process easy is absolutely essential to recruiting law students, most of whom chose law in the first place because it was the "path of least resistance." (An HLS placement official told Calvin Trillin that the large firms spend as much money in recruitment—travel, hotels, receptions, summer-clerk perks, and forgone billable hours—as the law school's annual budget.) Of course, Texas Rural Legal Aid has a hard time competing with Cravath in this game. Ninety-five percent of the groups which can afford to fly an attorney to Cambridge to spend a day or more interviewing are corporate law firms, corporations, or banks. Not coincidentally, that precise figure—95 percent—is also the proportion of second-year students who go to work for these employers in the summer.

There was, among the left, a philosophical debate as to who was to blame for the flow of students to corporate law: students or the system. The statistics, it was pointed out, could be read another way: firms, corporations, and banks come to Cambridge because there is student demand; public-interest groups and legal services have learned to stay away, in part because students won't take their low-paying job offers. Each of us faced tough moral choices, some said, but we were free actors who had to take responsibility for our decisions. No one was forcing us to go to a law firm. On the other side of the question were people like public-interest lawyer Douglas Phelps, who told *The Boston Globe*, "The obvious ones to blame seem to be the students. You want to say, 'This is so absurd, what you're engaging in.' Yet they're all victims of the system, largely perpetuated by the large law firms." One could hate the fact that liberal law students become lawyers for the wealthy and powerful but also understand that individual students aren't necessarily to blame. Everyone comes to law school under her own set of circumstances. Many take on enormous loans which must be repaid. Some were beaten down by law school, which made them highly vulnerable to law firm recruiters who told students that they were wonderful. Harvard had tried to address some of the concerns—the LIPP loan-forgiveness program was especially commendable. But Phelps was right: the whole structure was tilted toward the firms. Whoever was to blame, the fact was, Harvard Law students overwhelmingly chose corporate law.

And everyone gets a job. The tremendous employment success rate is partially because Harvard Law students have a name to sell, but it's also because of the legendary Harvard placement office. Besides publishing the comprehensive directory and coordinating all interviews, the office sends out newsletters, organizes student evaluations of previous summer jobs, coordinates overseas placement, provides statistics on how many Harvard students got offers the previous year and from which firms, gives workshops on interview strategies, and sponsors a series of panel discussions on various legal careers. A law student from New York's Cardozo Law

School once told me she salivated when she saw our placement office.

On September 30, I attended Director Byers's interview-strategy workshop. I almost didn't go, thinking back to the first-year placement meeting, but I was reluctant to miss out on anything. The meeting was smaller than the one first year, but Byers was equally blunt. He told us at the outset that grades are very important in the recruitment process. "The obsession is incurable," he said. In fact, he urged us to put our grades at the top of our résumés. He told us that those people who had taken time off or had a former career would have a tougher time getting jobs. I would have thought the opposite, but to the law firms, Byers said, these applicants may have too much perspective and not enough focus. He was also frank about the question of splitting summers. Many law students like to get a feel for two firms—"keeping options open" again—and split the summer between them, spending six weeks at one, six at another. Firms generally discourage the practice because they want to get a better look at the candidate and because the more firms a student sees, the less likely it is she will accept any one firm's offer for permanent employment. Byers said not to bring up splitting at the first interview. "Set the hook before you start to reel them in," he advised.

The placement office also warned against applying only to the "name" firms, a fairly hopeless task among students from a name school. The office gave us a list of firms which interviewed more than fifty Harvard students the previous year, with the intent to steer people away. But at Harvard the list had the opposite effect. Those firms that are popular must be the best, and inclusion on the list made a firm more, not less, desirable. And because there was so little to differentiate the firms objectively, reputation was everything.

I began my summer job hunt by doing research on about one hundred firms in the placement office's file. In the midst of my "shopping," I heard Ron Fox, the public-interest coordinator, talking to a student about legal services. I could feel myself turning red and buried my head in papers so he wouldn't see me. Then Seth came by and said hello. He had worked in a public defender's office the previous summer and I was embarrassed to see him, too, caught as I was with my hand in the corporate cookie jar. I started apologizing, saying I intended to work for a firm for only one summer, just to get it out of my system. He looked at me and said, "I'm looking at white-collar defense firms."

The real sellout, though, was not corporate law or white-collar defense work but investment banking. This was pre-crash and the hottest jobs were at Goldman, Sachs and Salomon Brothers. The previous year, *The New York Times Magazine* had done a cover story, "The Faster Track: Leaving the Law for Wall Street." It said that some of the best and brightest—the Supreme Court clerks—were going to the investment houses. The story featured large color pictures of mostly white, mostly male, law school graduates, busy at work in their new, lucrative profession. The banking firms, it seemed, paid two to three times the $70,000 law-firm salary associates were being paid and were even more willing to wine and dine you during the recruitment. Over the summer, I'd gotten an invitation from Goldman, Sachs to have dinner at La Ripaille in Manhattan, and now the placement office was advertising a seminar, "Lawyers in Investment Banking: Who Does It, When and How?" with representatives from Goldman, Salomon, Merrill Lynch, Alex Brown, and Morgan Stanley. The previous year, the group had gushed that its panel would include "several of the people featured in the recent *New York Times Magazine* article on lawyers and investment banking."

When I was an undergraduate, committed to doing public-interest law, I had met a Goldman, Sachs–bound Harvard Law student at a dinner party given by Marty Peretz. "If you're born with this," he said, looking around the Peretz house, "you can do public interest. I don't have this kind of money." He couldn't even afford to go to a law firm. What struck me was the boldness with which he had given up all pretense that he had gone to law school for anything but big bucks. The difference between Harvard Law students and Harvard Business School students was supposed to be that while both were after money, the law students felt guilty about it. Now, apparently, even that was gone.

I scoffed. I wasn't going to be like the guy who went to Goldman. No, I would settle for a law firm's measly $1,200 a week—a salary which, not coincidentally, was the direct result of the competition provided by investment banks. (The cycle worked like this: the investment houses were luring away the lawyers, so law firms had to raise their salaries and, to justify the salaries, required associates to work extra hours.)

It was almost as if the investment banks had redrawn the old lines. It was almost noble to go to a law firm, considering the financial sacrifice involved. The public-interest crowd had, in large part, given up trying to persuade people to do legal-services work. The Alliance for Public Interest Alternatives distributed a flyer saying, basically, "Okay, so you're going to a firm. At least ask about *pro bono*." An ad hoc group of law students circulated another note, requesting that their fellow students boycott "union-busting firms." These were not firms who represent management against unions (that would wipe out a huge chunk of the legal profession), but eight firms whose anti-union representation was most egregious. The flyer was not confrontational but sober, reasoned, even conservative in its rhetoric and, above all, self-conscious about not sounding self-righteous. "We don't want to pressure you into doing what's right," it said in essence, "only to inform you." The language of the bloodless neoclassical economists had replaced Marx's call for workers of the world to unite. The letter closed with the stirring challenge: "And the market for our talents and legal skills will work most efficiently if we each possess the fullest possible knowledge of both the options available to us, and the ramifications of our chosen professional activity."

At the Kennedy School, they were still fighting the good fight. A group organized a videotaped showing of Marian Wright Edelman's commencement speech from the previous June, and Rebecca and I went to get some of the old-time religion. Edelman, who heads the Children's Defense Fund in Washington, spoke movingly about the obligation to confront the important challenges facing society. "I hope you will view your job as a mission rather than just a career," she said. "I wish for you, above all, a passion of some kind in your life, to keep you going in good times and bad. Because you are going to find that money and jockeying for status and parties and awards and political game playing hold poorly as long-haul life anchors."

Yes, but we live life in the short term, I said to myself, and for now I had other plans. I marched over to Mr. Papalimberis's Custom Barbershop for my interview haircut. I asked for the corporate law firm cut. "Conservative," said Papalimberis, who had recently

won fame cutting Governor Dukakis's hair on the *NBC Nightly News.*
We talked about corporate firms in Boston. He recommended Hill
& Barlow, the Duke's old firm. Hill & Barlow is known generally
as Boston's leading liberal firm and was, for that reason, near the
top of my list. But Papalimberis wasn't fooled. "The conservative
cut," he said again.

October 6. After classes, I put on a jacket and tie and went to
an "informal" reception at the Harvard Faculty Club for a New
York firm, Kaye, Scholer, Fierman, Hays & Handler. I walked
over with George. We peered into the first-floor reception area,
where a number of people, dressed in jeans and sweaters, were
drinking cocktails. "I guess people took seriously the message to
'dress informally,'" I said. We felt a little silly in our ties and
jackets. But it turned out the casual reception was for the Harvard
philosophy department; the lawyers were upstairs, in uniform.

We casually sauntered over to the open bar and surveyed the
room. There were Laura Goldman and Stewart Ross, who had
been passionate Dalton supporters the previous spring, now ap-
pearing equally passionate in their pursuit of corporate careers.
There was Sam Roberts, who had worked for Congressman Schumer, the liberal Democrat from Brooklyn (and author of the libel
bill), engaged in intense discussion with the Kaye, Scholer people.
There was no embarrassment, no averting of eyes among the old
public-interest crowd.

George saw a classmate who had been talking with some attorneys
and asked her what she thought of them. She said they were okay.
"It's not what they say, it's how they say it," she advised.

A young Kaye, Scholer associate spotted George and me and
introduced himself as Brad. He gave the firm pitch, making jokes
about how well the firm eats and about the half-billion-dollar "deals"
it does. I had no real idea of what a deal was, but I feigned understanding. Brad asked us if we had any questions. A classmate
from my first-year section chimed in, "What's a Street firm?" Immediately our friend Brad got defensive. The Street firms are the
high-powered Wall Street firms, like Cravath, Davis Polk, and
Shearman & Sterling, he explained. Kaye, Scholer was among the
fifteen "second-tier" firms, he said, which are less prestigious but
more fun to work at. "We eat well," he said again, nodding and
smiling.

Brad asked me what area of practice I was interested in. I thought it would be rude to say none, so I told him I didn't know. Brad paused. I had thrown a monkey wrench into the system. He turned to George, who told Brad he had done real-estate work the previous summer for O'Melveny & Myers. Brad looked relieved. He called over a Kaye, Scholer real-estate lawyer and turned away. Lacking a pigeonhole, I was left standing listening to George and our new attorney talk real estate.

The next afternoon, I was at the Charles Hotel for my first law firm interview. It was with Covington & Burling, a premier Washington firm. Valinda Jones greeted me. She was attractive, well-mannered, polished, but not oily in the way I had imagined corporate lawyers to be. The law firms, as if by alchemy, turn geeky Harvard Law students into suave lawyers. Or maybe the money does it. Valinda dove into my résumé: my time in Africa, my senior honors thesis, my work for Senator William Proxmire and Democratic Congressman Robert Torricelli—and the fact that I was writing a book about Harvard Law School. I decided that I could not and should not hide my liberal bent in these interviews, and explained that the central question of my memoir was whether a liberal could, in good conscience, work at a corporate law firm.

Valinda said that she considered herself liberal and that Covington was a good place for liberals who want to move into government later. She quoted from the firm résumé, which stressed Covington's commitment to public service, its location "on Pennsylvania Avenue midway between the White House and the Capitol," and the previous positions of its lawyers, including United States senator and Special Counsel to the President. The firm's alumni included liberals like Harvard professors Abe Chayes and Roger Fisher, and Yale Law School's Burke Marshall, who headed the civil rights division in Robert Kennedy's Justice Department. Covington, though, also represented the nation's leading defense contractors, the Tobacco Institute, and other, less than progressive corporate interests. Valinda's answer to the dilemma—"In life, you learn to make compromises"—was more description than justification. As I left, she asked nonchalantly for a copy of my transcript, as if it didn't really matter. The obsession was incurable.

I headed on to my 6:20 interview at the Sheraton Commander with Choate, Hall & Stewart, an old-line Boston firm. I interviewed with an associate, George Ticknor, who had gone to Harvard. He picked up on my thesis and mentioned that he had worked on Joe Kennedy's campaign for Congress. We discussed the race and agreed that Joe Kennedy had engendered the same animosity among the intelligentsia and the same admiration among the working class his father had. We agreed that an appeal to blue-collar and "new-collar" voters was essential for Democrats. We thought alike and by the end of the interview were completing each other's sentences. George Ticknor's life seemed ideal; he made a good salary and used his position in the legal community to further causes he cared about. Neither he nor Valinda was a Neanderthal corporate slave. They were bright, friendly, sensitive, liberal corporate lawyers. They were so much more appealing than the Luke Houghtons, and more influential. They were working within the system, doing progressive things after hours, and positioning themselves to be tapped should a liberal Democratic governor or President choose to do so. That was critical: the lawyers who get the high-level government jobs, even in Democratic administrations, are invariably attorneys from corporate firms. While they're waiting to be called on, they build a nice nest egg, earn the respect of their peers, and have the resources to do interesting *pro bono* work when they find the time. It was much more pleasant to be Warren Christopher (Deputy Secretary of State under Carter) or Bill Coleman (Chairman of the NAACP Legal Defense Fund) and earn half a million dollars annually as partners at O'Melveny & Myers, I was learning, than to work with Ralph Nader at $18,000 a year—and very few people will criticize you. Actually, quite the opposite was true.

On October 9, I interviewed with the Washington firm of Williams & Connolly. Williams was Edward Bennett Williams, the great defense attorney and Democratic political operative. He had won me over in 1980 when he gave an important speech for Ted Kennedy's candidacy at the Democratic National Convention. Like Covington, Williams & Connolly was an elite firm from which one could leave to do public service. (Joy's friend Ann Kennedy was at W&C, and had just left to work on the Dukakis campaign.) Some of the firm's paid work even coincided with a liberal politics; its representation of *The Washington Post* in free-press cases, for example, provided a nice blend of practicality and principle. At the same time, the bulk of its work involved defense of white-collar

criminals. My interviewer was honest enough to admit some "cog-
nitive dissonance" between being a liberal and working for a firm,
even one like Williams & Connolly. Later that afternoon, I interviewed with Sullivan & Cromwell, a New York firm which made
no pretense about being either liberal or humane. The attorney
with whom I interviewed was an unapologetic conservative. He
said he was at S&C for the money and that working for the D.C.
branch office meant he could drive a Porsche and own a three-
bedroom house in the suburbs, things he couldn't afford in New
York. I laughed nervously at this bit of witty cynicism. He said
he was dead serious. Harvard Law School had been a bitch, he
said, and now he was spoiling himself a little.

October 13. Three more law firms. At 2:20, I interviewed with
Boston's Nutter, McClennen & Fish. "Why did I want to work for
Nutter, McClennen?" my interviewer asked. Because, I said, I
thought it might be the elusive liberal firm for which I had been
searching. The firm was founded by Louis Brandeis, the great
Supreme Court Justice who provided a model for so many of us
who look to law as an engine for social change. Today, James
Roosevelt, F.D.R.'s grandson, practiced at Nutter, McClennen,
and the firm was civic-minded enough to sponsor the *MacNeil/Lehrer
Newshour*. The Nutter attorney simply smiled when I mentioned
these things. At 6:40, I interviewed with a small Boston firm—
Withington, Cross—in a cramped room in Griswold Hall. There
were no hors d'oeuvres laid out, no soft couches, and the pay was
a miserable $675 a week. But Withington had given 80 percent of
the Harvard applicants job offers the year before and you couldn't
find a better safety firm than that. My interviewer said he saw no
conflict between liberal politics and the practice of corporate law;
the two were entirely divorced in his mind. He held the lawyer's
ethos in its purest form: everyone-has-a-right-to-her-day-in-court.
He said, "Who are lawyers to say what is right and wrong? Besides,
what does filling out a corporate tax return have to do with politics?"
On the spot, he invited me for a callback interview on October 28,
which I penciled into my calendar book. Interview number three
was back to normal. It was at the Charles Hotel with a tax attorney
from Weil, Gotshal, a large New York firm which paid a large

New York wage. I asked the Question. He sympathized with me. He was a liberal himself and said he had never dreamed of becoming a tax attorney. But now he claimed to have few qualms about spending his life minimizing the tax contribution of enormous corporations. "Congress is to blame," he said. "They write the laws." Ah. Lawyers Only Implement the Law—it's not their problem if the law is wrong. But he took this twisted reasoning a step further. He had actually convinced himself that by exploiting tax loopholes to their logical legal extreme, he might spur Congress to reform. A rather attenuated public good.

Afterward I went straight to Langdell to attend a forum on Critical Legal Studies. I felt embarrassed in my gray suit, but this was, of course, recruiting season, so several other students there were similarly dressed. The panel discussion, sponsored by the Harvard National Lawyers Guild, was entitled "What Is CLS Anyway?" and featured leading left-wing professors: Dalton, Derrick Bell, Gary Bellow, and, of course, Duncan Kennedy.

When I arrived, Kennedy had just begun to speak. He described himself as a radical. "Liberals and conservatives are like the yin/yang. They complement each other, and the system is stable," he said. To reassure the liberals in the audience, Kennedy cautioned, "I'm totally on the side of the liberals. I have liberal parties for local candidates. I'm in liberal groups like the ACLU." But, he said, his vision went beyond the traditional liberal one. Given that it was recruitment season, Kennedy focused his comments on the liberal or radical attorney and laid out his theory that there were three life patterns for lawyers with progressive instincts. "Model one is passive consumptionist," he said. It's the liberal professional who votes with her money. She is liberal in politics, writes checks for liberal causes, but spends her day representing corporate clients and rich folk. The second model is one where the professional life is a base. The lawyer is productive, not merely consumptive, in that she sits on boards of liberal groups, organizes petition drives, and supports liberal candidates. She is the corporate lawyer by day, Kennedy said, "but when night falls . . ." Laughter. Finally, Kennedy said, there is "the professional as political," who says, "Liberalism begins in the workplace. It's not something that will happen elsewhere." That, Kennedy proclaimed with great pride, "is a radical idea." But as Kennedy continued, it became clear that his message was actually quite modest. Although he had no love for the firms (they were at best "socially inconsequential"), he was not insisting that liberal lawyers give up corporate jobs for legal aid or government work, but merely that they fight hierarchy within the corporate arena. This was a rehash of his essay published in the alumni magazine, which urged that young associates "sabotage . . . the bad guys" and fight illegitimate hierarchy by, among other things, refusing to smile at the senior partners' jokes. Maybe Kennedy's emphasis, given the career statistics about Harvard Law School graduates, was realistic, or maybe it was just cynical. *The New Republic* labeled it "radicalism for yuppies." Was I really more radical than Duncan Kennedy in thinking that maybe liberals shouldn't be corporate lawyers? As my behavior moved right, was my mind moving left?

The next afternoon, at 3:00, I was back at it, with four more appointments scheduled. My first interview, with Boston's leading litigation firm, Hale and Dorr, took place at Lincoln's Inn, the HLS social club that took its name from the Lincoln's Inn referred to in Dickens's *Bleak House*. The interviews were, indeed, straight out of Dickens, as the law became a tangling fog and the firms began to blur. Hale and Dorr, home to James St. Clair, Nixon's Watergate attorney, seemed no different from Hill & Barlow (Mike Dukakis's liberal firm). New York's Debevoise & Plimpton seemed no different from Cadwalader, Wickersham & Taft. I walked from interview to interview, dazed, and ran into a friend from my orientation group who'd worked with inner-city kids after college. He was now checking out Boston firms, caught in the same moral fog.

October 15. At 2:00 p.m. I interviewed with Margaret Ayres, a Carter appointee now working at Davis Polk's Washington office. Ayres declared herself an unabashed liberal, biding her time for the next Democratic administration. She said proving yourself in the private sector was key to getting plucked for top positions where you can have a real impact. (This was apparently a common Davis Polk aspiration. The office was headed by Richard Moe, who'd been Mondale's Chief of Staff.) Later that afternoon, Rebecca and I went for a long drive. We traveled north, up to Marblehead on the coast. Rebecca loves the ocean and we looked longingly at the houses lining the water. I wanted her to have one, and the strange thing was, it was all eminently possible if I so chose.

The next afternoon, I was back at the Charles Hotel interviewing with Skadden, Arps's Washington office. I told the attorney I was looking at law firm jobs for the summer but ultimately wanted a career in public policy. He told me if I went to a firm, everyone would be like me and that I'd like them, realize they didn't have horns, and stay. My next two interviews blew apart the theory. The first was with a corporate partner of New York's White & Case. In no time, he let me know that his daughter went to St. Paul's, that his father was a partner at Hale and Dorr, and that his politics were not liberal. I found myself kowtowing, criticizing the crits (which was genuine) but failing to balance that with my criticism of conservatives. An hour later, I was pressed against the back of my chair as a partner in Skadden, Arps's New York office leaned forward and told me about how Skadden was an upstart firm, shaking the legal community, not least the complacent, stuffy, old-line firms. He leaned closer and said, "M&A"—Mergers & Acquisitions—"is fun." His pep talk was all about "can-do," "hustle," "doing deals," and legal "entrepreneurship." He bragged that Skadden was the first American firm in Tokyo and that his work enabled him to travel at least two days a week. He said the leisurely three-hour lunch would be the downfall of the old-line firms and generally reveled in the crazy, unpredictable hours, trying to turn what might, to the untutored ear, be a fatal drawback into a convincing reason to practice at Skadden. I feigned interest, even though part of what I wanted from a law firm was a relaxed, genteel, pipe-smoking atmosphere. If you were going to be a rich lawyer, you wanted to have more dignity than a traveling salesman.

My last interview of the day was with Brown, Rudnick, a low-key Boston firm. The attorney was a calm, sensitive guy who had a new twist on why liberals could practice corporate law. He said he was there just to make some money before going into politics. That way he wouldn't have to be beholden to any fat cats. He seemed genuine in his desire, but I wondered how many other lawyers had said the same thing and then just stayed.

October 17. At 3:00 I interviewed with Paul, Weiss, New York's leading "liberal" law firm (according to none other than the impeccably liberal Arthur Schlesinger, Jr.). For the first time in two weeks, I was nervous. I had been numbed by the interviewing process—so many interviews made no one seem particularly important. But Paul, Weiss was different. If there is such a thing as a liberal corporate law firm, Paul, Weiss was it. The firm counted among its present and past partners Ted Sorensen, Ramsey Clark, and Arthur Liman (of the Iran-contra congressional investigation). But the Paul, Weiss interviewer turned out to be just another lawyer, which made me wonder if this was just another firm. When I got home, I reread a piece Jack Newfield had written blasting Sorensen's transition from Kennedy speech writer to Paul, Weiss attorney. "Sorensen might have spent the years since Dallas differently," Newfield wrote. "He might have spent time in Bed-Stuy, or in the Mississippi Delta . . . He might have worked for Ralph Nader instead of General Motors . . . He might have renewed his humanist reflexes by joining a cause . . . But Sorensen just served corporation clients." It was powerful stuff, but in truth, I was coming to realize that I come down somewhere in between Arthur Schlesinger and Jack Newfield. The two men, both biographers of Robert Kennedy, represented the two approaches to life with which I was struggling. While Schlesinger was Establishment, which is to say, responsible and influential, Newfield was more romantic, passionate, but perhaps less effective. I felt more confused than ever.

October 19. The stock market crashed, with the Dow falling 508 points. *Newsweek* would later declare this day the end of an era: the unreal, materialistic, greedy 1980s. But the crash didn't seem to deter any of us. (If anything, it made law look more reliable than investment banking.) I myself marched forward to interviews with two more large New York firms: Milbank, Tweed, Hadley & McCloy and Shearman & Sterling. The Milbank, Tweed attorney was Roger Oresman, a kindly, grandfatherly partner, complete with bow tie. We talked of politics and Oresman spoke of law as a profession not a business. He mused about how he had first come to Harvard fifty years earlier, and spoke like my father in ringing phrases about the commitment to public service that was part of the Harvard tradition in those days. He invited me for a second interview on the spot, which naturally made me even more favorably disposed to his firm. My next interview, with a young attorney from Shearman & Sterling, was quite different. The Shearman attorney spoke not about law as a profession but of the excitement of making the front page of the *New York Times* business section. It was, I guess, a generational difference.

On October 20, I happened to have interviews with two firms that, like Williams & Connolly, did work that combined principle and profit. Bingham, Dana & Gould represented the *Boston Globe* and Cahill Gordon, *The New York Times*. Either firm offered the opportunity to defend the First Amendment and take home a fat paycheck in the process. No trade-offs.

That was the idea, at least. But the Cahill lawyer I interviewed with was honest enough to say that unless you were Floyd Abrams, you wouldn't spend much time on First Amendment work, even at a firm like Cahill. Moreover, you were still your client's servant, and even a client like CBS isn't always the master you want. Later that afternoon, by coincidence, Henry Kaufman of the Libel Defense Resource Council spoke before Lewis's class and dramatically (if unwittingly) showed how even First Amendment lawyers can be little more than hired guns. Again and again, we asked him what he thought of various First Amendment issues. He would not say what he believed but only what his media clients thought. He had apparently allowed his opinion—and identity—to be eclipsed by theirs.

Interview number thirty (!) was special, because Washington's Wilmer, Cutler & Pickering was a leading liberal firm and, better yet, located in the nation's leading political city. My interviewer, John Payton, said a liberal law student shouldn't feel guilty about going to a big firm, because the public-interest places—the NAACP Legal Defense Fund, Ralph Nader's Public Citizen Litigation group, and others—don't take people straight out of law school. They don't have the resources to train people the way the big firms do. Of course, Payton's reasoning didn't explain why *he* was still at Wilmer, Cutler several years later. Payton presumably had acquired the training and developed the skills to be taken by LDF and Public Citizen. So why did he stay? I didn't have the gall to ask, but I later learned that Payton was what Duncan Kennedy had called the daytime/nighttime lawyer. By day he represented the law firm's clients, but by night he was the Great Liberal Lawyer, championing civil rights. (Payton was later one of the attorneys who argued—and lost—*Croson v. City of Richmond,* in which the Supreme Court ruled that affirmative-action set asides were unconstitutional. He subsequently left Wilmer to serve as corporation counsel for the District of Columbia.)

Payton was, of course, following the model set by one of the firm's name partners, Lloyd Cutler. If ever a lawyer personified the corporate lawyer of the liberal Democratic establishment, it was Lloyd Cutler. Mark Green, whose book on Washington lawyers devotes a chapter to "The Paradox of Being Cutler," wrote:

> He represents the American drug industry *and* the Lawyers Committee for Civil Rights Under Law, counsels the violence-prone automobile industry *and* the President's Commission on Violence, innovates in the civil liberties area *and* belongs to the discriminatory Metropolitan and Kenwood clubs, and advocates a Justice Department more independent of outside pressure while he occasionally lobbies it into submission.

Michael Kinsley is even more suspicious of Cutler's two sides and has argued that his advocacy of liberal causes only made him a more dangerous lobbyist for corporate America. "The more sympathetic you seem to the general cause of progressive reform," wrote Kinsley in *The New Republic,* "the more sympathetic legislators and regulators will be to your suggestions for 'compromise' or 'delay' in particular cases."

But in the end, I thought, it didn't really matter what commentators like Kinsley and Green said. The people who called the shots—like Presidents and senators—were glad to overlook the Cutler Paradox. Jimmy Carter hired Cutler as special counsel. He named corporate attorney Griffin Bell as Attorney General and appointed corporate lawyer Joseph Califano as Secretary of the then-Department of Health, Education and Welfare. O'Melveny & Myers partner Warren Christopher was named Deputy Secretary of State under Carter. The list goes on.

On October 28, I interviewed with Cravath, Swaine & Moore, the Harvard of law firms. Cravath is the one firm with guaranteed name recognition, largely because it has set the pace for exorbitant starting associate salaries. When Cravath raised its starting salary to $65,000 in 1985, the news made it all the way to Kenya. (I read it in the *International Herald Tribune* and promptly calculated that the amount represented roughly what two hundred Kenyans make in a year.) Being in the middle of the class, I didn't have a prayer of getting an offer from Cravath, even if it was easy to get an equivalent salary. In the fall of 1985, of 104 Harvard students who applied for jobs at Cravath, ten got offers and ten accepted, an unheard-of ratio of offers to acceptances. (Fifty percent acceptance of offers is very, very good.) But I applied anyway, in part because I didn't want to face the fact that my grades had closed doors. The young Cravath attorney was very polite considering that I, like most of his interviewees, didn't have a chance of getting a job.

In the middle of all this interviewing we discovered that Rebecca was pregnant. Perhaps I had taken the admonition "Make love not Law Review" a bit too seriously. We went through all the emotions expectant parents experience: exhilaration alternating with fear, nervousness mingling with giddiness. Suddenly we needed to be Responsible, far earlier in life than we had anticipated. (Most of our friends were still looking for dates on Saturday nights, so our new baby would make us pioneers of sorts.) Money would be needed to pay for day care. Our baby would have only the best.

It was with this in mind that I began, in the beginning of November, the second-round interviews. I had received callbacks from about half the firms with which I'd interviewed, and now I had to pare down the list, deciding which were worth the time a second interview demands: one afternoon for Boston firms, a full day for firms in other cities.

The first callback interview, at Choate, Hall & Stewart, was, happily, only a subway ride away. I met with four attorneys, all of them very friendly, genuine, reassuring people. They were "just like me," which is to say white and male and clean-cut. The firm was divided into five departments—Business, Litigation, Real Estate, Health Care, and Tax/Fiduciary. As for *pro bono*, one partner told me he worked on a golf tournament at his country club in Brookline.

They made me an offer a few days later. It was a Solid Firm. Founded in 1899. Counted among its alumni was Archibald MacLeish, the Pulitzer Prize-winning poet and playwright, assis-

tant Secretary of State, Librarian of Congress, and Harvard professor. Of course, MacLeish did all these things because he had the
guts to leave corporate practice, turn down an offer of partnership,
and sail to France to write poetry. Still, I was relieved. The job
would pay at least $1,000 a week and the firm had a respected
name. I told George Ticknor I would let him know soon.

November 3. I caught the Eastern Shuttle to New York for my
interview with Sullivan & Cromwell. When I arrived at LaGuardia,
I told the cabby "125 Broad Street."

"Are you a lawyer?" he asked.

"Law student," I responded. "I'm interviewing at Sullivan &
Cromwell."

"I could tell," he said cryptically. His nephew, it turned out,
was at S&C and hated it.

I explained that I was actually more interested in doing government or public-interest work, but I wanted to try working for
a firm for a summer to see what it was like. He smiled. As I
paid the fare, he said, "Good luck . . . if that's what you
want."

I took the elevator to the thirtieth floor and checked in with the
receptionist. The offices were elegant, luxurious but tasteful. I
waited in the lobby, feeling genteel. A young attorney came by
and told the receptionist, "I'm having root canal done in the suburbs. I'm bringing some work home with me." A few minutes later
a friend from my first-year section walked by with an S&C attorney.
I waved and grinned sheepishly.

My first stop was with Rob Lacy, a litigation partner. He looked
very, very conservative: white shirt, very short hair (too short,
really). We talked for a long while about what his average day was
like and why he had decided to work at Sullivan. I asked about the
firm's *pro bono* program. Very active, he said. He pointed out that
an attorney named Robert Hayes had done a great deal of work
for the homeless as an S&C associate. (In October, *The New York
Times* had done an extensive story on Hayes. In 1982, he had left
Sullivan & Cromwell and started the Coalition for the Homeless,
a public-interest group dedicated to improving the plight of street
people. "Having put aside his career with the prestigious Wall Street
law firm of Sullivan & Cromwell," the article said, Mr. Hayes
"works out of a dingy suite in midtown Manhattan, almost always

on the attack, filing new suits or issuing blistering appraisals of Mayor Koch's latest efforts." The point was that S&C wasn't right for Hayes; in order to do the work he cared about, he had to leave.)

When our hour was up, Mr. Lacy escorted me to the office of Bob Lack, a litigation associate. The journey was a silent one, through cold hallways. Not a word was exchanged among the attorneys passing one another; not a peep from the secretaries; no one spoke to anyone. Even the young S&C messengers, wearing blue-and-gray uniforms, scampered about silently. Lacy handed me—and my evaluation sheet—to Lack. Lack asked why I was looking at S&C and I told him there was a dignity, an established quality which made Sullivan less harried than a firm like Skadden, Arps, which was scrambling to be at the top. He smiled and said that law students who think of S&C lawyers smoking pipes and pondering deep issues of law were in for a surprise. "People work very hard here," he said. I turned the tables and asked him why he had chosen the firm. He said that he wanted to prove himself in the private sector and then go into the public sector at a high level. Where had I heard that before?

My third stop was with Earl Weiner, a general practice partner, complete with suspenders. I asked about *pro bono*.

Well, we have Robert Hayes.

"Why should I come to Sullivan over some other firm?"

"There are advantages to being at a blue-chip establishment firm."

Well, yes, but . . . you're not supposed to come out and say that, are you? It would be like saying "I'm rich," or "I come from an old family."

As I left, I saw the word "sensitive" scrawled on my evaluation form. I knew I was doomed.

The last interview was with Dick Carlton, the hiring partner and a litigator. By this time, I was having trouble keeping my eyes open. Carlton sat me down and asked, "So, what can I tell you about Sullivan & Cromwell?" I thought I would collapse.

I summoned up strength from somewhere and coughed up a Standard Question whenever his monologue began to wind down.

Carlton said he was rather happy with his life at Sullivan, that compared with the rest of his law school class, he was doing the most exciting stuff. "I'm doing more 'major' cases than anyone in my class," he said. Major cases? What does that mean? "Nothing under $150 million," he explained.

Carlton asked why, after doing well at Harvard College, I had gotten so many Bs at Harvard Law. Almost all the other lawyers I had interviewed with were embarrassed to ask for my grades. They would awkwardly request my transcript "for the files." But Carlton had no shame. I thought about the ending of *The Paper Chase*—when Hart makes a paper airplane of his grades and shoots them into the Cape Cod waters in a triumph of sanity—and how misleading that was. I told Carlton I had spent a good deal of time my first year working to update my senior honors thesis for publication.

"Are you sure you want to practice law?" he asked.

"After investing so much time and money, I feel I have no choice," I said feebly. I was angry. I had, throughout the afternoon, become convinced that Sullivan & Cromwell represented the worst of corporate law and that I did not want to work there. But now, with the discussion of grades, Carlton had taken the offensive. I wanted to reject them, but my grades had put me at their mercy.

The conversation lagged. I threw out my *pro bono* question. Robert Hayes, he said. Goddamn Robert Hayes. Hadn't anyone done any *pro bono* in the five years since Hayes had left?

Carlton was showing me to the door when I remembered that I had left my Accounting book, which I had brought to study on the plane, in the closet. I groaned about accounting, expecting, finally, to find the same common ground as when people complain about the dentist.

"Some of my most fascinating cases have been accounting cases," said Carlton.

A week later, I was at Logan again, awaiting the same shuttle to take me on the same trip to the same airport, where I'd get into another cab to see another set of law firms. From lack of experience, I had tried to be efficient by scheduling back-to-back interviews with two New York firms—Cahill Gordon & Reindel and Milbank, Tweed, Hadley & McCloy. For some reason, the Cahill people had the impression that I was interested in doing corporate law, so they arranged for me to speak only with corporate attorneys. All were quite progressive, many of them attracted to the firm for its outsider mentality. (It was originally thought of as a Catholic firm, one attorney told me.) They took me out for a fancy lunch before I dashed off to Milbank.

Where Cahill was upstart, Milbank was Establishment. Its major client was the Rockefeller family and its alumni included the president of Barnard College and former Cabinet official Elliot Richardson. My first interview was with Patricia Irvin, a corporations partner. As I entered her office, I found myself amid a hundred drooping flowers. Irvin had just been named the first black partner at Milbank and was only the fourth black woman partner in a major New York firm. Her success had made the papers. I asked her about the social value of corporate law and she smiled the smile that comes with familiarity, with recognition that two people think alike. She told me that as a law student she had applied to Milbank because she knew she didn't want to work in a Wall Street firm and Milbank didn't have a Wall Street address! She said she now enjoyed her job, enjoyed the people, earned a nice living, and felt as though her position in the Establishment helped her to do things for causes she cared about in a way she could not as a public-interest advocate. At Milbank she had the resources to do *pro bono* and could help raise $400,000 for a cause. As she had told a reporter for *Manhattan Lawyer*, she could have her cake and eat it, too.

Next, I spoke with a Milbank litigation partner, Joseph Genova. Of the sixty-odd lawyers I met during the interviewing season, he was tops: the most perceptive, most sensitive, most intelligent. He looked like my first-year Contracts professor, Rakoff, and seemed to share Rakoff's sense of what his job meant to society, what responsibilities and duties it entailed. He headed the *pro bono* program at Milbank but was a bit more cautious than Irvin. "If you can't have your cake and eat it, too, at least you can have the icing," he said, rather cryptically. "It's difficult enough to balance private practice and a family," he said. "To add *pro bono* work in makes the combination nearly impossible."

Afterward, there were three more interviews, including one with a bearded liberal who had worked for an environmental group called Friends of the River and was now a bankruptcy associate. But I kept thinking back to Genova's comments. For the first time, I started to feel sorry for Lloyd Cutler and Ted Sorensen and Patricia

Irvin and all those limousine liberals who seemed to have it both ways. I had always been angry that the Cutlers didn't have to make choices, like everyone else, between doing well and doing good. But, in a way, they do. They have to work twice as hard if they want to bill their share of corporate clients and do the *pro bono* work that they find fulfilling. That's eighty hours a week. What about family?

When I arrived at LaGuardia for the return trip to Boston, I was exhausted and starving. Seated in the lobby were my classmates Joel Lewis and Lisa Chen. I asked Joel if he thought Milbank would pay for my hot dog and he said to go for it. His firms had agreed to pay for a fancy Manhattan hotel room the night before; no one was going to object to a $2.00 hot dog. It was kind of fun buying the hot dog. It was free food and also a way for people like Joel and me to say to hell with the firms—our version of not laughing at the senior partners' jokes. Joel had worked in D.C. for the Lawyers Committee for Civil Rights under Law the previous summer but was now in pursuit of a high-priced firm, so we were both following the same path from public interest to private. Lisa's transition was even more striking. When I had Legal Methods with her first year, she had sported a half-shaved head, and now she was just another law student looking for a corporate job. It was at once embarrassing and reassuring, the three of us, in LaGuardia, catching a late-night shuttle: embarrassing that we had changed, reassuring that each wasn't the only one.

When Joel and I found seats together on the plane, I told him we were selling out, in part just to hear him say we weren't. And he did. "You'd be crazy not to try what 95 percent of your classmates are doing," he said. Of course, there is circularity to that thinking; if he didn't go corporate, I might not go corporate, and Seth Rubenstein, who had done public-defender work, might not go to Arnold & Porter, and Ed Murphy of Ralph Nader and Ed Markey's offices mightn't have gone to Steptoe & Johnson, and Barbara Chandler, who had worked in the Massachusetts attorney general's office, might not go to Hogan & Hartson. We were all, as Duncan Kennedy put it, acting "within the channels cut for [us], cutting them deeper."

Joel said he had spent the day at both Cahill and Cravath. At Cahill, he had met Floyd Abrams. At Cravath, he had met with

F.A.O. Schwarz, Jr., the former corporation counsel for the City of New York and heir to the toy empire. The treatment was typical for *Harvard Law Review* editors. Jones, Day's Erwin Griswold— former Solicitor General and dean of HLS, a man after whom a law school building is named—was among the legal giants known to fawn over second-year Law Review during recruitment season.

But if the law firms were guilty of placing too much importance on credentials, law students were just as picky when choosing firms. There was really very little that distinguished firms other than reputation. For this reason, I went to my interview with Boston's Ropes & Gray two days later with high expectations—it was, according to *Boston Magazine*, "the city's richest and most traditional" firm. Founded in 1865, its clients included such giants as the Bank of Boston, John Hancock, and Harvard. (The relationship with Harvard was symbiotic: 60 percent of the firm's lawyers were HLS graduates.) Behind the name stood a great deal of substance and an alumni roster that included Archibald Cox, Dean James Vorenberg, Judge Charles Wyzanski, and Elliot Richardson. In short, Ropes & Gray was a safe choice. It was like Harvard: solid, established, well known. It wouldn't close any doors. My classmates would have heard of it. It would rank well on the Cocktail Party Index. But it was a safe bet for another reason as well. Because Ropes made little pretense of being a progressive firm, there was also little danger of a liberal like me getting coopted into taking a permanent position. My interviews were all very civil and I knew that if I got an offer I would be set for the summer.

In the meantime, I had one final interview with Bingham, Dana & Gould, located on the thirty-fifth floor of the Bank of Boston building. I was attracted to Bingham's practice for many reasons: its First Amendment work for *The Boston Globe* and *The Atlantic*; its reputation as an established top-notch firm; and, not least, its phenomenal ratings in the annual *American Lawyer* survey of summer associates. The magazine reported that among other things Bingham's Monday-lunch series featured "amazing desserts."

The first people I spoke with were Zachary Karol, a litigation partner who'd argued a religious freedom case before the Supreme Court, and David Engel, a former Stanford professor. But I was most struck by my third interview, with Rory Fitzpatrick. When he read over my résumé, he brightened and said he had worked on the '68 Kennedy campaign. We fell into a long discussion about Robert Kennedy's concern for blacks and Indians and migrant workers and the hungry in America, and we forgot, for a while, that he was a lawyer in a big Boston firm and I was there because I wanted to do the same thing.

I received an offer from Bingham that evening, but more importantly, I also received the desired offer from Ropes & Gray, which I accepted. Thank God. The long process which had begun six weeks earlier was now, thirty-four interviews later, finally over. Despite my grades, I had landed at my first choice, a well-known Boston firm that would pay far more money than I deserved. No more long interviews or patronizing rejection letters. Arthur and I joked about sending the firms who had given us offers rejection letters like the ones firms send to students.

Dear Sir/Madam:

I very much enjoyed seeing Sullivan & Cravath. Your firm's qualifications are excellent. Unfortunately, I have limits to the number of firms for which I can work, and competition among law firms for my talents is intense. I have given careful consideration to your firm but must decline. I am unable to accept offers from many firms, which, like yours, have excellent credentials.

I appreciate your interest in me. Should you have an interest in me next year, please arrange to talk with me in the fall. Good luck in your search for summer associates.

Thank you for your interest and best wishes for continued success in the legal community.

> Sincerely,
> Richard D. Kahlenberg

But mixed with my relief was a gnawing feeling of shame. I thought about *Gideon's Trumpet*, Ralph Nader's speeches, and old conversations with people who advised me not to attend law school because I would just end up practicing at a big firm. I thought about my first visit to HLS in 1978, and how my father had pointed to the Latin inscriptions about knowledge, power, and justice on the walls of Langdell Library. I remembered my law school application essay, with its fancy talk about my commitment to public service and to public-interest law. I thought back to the first meeting of the public-interest group in my first year when I had indicated my interests were civil rights and consumer affairs. And I remembered Minow's sermons about not forgetting why we came to law school. I even thought about Bingham, Dana attorney Rory Fitzpatrick. Sure, he'd sold out, but at least he'd waited.

Then again, maybe I was just being too hard on myself. This was only a summer job, nothing permanent. I had to make some money—if not for me, then for Rebecca and the baby. And the corporate lawyers I had met didn't have horns; they were, on the whole, kind, sensitive, and interesting.

In February, my sister Joy had a baby and the whole family congregated at her house in the quiet Boston suburb of Newton. After dinner, my father and I went for a walk around the neighborhood. We talked about Joy's baby and the child Rebecca and I were expecting and about the difficult choices that lay ahead. I told him that we hoped to raise our family in a community like Newton. I didn't want to drive a Mercedes or go to expensive restaurants or wear $800 suits. But I did want a house in a safe neighborhood, where our child could play and receive a solid education—where we could go for walks at night. I could probably get all that eventually doing public-interest law, I said, but not as soon or as easily as I would if I worked for a firm. Then my father, Harvard class of '52, who could have gone for a high-paying career but instead chose the ministry and teaching, a man who endlessly quoted Harvard's Dean Wilbur Bender about privilege incurring obligation, told me that perhaps he had imparted too much liberal guilt.

No other students seemed to share my embarrassment or shame about working for a big firm that summer. According to the school newspaper, Matthew Hall—the activist *par excellence*, leader of the protest against Bork, apologist for the attack on Adolfo Calero, and revolutionary who spearheaded a petition drive against the Moot Court scheduling first year—was now looking for law firm work. Hall had spent the previous summer clerking for the Chief Justice of Sandinista-led Nicaragua. But now Hall was writing a letter to the editor saying he had canceled an interview with Akin, Gump when he found·out they were union busters. In Hall's attempt to score liberal points by opposing an anti-labor firm, he apparently didn't think anyone would wonder what he was doing applying to Akin, Gump in the first place. As it turned out, Hall ended up splitting the summer between two Los Angeles firms. At $1,100 a week, the firms presumably paid better than the Sandinistas.

Everyone was going to firms, even the most vocal radicals. And if everyone did it, it had to be right. Right?

C H A P T E R

7

Judicial Clerkships

Before the dust had settled on the summer job competition, a new contest began. The dual quest for money and status was replaced by the unadulterated pursuit of prestige as second-year law students began gearing up to apply for judicial clerkships, those few precious jobs which would begin a year and a half later after graduation. These high-powered positions were part of a strange system that has developed over time in the American judiciary. Youthful law school graduates are hired by judges to research (and often write) judicial opinions involving the most complex and weighty issues of their time. When one considers the extent to which clerks are responsible for crafting legal opinions involving billions of dollars or even fundamental rights, the corporate jobs to which the clerks subsequently graduate after their clerkships terminate may rightfully be seen as a step down. Despite the relatively low pay (averaging about $27,000), a judicial clerkship is not only extremely challenging, it is an additional badge, like Law Review, that will advance one's career until retirement—to say nothing of postponing real life for another year.

In early January, I received a 34-page packet from Margaret Tuitt of the placement office on how to get a judicial clerkship. Her packet had it all: how to choose a court and a judge, how to get information, how to apply, and general advice on timing, interviewing, procedures, forms, and addresses. I was struck by how different the process was from that for getting a law firm job. The competition was much more keen. Many judges warned that students in the bottom 90 percent of the class need not apply. They wouldn't tolerate qualified students who shopped around. "Never apply for clerkships which, if offered, you are not prepared to accept," Tuitt advised. Judges required prospective clerks to fly out for interviews at their own expense. And, worst of all, judicial clerkships required letters of recommendation from law professors.

Recommendations are always awkward. (Who wants to bother busy people?) Moreover, this requirement drove home the depressing fact that I didn't know any of my law school professors. Tuitt anticipated this concern, which is obviously a common one at HLS. "The problem of not knowing a professor should not deter you," she wrote. "Many of you are not well acquainted with your professors (who are aware of this difficulty) but they are generally willing to write recommendations for students whether or not they know them personally." Tuitt had the answer. "You should simply ask one or two faculty members in whose courses you have done well to write recommendations." Great advice—except there weren't any of those, either. My only hope was to do well on my first semester 2L finals, but I wasn't even sure if the grades would come out in time.

The professorial role in clerkships, though, went beyond simply writing recommendations. Attached to the memorandum were the names of judges who used faculty contacts to interview, screen, or even select applicants on their behalf! Estrich advised for J. Skelly Wright of the D.C. Circuit and Justice John Paul Stevens of the Supreme Court. Tribe was connected to three D.C. Circuit judges and Justice Harry Blackmun. Professor Lloyd Weinreb made the final decision on clerks for Judge Lumbard of the Second Circuit. With respect to timing, Tuitt said the American Association of Law Schools was asking judges to put hiring decisions off until April 1, but it was unclear whether or not judges would abide by the guideline. Tuitt's memo ended with a list of judicial clerks from the class of '87 and students from the class of '88 who had received clerkship offers. The hottest clerkships—those with the Supreme Court, D.C. Circuit, and Second Circuit (New York)—went almost exclusively to Law Review editors. In the previous two years, of the fifteen HLS students with D.C. Circuit clerkships, fourteen were members of the Law Review. I knew I was sunk.

But something inside me didn't want to give up without a fight. My failure to make Law Review had put me in the mediocre majority and only a clerkship could help me escape. I set out on my quest with great energy. At the placement office, I discovered that there are 144 federal judges in the locations where Rebecca and I were interested in living: New York, New Jersey, Philadelphia, and Washington. Since most people don't apply for more than twenty clerkships, I started to narrow the field of choices. At the outset, I knocked out almost all the judges nominated by Republicans, unless there was some reason to believe they had become an Earl Warren or a William Brennan. As I talked to friends, though, I found out that no one else looked at ideology. Reagan had appointed almost half the sitting federal judges, and to discount all of them—as well as the Nixon, Ford, and Eisenhower appointees—left a student with a small slice to choose from. My liberal friends said that most issues judges deal with aren't political. When it came to accepting judicial clerkships, legal realism (to say nothing of CLS) was conveniently discarded in favor of the idea that law was neutral, nonideological, and nonpolitical after all. Funny: if a judge's ideology didn't matter, why had my classmates fought so fervently for or against Robert Bork?

I pored over the *Almanac of the Federal Judiciary*, which contained biographical snippets. The sketches listed education, career history, publications, *pro bono* activities, noteworthy rulings, media coverage, and, most important, lawyers' evaluations. I prepared a 5 × 8 card on each of the fifty-three judges from my preferred geographic areas who were appointed by Democrats. In addition, I looked into five New Jersey supreme court justices and seven Republican appointees described as "independent and liberal." I created plus and minus columns for each judge and then ranked them as either As (20), Bs (22), or Cs (23). The problem was that my As—the bright, well-educated, liberal, high-profile, highly rated judges from Washington and New York—were also everyone else's As.

While I was still figuring out which judges to apply to, Arthur informed me that the D.C. Circuit clerkships were beginning to go and that one student had already accepted a position. The Law Review, it seemed, was not only a requirement for getting the hot clerkships, it was a prerequisite to knowing what was going on with them. Law Review editors were obsessed with getting clerkships, Arthur said. "It's all we talk about at the Review." He told me that a clerk for Judge Alex Kozinski was advising him. "Kozinski is a feeder judge," Arthur said.

"What?"

"Feeds the Supreme Court."

"Oh."

So much had already passed me by. Clerkships involved a set of rules that were widely ignored (April 1 couldn't be counted on) and a network of which I was not a part.

On February 23, first-semester grades were released. Whatever hope I had for a clerkship hung in the balance. I headed over to Austin North to discover my fate. The second year had not brought new dignity to the process: A–K still lined up, single file, waiting for the computer printout containing our grades. In front of me in line was a friend from first year. We made small talk about our courses as we inched forward toward the front of the room, but our minds were elsewhere. When I was handed my computer print-out, I took a deep breath before unfolding it. Two As and a B+! I was ecstatic. These were the first As I had received at HLS. And they were from the professors I respected most—Tribe and Lewis!

Or was this a mistake? The student directly ahead of me in the alphabet was Dean Kaban, who two weeks before had been elected president of the Law Review. These must be his grades, I thought. (No, his were probably better. He wouldn't have gotten a B+.) I realized then that Harvard Law had beaten me. It had shattered my academic self-confidence so completely that I no longer believed myself capable of earning the type of grades that I had taken for granted before law school.

Immediately, I called Anthony Lewis for a clerkship recommendation. He said he'd do it. I went to Larry Tribe's office and explained my situation to his secretary. She said he wrote only for people he knew. I fired off a letter to Tribe saying, "I realize that you may feel uncomfortable writing for someone whom you do not know well. But to be candid, I cannot say I really know any of my professors at the law school, so even a brief letter from you discussing my exam would be greatly appreciated."

Two days later, I presented myself at Tribe's office hours. I was very worried, given what his secretary had said, and given the rumors that people had been turned down by other professors. I was ready to plead on my hands and knees. When the secretary said he was available, I went into his office and introduced myself. I explained that I didn't know any of my professors and hoped he would help me. Tribe said yes, he would write a letter in the limited context he knew me. I was taken aback, said thank you, and left. I hadn't even taken off my coat.

Later that afternoon, I cranked out eighteen letters. Rebecca and I had decided by then that since we eventually wanted to move to Washington, it wasn't fair for me to work for a judge in another city and then uproot the family a year later. This put me in a rather embarrassing situation. The D.C. clerkships were the most competitive in the nation, even harder to get than the New York spots; I would have to reveal to Lewis and Tribe that I thought myself in the running for clerkships normally reserved for the top Law Review students from Harvard, Yale, and Stanford. Nevertheless, my list included the four D.C. Circuit Court liberals: Patricia Wald, Abner Mikva, Harry Edwards, and Ruth Bader Ginsburg (all of them feeders). I also listed twelve D.C. district court judges, including Gerhard Gesell, who'd sat on the Pentagon Papers case, and John Sirica, of Watergate fame. As a backup, I applied for positions with the two best judges on the D.C. Court of Appeals (the D.C. equivalent of a state court): John Ferren and James Belson. I braced myself for humiliation.

Patricia Wald's office wrote back first to say, "We generally begin to process applications around April 1." That didn't jibe with what the Law Review people had said. The next day, Gordon Pope showed up in Corporations class in a suit. He was going down to interview with Harry Edwards. On March 8, I received a letter from Edwards saying he was unable to offer me a position. The rejections began to pour in: Judge Gesell, Judge Ginsburg, Judge Mikva. Arthur, meanwhile, received four informal offers from D.C. Circuit judges, who were not making final offers until April 1.

At 8:00 a.m. on the first, Arthur received a call from a D.C. Circuit judge offering him a job. Just as law students get prestige from the judges they clerk for, so, too, is a judge's status elevated by hiring the most promising law students. Arthur turned her down in favor of Judge Ken Starr, a young Reaganite. I marveled that he was in a position to disappoint powerful judges, just as later he would be in a position to reject assistant professor tenure articles.

On April 8, I finally got an interview. It was from Judge Belson of the D.C. Court of Appeals. We arranged an appointment for April 15. When I told Arthur, he seemed surprised that I had even applied. "You'd rather take a state level job in D.C. than a federal one elsewhere?"

"Well, I have the family to think about."

The truth was that I wanted a federal D.C. clerkship, so I called all the judges who had not yet rejected me to say I would be in Washington on April 15 and available for interviews. The responses were not encouraging. Judge Penn's office said, "Call on the fifteenth." Judge Bryant's and Corcoran's offices didn't answer the telephone. Judge Gasch's office said they didn't care if I was in town. Judge Robinson's office said I was the fiftieth caller and no, they were still reviewing applications. Judge Pratt didn't interview candidates until June. And the three Judge Green(e)s—Harold Greene, June Green, and Joyce Green—had already selected clerks. Judge Ferren, from the D.C. Court of Appeals, said yes: if I was coming to see Belson, I should stop by and see Ferren, too.

April 15. I flew down to D.C. (at my own expense) to interview with Belson and Ferren. As I arrived at National Airport, I saw the wonderful view of the Capitol dome and knew I was in the right place. In the morning, I visited Congressman Schumer's office to get some information on the Schumer libel legislation and started to wonder if I wouldn't be a whole lot happier on the Hill than doing a clerkship.

At 1:30, I met with Judge Belson. He seemed kindly and genuine, a solidly moderate man out of Georgetown Law and the law firm of Hogan & Hartson. I said that I wanted a clerkship to influence public policy without the contamination of special-interest lobbyists. This was my old antidemocratic line, and it wasn't clear how well it went over.

Afterward, I met with one of Belson's clerks, a nervous, talkative, self-proclaimed Reaganite. I told him I was also interviewing with Judge Ferren and asked him to compare the two.

"Ferren walks around without shoes. Belson doesn't. In fact, Belson doesn't own a pair of jeans. Ferren rides a bike. Belson doesn't sweat. Ferren's clerks call him John. Belson's clerks, even one who is now forty-five years old, call him Judge." The clerk showed me the D.C. courtroom and the alcove from which the judges enter the chambers, from behind a set of curtains, to hear oral arguments; this made the whole clerkship seem real.

At 2:00, I met John Ferren, who looked like a young public-spirited judge. A 1962 graduate of Harvard Law, Ferren had been the director of a federally funded neighborhood law office at HLS and subsequently founded the public-interest division within Hogan & Hartson. As we talked, Ferren made me feel relaxed. He said he almost quit law school after a year to get a degree in history. Then he asked me what my greatest weakness was. In a disastrous fit of honesty, I said that I was not fascinated by law, that my real interest was politics. A few weeks later, the rejection letter came.

The end of the story is that I didn't get any clerkship, not even a devalued state clerkship. I'd have had a better shot if I had applied to judges of all ideological stripes and, also, looked at positions outside the Washington, D.C., area, but even with a better strategy, my first-year grades would probably have done me in. If grades were an "incurable obsession" for the law firms, the judges took their importance to new heights. Arthur, who had worked damn hard to get the grades he did, became the first law student in the country to receive a Supreme Court clerkship offer that year. Justice Scalia chose Arthur, and when Scalia came to Harvard to give a speech in the spring of third year, Arthur was invited to the pre-lecture dinner and sat at the head table between the Justice and Dean Vorenberg. I was happy for Arthur, even though I naturally would not have minded it had the pleasure been a little less vicarious.

CHAPTER
8
Learning Real Law

My second-year spring term was a mix of the respectable—Taxation and Corporations—and the disreputable—Poverty Law and Dickens and the Law. Tax and Corps were recommended courses; the others were decidedly not.

Taxation, with Professor Ault, had all the problems of first-year courses—a gigantic class, uninterested students, mundane subtopics—without the humanizing elements of the Experiment. Ault, who looked and acted like a Marine sergeant, was of the old school of education by humiliation. Worse yet, he wasn't even good at the Socratic method. Ault framed his questions poorly and then blamed the students who couldn't answer them. The only good thing about Tax class was that learning the loopholes might come in handy in years to come.

I sat with Arthur and George near the back of the class, but there was no escaping Ault's Socratic method. He went straight through the alphabet, from beginning to end. George got called on the second day of class, but when Ault asked him some tricky questions about the taxation of employee benefits, George performed exceedingly well. Other students weren't so lucky. Ault's prey were forever being crushed by his snide comments. George scrawled "son of a bitch" on his notepad on more than one occasion, even though he assumed he was now personally beyond Ault's reach. But in Ault's class, you were never safe. In late February, we were up to Epstein in the alphabet, when George, who was half listening and half reading the *Aeneid*, got called on again. The question involved Section 119 of the IRS Code, George's area of expertise from the second day of class. Was Section 119 a tax expenditure? "Who did we ask about employee benefits—someone back there," Ault said, pointing to our section of the room. I nudged George, who panicked. "I'm sorry, could you repeat the question?" Ault did and George came through again, the picture of grace under pressure. I told George he was ready to join the stars of the class, the select few whom Ault always went back to when no one else could answer the question.

I, of course, never said a word in class, and on March 16, when Ault wrote "Kahlenberg—Levin" on the board, identifying the victims for class discussion the following week, I panicked. Janey Jackson was presently on the hot seat, but, I wondered, what if he accidentally leaped beyond her into next week's group! He didn't.

March 21. I woke up at 6:30 in the morning to do last-minute reading for Ault's class, going over the material one more time. I had worked all weekend and was completely obsessed by now. I hadn't had to perform before a huge class since the first day of first year and my stomach churned. All weekend I had had trouble concentrating; when I read, all I could think of was Ault's face, his sneer, his horrible voice questioning me, nailing me. The material was extremely complex, so I bought an Emanuel's study aid to sort it out. The problem with Ault's class was that you never felt well enough prepared. He could pull a question out of left field. A friend told me he had recently co-judged an Ames case with Ault in which Ault had mercilessly destroyed a hapless first-year student. All weekend my head pounded.

I knew I had to go to class, though I dreaded it. As the hour of class approached, I began to feel flustered, panicky. I went into the bathroom and threw up. As I stared into the toilet at my vomit, something in me snapped.

No! I was simply not going to go. I called George and Arthur to see what they thought. George wasn't home. Arthur said he thought I should be more confident, but that he could understand my not going. I strengthened my resolve: I was sick of doing things just because I was expected to. The pain was not worth it. I felt a tremendous weight lift from my shoulders. I wasn't going to con-form. It was a small step and a cowardly one. If I had really been brave, I would have gone to class, and when Ault had called on me, I would have said, "No, I prefer not to." But I couldn't have pulled it off. Professors at Harvard have an unquestioned authority.

Rebecca called to wish me good luck. I told her I wasn't going and hoped she wouldn't be ashamed of me. She was supportive, as always. At 10:10, I looked at my watch and knew Ault was, at that moment, calling on me. I became tense, even in the safety of home. During the break in the middle of class, George telephoned me. He said I had been called on and that my absence, and a few other people's, had thrust students who had not expected to be called until later in the week onto the hot seat. Arthur had bailed out at the break, George said, because he was not prepared to speak, and it looked as if he might be called on.

Later, when I played squash with George, he told me that I should have conquered my fear. He had a point, of course. This episode wouldn't help my anxiety about public questioning. But my hatred for Harvard Law only grew as I realized that this school didn't have to put people through this hell, that there were other, more effective teaching methods. In my own timid way, I had, as Dunc urged, resisted!

It wasn't until after spring break that I returned to Tax class. I walked in late and sensed that people were looking at me funny; I swear that Ault stopped teaching when I entered. George called me the "tax evader." Very cute. Class went on, but my imagination was on fire. And this continued throughout the semester. Four weeks after my delinquency, my stomach tightened as Ault called on Jack Davison. That's D! Perhaps he was going back to the miscreants. But Davison was an aberration, as Ault plowed through the rest of the alphabet, destroying people left and right.

That is, until the S's.

On the morning of April 19, Ault called on Joe Sisorelli, a friend whom I played squash with first year. Sisorelli was a kind of wonderfully crazy guy who did things like proposing to his girlfriend on a Times Square billboard. Ault asked him some intricate question and Joe said, "Well, I'd be glad to answer. But first, could you tell me where you got that great haircut?" The class erupted with laughter. Ault had, finally, been stopped. No longer could he terrorize the populace. He had taken himself just a bit too seriously and been called to task. After class, people swarmed around Joe and congratulated him. The next day, Ault came back and called on Sisorelli again, but his powers of intimidation were gone.

After Tax class, my Corporations course with Professor William Simon met in the same room. The juxtaposition was jarring. Where Ault was authoritarian, Simon was communal. Where Ault plowed through the casebook, Simon claimed the case method was fairly inefficient for 2Ls. A self-described "flaky leftist" visiting from Stanford, Simon was a very hip ("Call me Bill") Californian. I don't even know if Ault had a first name. It was always just "Ault." Simon said he would call on people but that we could "conscientiously object" to this form of "conscription." We were a different kind of class—small (about half the seats were empty) and largely foreign-born.

The first day, Simon reassured the hard-ass conservatives in class that he would teach all the basic corporations law. He promised we'd learn all about "LBOs" and "M&A" and become literate for cocktail parties. But he said he'd supplement the traditional curriculum with some material on worker ownership and cooperatives. The conservatives were also comforted by Simon's having spent three years with Boston's old-line firm Foley, Hoag & Eliot.

The worker cooperatives stuff was very interesting. We got beyond the they-seem-like-a-good-idea stage and looked at how these projects actually worked in practice. In particular, we discussed the paradox of success: if a cooperative becomes successful, the workers become capitalists and want to hire other workers, which rather defeats the whole idea. The majority of the class, however, seemed most interested in the discussion of takeovers and mergers. We had come of age when a whole new vocabulary sprang into common usage in corporate America, and now we were being let in on what all those words meant: "scorched-earth tactics," "shark repellent," "poison pills" (both the "flip in" and "flip over" varieties), "crown jewels," and "white knights." There was talk of another term, "social responsibility," but the question was not whether corporations *should* consider it but whether they *could*. To base a decision on social responsibility rather than profit could be illegal if it was seen as a breach of the fiduciary duty to the stockholder.

The corporate mentality was completely foreign to me. Both my sisters followed my parents in working for nonprofits. Trudi worked with children with disabilities and Joy with a Democratic governor. There was no drive for profit in my blood. As the semester wore on, it became clear that corporate law was really all about the struggle between shareholders and managers, neither of whom I found particularly sympathetic. In the end, even cool, hip Bill Simon couldn't overcome the fact that if the battle was between (mostly) rich stockholders and rich managers, many students—myself included—didn't really care.

What I did care about—or thought I did—was my third class: Poverty Law. The course was taught by Gary Bellow, who, unlike most of the CLS crowd, actually practiced law on behalf of the poor. Bellow was hefty, his hair greased back in a style that said he wasn't some Ivy League wimp with liberal guilt. The class took place in the same room where Ron Fox held his seminars, and attracted the usual crowd of lefties: Houghton in his Amnesty International T-shirt and all the rest.

Bellow sought to give these idealists a little dose of the real world. He began the first class by telling us about the migrant workers he had represented in Southern California. He told us about kids who lived in makeshift tin cabins and had burns on their arms from exposed pipes. He explained the way that auto dealers in California routinely screwed migrant workers. The dealers would sell cars to migrants on credit and, if they faltered once, would repossess the cars and schedule the hearing in a faraway site. The migrants, unable to contest the case, would lose whatever equity they had in the car by default.

As the semester wore on, my feelings about Bellow alternated from good to bad. I nodded when he told us how lucky we were: 55 percent of the people in our country have no savings at all, he said, and only 3 percent of American families make more than $75,000 a year, the starting salary for an HLS graduate. "What is enough?" he asked.

But if poverty law was the right field to go into, Bellow never convinced us that it was interesting. He said that poverty lawyers should use arbitrary rules to benefit their clients, exploit the loopholes, because "the poor do not have resources, all they have are the rules." But the rules were boring. It was not interesting to know that when a rule says you have ten days to file, you do or do not count the days at both ends. But that was what poverty law entailed: knowing the arcane rules involved in such things as meeting income and the asset requirements of various programs. During a break one day, I heard one student tell another, "This is as bad as tax." Maybe we were just painfully naïve, but we still held out the hope that doing good, if not remunerative, could at least be interesting.

The final day of class, Bellow left us with the somewhat weary but also determined message that "it is important to do things on the margins." The margins! If the margins weren't interesting enough for me—a liberal willing to work within the existing system—they certainly weren't enticing to the left-wingers.

Instead, the radicals focused their attention on organizing demonstrations. The left had, for a time, renewed its hope that Clare Dalton would be tenured. Following the faculty vote in my first year, twenty-one professors had asked Bok to review her case. Bok had appointed a special panel, chaired by Archibald Cox, to see whether she should be tenured. Its answer was no, a recommendation which Bok ratified in mid-March. Cox, the Watergate crusader who had argued for the University of California against Bakke, was now the villain. He was, the left said, just another St. Paul's–Harvard elitist out of touch with the concerns of women and minorities. The halls were suddenly filled with posters saying D IS FOR DIVERSITY. There was talk that Dalton would file suit, "apparently," as *Newsweek* put it, "in the belief that the law is not wholly corrupt."

The other great cause on the left that semester was the effort to get the Law Review to adopt an affirmative-action program for women. I had assumed that the Law Review's affirmative-action program already included women, but it did not; and after a contentious meeting on the issue in mid-April, the Law Review voted to keep it that way, the Women's Law Society's protest notwithstanding. Arthur said some of the strongest opposition came from the women on the Review, who didn't want people to think they hadn't made it on merit.

———

In general, Rebecca and I had as little to do with Harvard Law School as possible that spring—what with preparations for the baby—but we both did go to Ames Hall to see Scott Turow when he came back to speak in late April, ten years after the publication of *One L*. Nick Littlefield, an assistant U.S. attorney turned defense lawyer, introduced Turow, a former student of his, who had also parlayed his work as an assistant U.S. attorney into a lucrative practice—as partner at Chicago's Sonnenschein Carlin Nath & Rosenthal. I was surprised that Turow, who was a phenomenally successful writer, didn't have a more imposing presence: short and balding, he looked rather like any other corporate lawyer on the make. Turow began by analyzing the sad state of the legal profession. He noted that lawyers were often despised. "Lawyer jokes have evidently supplanted ethnic humor," he said. Most lawyers were not happy. They worked hard hours—"It is a stressed-out existence"—but they didn't see any social utility in that work. "There is a sense that they're not doing anybody any good." The attitude was: "What do I care whether his robber baron wins or mine." I nodded my head: he's finally gotten at the heart of the problem, I thought. But then Turow dropped this reasoning, perhaps because his own status as white-collar defense lawyer made the whole theme seem a little hypocritical, or worse, because he found the argument embarrassing in its idealism. Turow's real theme was that law schools should be more practical, more trade-oriented. "Law professors generally don't want to practice law," Turow said. "That's why they become law professors." Accordingly, law school "does not teach you to think like a lawyer, it teaches you to think like a law professor." True enough, but what did the first theme have to do with the second? If anything, I wished the curriculum were broader and less trade-oriented—a continuation of a liberal arts education, giving one tools to tackle important social problems.

The school year ended, as all do, with exams, and with the competition Turow had chronicled so well. Tax was going to be tough, and when Arthur said he was organizing a private Law Review outline and would like me to join, I said I'd be glad to. Bev Sacks from my orientation group was running the "public" tax outline and asked me after one class if I would contribute to it. I said I was already working on one, just as Arthur walked up to us.

Bev smiled knowingly. Later, I picked up the 110-page Le Palm outline from the copy center. Ault's name was crossed off each page as if by a government censor, presumably to keep the outline fully private. It was a fantastic outline, and even included some old Ault exams from his days of teaching at Boston College. It was all so . . . unjust.

CHAPTER

9

Dickens and the Law

In addition to Corporations, Taxation, and Poverty Law, I took one very special course in the spring semester of the second year: Dickens and the Law, taught by child psychiatrist and social commentator Robert Coles. On the first day of class in early February, I walked into ILS-2 and there he was, seated, wearing the same blue shirt with sleeves rolled up too high, the same hiking boots I remembered from my college days.

"Hello, Professor Coles." I smiled.

"Hello, Rick," he said warmly.

I quickly took my seat and readied myself for a quintessentially anti-law school experience. Coles made some introductory remarks. We would study four Dickens novels—*Bleak House, Great Expectations, Little Dorrit*, and *A Tale of Two Cities*—and talk about what Dickens (and we) thought about the law, "about who gets justice and at what price." And then Coles stopped. There was silence.

People didn't know how to react to him, to this silence, to his rebellion against structure and organization. Coles just wanted us to talk, which would be a hokey idea with anyone but him. We moved from topic to topic: the law's reliance on precedent (in contrast to medicine, which tries to put aside precedent); Dickens's metaphors of law as fog, law as a dinosaur; the fact that Dickens was read in his day by nonintellectuals, that Dickens himself had never gone to the English equivalent of high school—"Admitted by no one, no place." Slowly, the students began to chime in. One woman sat doing a crossword puzzle, but in general there was a great deal of discussion and laughter, a general sense of relief, from the twenty of us present.

A few of us who had had Coles as undergraduates knew what to expect. I had taken both The Literature of Social Reflection (dubbed "Guilt 105") and The Literature of Christian Reflection. Coles would bound into the classroom in an old, beat-up parka and then begin to speak in a rough voice about Walker Percy and James Agee and Dorothy Day and Erik Erikson, all of whom he knew personally. Coles tried to teach us through novels because he had more faith in the humanities than abstract social science—novels filled with moral dilemmas and questions. He attempted to help us examine our privileged existence by questioning his own—his large house in Concord, his BMW. Some students disliked his lectures, said they lacked structure and focus, but most of us loved to hear Coles just talk for an hour about what was on his mind that day. I will never forget the undergraduate class when a member of the *Harvard Lampoon* burst into the room during the middle of a lecture and began imitating Coles's very distinct lecture style as part of the *Lampoon*'s initiation rite. Coles, unaware of the student's purpose, quietly asked him to leave. The professor then stood, in silence, for minutes that seemed like hours, visibly distressed. After the silence became unbearable, someone yelled out from the back row, "We love you, Doc." Four hundred students suddenly jumped to their feet, clapping furiously. I had never seen anything like it at Harvard.

I did not meet Coles personally until I interviewed him for my thesis senior year. I still remember the day I heard from him and another Kennedy associate, Adam Walinsky. Walinsky, now a corporate lawyer, had his secretary write to me in the lawyerly style of Dickens's Kenge: "In response to your letter of November 20, 1984, Mr. Walinsky will try to make himself available for an interview some time next month, but cannot guarantee a date at this moment." The Coles letter had a different tone: "I knew and loved Robert Kennedy—worked with him in those last, precious years of his life, and wrote the last speech he gave, and still mourn his death: he was the first and last politician to win the real trust, as you say, of people hitherto and henceforth politically 'apathetic.' I'd be glad to talk with you. Please call, and we can get together."

We did get together, and Coles spoke of an enlightened populism, which I found profoundly more persuasive than the standard high-minded liberalism. Now, in class, Coles returned to that theme. In *Bleak House*, Dickens writes of Mrs. Jellyby, who is so concerned with events in Africa that she ignores her own children. Coles wrote on the blackboard the title of the chapter where Dickens introduces Mrs. Jellyby: "Telescopic Philanthropy." Coles said, "There is plenty of that in Cambridge," and we all laughed.

The next week, the class was led by two students who had agreed to take charge of the session. They began the discussion by asking each person to talk about which *Bleak House* character she found most interesting. One student said he found Richard Carstone intriguing because he could identify with Richard's not knowing what career to pursue. Richard tries medicine, then law, then the military, but never finds his niche. Heads nodded in sympathy. Students spoke up, one saying he'd rather be a photographer, another a writer. No one present, it seemed, really wanted to be a lawyer. "You know, it's not too late to change," Coles suggested. His own career had spanned several professions: psychiatrist, writer, political activist and speechwriter, professor of literature. "Studs Terkel went to law school," he added.

A few students said they found the narrator of *Bleak House*, Esther, infuriating because she was so unbelievably selfless. Coles seemed interested in this pervasive cynicism and asked, "Is Jesus' life credible?"

The room fell silent. It was the first time in a year and a half I had heard mention of religion, much less Christianity, at the law school. Religion was anathema, the antithesis of pure reason and rationalism, for which the law school stood. From a literary standpoint, the comment was perfectly reasonable. Christianity was central to Dickens's moral awareness. But Coles had broken a taboo and we didn't know how to react. I noticed that a few people squirmed uncomfortably.

Neither Rebecca nor I was particularly religious, but we were both raised with religion and wanted "God" to be part of our ecumenical wedding service. A part of me was interested in hearing Coles talk from the perspective of the Christian left. That was the faith of my childhood, the tolerant, progressive Christianity of Reinhold Niebuhr, which had been lost in all the publicity about

Jerry Falwell and Jim Bakker and Pat Robertson. But what was to me familiar was apparently disturbing to others in the class, for Robert Coles was an intellectual with liberal credentials who couldn't be written off as a bumpkin born-again fundamentalist.

A number of students said they found Mrs. Jellyby interesting and railed against her telescopic philanthropy. Taking their cue from Coles, they regurgitated, one after another, his talk about Brattle Street liberals. They had learned that this was what Coles wanted to hear. When it came to me, I found myself in a strange position.

"I'd actually like to defend Mrs. Jellyby," I said. "I think Dickens's critique of her is basically right. It's important to attack the radical chic, especially in Cambridge. But what bothers me is what we do with the critique. Mrs. Jellyby is an easy target; it's easy for all of us to laugh at her. But does she become just one more rationalization for going into corporate law? Does she make us into cynical conservatives?

"People say that Ralph Nader is not a nice person to work for. That he's horrible to the people around him. But he's done a lot of good, too, and to focus on his shortcomings may just be a way to let us off the hook for being less than he is."

I looked over at Coles for approval. He was looking down, thinking. No one followed up on the point. The fellow next to me spoke about his favorite character, but I didn't hear.

The following week, I began to think the Coles class was evolving into a class on "What's Wrong with Harvard Law School." The main complaint was that we students were ignored. "Sometimes I feel as though the law school grinds on and the students are just extras," one student said. "As if the real purpose of the university was to allow professors to do their thing, and that the students were just here to make it seem like a university." The "extras" comment struck me as right; I thought back to how Professor Dalton's Contracts exam first year had asked students to provide legal theories in defense of a professor denied tenure, and how I had wondered whether she was using the exam for her own purposes. Other students chimed in, complaining that most professors never hand back exams, and those who did usually gave no comments. Susan Estrich was said to have joked that if she graded an exam in eight minutes or less, she allowed herself a Twinkie—and that she ate a lot of Twinkies.

Then someone asked, "If we all hate it so much, why don't we quit?" Every year a few first-year students decide after a week or two that the law is not for them and leave. People admire but do not respect them. For all my alienation, I never once considered leaving. So what keeps us in law school? Some students said it was the money. Having invested so much of it into the education, there's no alternative. Thus, the decision to go to law school, which was designed to keep options open, in fact closed them. But Coles, putting his finger on the best reason why we stay, asked, "Aren't there any Atticus Finches here?" These second- and third-year classes were filled with skeptics and cynics, but Coles was right: every once in a while many of us did see ourselves in *To Kill a Mockingbird*, defending the innocent victim of racial prejudice, or as Ralph Nader taking on GM. It was nice to be reminded of that.

The class discussion of *Bleak House* inevitably moved to Tulkinghorn, the high-status lawyer many of us would become. Dickens points out that Tulkinghorn gets his sense of dignity from the fact that his clients, the Dedlocks, are so wealthy and powerful. I thought about the countless interviews in which I had listened to lawyers tick off their firm's clients with great pride and about a lengthy *New York Times* obituary of a partner at Cravath which stressed not what he had done but who his clients were. I realized that Dickens haunted us with his relevancy.

At the next class, someone brought beer on Coles's recommendation that alcohol can enhance discussion. The brew made for a giddy atmosphere, as if we were naughty kids doing something we ought not to. So it was fitting that the youngest member of the class—an undergraduate who had weaseled his way in—really opened the discussion. While we were talking about the different ways the law treats the poor and the rich, this student asked, "Why not have lawyers paid for by the state?"

One law student laughed: "Life is unfair; law is just a reflection of that." As if that were the end of the matter.

Coles then asked, "But doesn't law have a higher standard for itself?"

We never resolved that question, but I left class thinking about the undergraduate's freshness, and about a passage I'd read from *Great Expectations* concerning a child's sense of injustice—how it is keen, not dulled by rationalization and "maturity."

> In the little world in which children have their existence, who-soever brings them up, there is nothing so finely perceived and so finely felt as injustice. It may be only small injustice that the child can be exposed to; but the child is small, and its world is small, and its rocking-horse stands as many hands high, according to scale, as a big-boned Irish hunter. Within myself, I had sustained, from my babyhood, a perpetual con-flict with injustice.

Had a year and a half at HLS served to numb the righteous anger with which we came to law school?

A week later, the class discussion focused on Wemmick, the law clerk in *Great Expectations*, whose awareness of injustice could be neatly turned on and off. During the day, Wemmick was brusque and arrogant, but at night, once he crossed his drawbridge to home, he was the kindest, most gentle son to his ailing father. In this one character and his bifurcated life, Dickens captured the central phe-nomenon of Harvard Law. During the fall interviewing season, how many corporate lawyers had responded to my question "Can you practice in a big private law firm and still be a good liberal?" with Wemmick's answer: "The office is one thing and private life another"? Coles said that the sociology of suburbs—the need for business executives to escape from their urban work lives—was bound up with Wemmick's drawbridge; and he added the sobering thought that the Nazi concentration-camp guards, who went home and were good, kind fathers to their kids, were only a more extreme manifestation of the compartmentalization seen in our lives every day.

A dark-haired woman, who peppered her comments with ref-erences to pop psychology, said she found Wemmick's approach misguided, because a job should be "an extension of oneself." A number of students jumped all over her. They countered, "Sure, it's nice to say a job should be fulfilling and consistent with one's personality, but most people don't have that luxury and work because they have to put food on the table." The dark-haired woman, like Mrs. Jellyby, was easy to ridicule, but in the context of Harvard Law School, I thought she was right. Fair or not, we did have the luxury of making our careers more than a way to subsist, and with that ability, I thought, came some obligation to make our careers reflect our values.

There will, of course, always be defenders of Wemmick. In college, I had gotten into an argument in the pages of *Harvard Magazine* about yuppies. John Moore, a student who was interviewing with investment banks, had said, "My occupation tells you nothing about who I am . . . You don't see me at confessional; you don't see me working with the Big Brother program; you don't see me criticizing the policies of the Reagan Administration." My response was that investment bankers and high-priced lawyers didn't have much spare time to do any of that. When you devote 80 to 90 percent of your waking hours to helping rich people stay that way, there just isn't much time to be Mother Teresa on the side. "How can you possibly divorce your career from your values?" I had asked. With Wemmick's drawbridge, Harvard Law students now answered.

April 14. The topic of discussion was: Why do we read *A Tale of Two Cities* in this seminar? What did it have to do with lawyers? To me, the answer was simple. *A Tale of Two Cities* is straight social criticism, which is the grist of law. My question, in fact, was the opposite: Why didn't Harvard Law School better equip us to take on the social problems Dickens portrays? I had come to law school expecting it to be a sort of continuation of a liberal arts education, a place to hone the analytical tools necessary to tackle important public policy questions. Now I often wished I had gone to the Kennedy School with Rebecca. The students and professors there seemed much more ready to tackle the Big Problems, while we were bogged down in the technicalities.

The discussion then turned to Lucie Manette in *A Tale of Two Cities*, who, like Esther in *Bleak House*, seemed to many in the class to be too good to be true. The dark-haired woman looked exasperated. She told a story about a friend in an immigration law course who said she took the class "because I want to do some good" and was met with a roomful of snickers. "This is the kind of comment you could make in high school and no one would laugh," the dark-haired woman said. "But here, it's guaranteed to evoke laughter—as if you're running for Miss America." Amen, I thought.

But the class intelligentsia disagreed. One student said the reason young people don't laugh at idealism is that they are unsophisticated and naïve about the necessity of compromise. They just speak in platitudes without thinking of the consequences. I shook my head. Hadn't he been reading Dickens, whose message was the very opposite? Hadn't he read Erik Erikson on the importance of not losing one's indignation? A second student added that talk about doing good was relative. The individuals who had recently hijacked a Kuwaiti airliner thought they were doing good, she pointed out. It was a nice rationalization: We don't know what's good, can't know, and therefore "who are we to judge?" Let's throw up our collective hands.

The last Dickens class met in early May. In the sun. Outside. With beer. The kind of class you would see pictured in the Harvard Law School admissions packet but in reality rarely met. Maybe it was the beer, but finally someone said what had needed to be said for weeks: he was planning to work for a big New York corporate law firm after graduation; for all the talk about how horrible lawyers were, and particularly those working in corporate firms, that's where he was heading. He wondered aloud whether he was the only one.

One student said he had, the day before, decided to give up a writing career and accept an offer from Weil, Gotshal & Manges, a big New York firm that (another student piped in) ranked among the top ten firms in the country.

"How do you rank them?" Coles asked.

The student dodged, saying they just have reputations, like prestigious universities. But of course Dickens had provided the answer in the character of Tulkinghorn; in twentieth-century America, prestige stemmed from representing the largest Fortune 500 companies.

The Frustrated Writer didn't quite make clear why he had, as he put it, "sold out." He said it had something to do with a lack of confidence that he could make it in the long run as a freelance writer. He said he was upset with his decision because he knew he would have to give up his writing. Someone asked why he didn't go to a smaller firm where less demanding hours might allow him to combine law and writing. It seemed he'd already sacrificed some prestige in turning down Sullivan & Cromwell, and to descend farther down the status ladder was asking too much.

It was an awkward moment, because the Frustrated Writer was not alone. Most of the 3Ls were going to be corporate lawyers. Were we just a bunch of hypocrites? We looked to Coles for the answer, as a student asked him about his frequent criticism of psychoanalysis, which seemed to parallel our criticisms of lawyers and law school. Why didn't any of us get out? Coles said that psychiatry, at its best, could help people figure out their problems. (And so, too, I thought, might lawyers counsel vulnerable people in trouble.) For all our complaining, both our professions had redeeming virtues.

Coles ended the class with an attack on CLS. Rather than writing incomprehensible treatises, he asked, "why don't they open a soup kitchen? Get down on their knees? This is what *Little Dorrit* is about." But I wondered, could the same thing be said of our Dickens class? The danger was that all our talk, which made us feel awfully guilty, wasn't enough.

Still, it was something. Although this type of open-ended seminar was looked upon by most law students as a quaint exercise of little relevance, what could have been more important as we decided now, finally, what we would really do with our lives? At its best, the Dickens seminar provided a reservoir of ideas which we could draw upon in times of moral weakness.

Coles came to represent and symbolize for me the counterpoint to Harvard's left, whose failure may have as much to do with driving people to corporate firms as the lucre those firms offer. Coles was populist where the left was elitist, plainspoken where it was incomprehensible and pretentious, idealistic—even spiritual—where it was cynical and dry. When Dickens and the Law ended, the students clapped and cheered Robert Coles in the open air. Coles was the real-life Atticus Finch for whom we had been searching, even if he was an Atticus Finch with a BMW. The only problem was: Bob Coles wasn't a lawyer.

CHAPTER

10

Ropes & Gray

Juice and coffee were waiting when I arrived, but what caught my eye were the muffins. They were large, moist, delicious, sugary muffins, just the kind you'd expect from Ropes & Gray. I smiled. The U.S. Attorney's Office never gave us anything, not even dry toast. Maybe I was making too much of it. But then again, Michael Kinsley entitled an entire book of essays *Curse of the Giant Muffins* —referencing Solicitor General Rex Lee's complaint that as a public servant he had to think twice about buying Giant brand or Thomas' English muffins. In a symbolic sense, the pricey muffins were the strongest thing Ropes & Gray had going for it.

The other summer associates began filing into the conference room and I was surprised to find that I knew some of them from college. Rob Shapiro, the bow-tied coordinating attorney, welcomed us and previewed the upcoming summer events: the firm outing at the Essex Club, the tennis tournament at Longwood, the lunches we were invited to at the Meridien Hotel and the Harvard Club. He told us, for the first time, what our salaries would be ($1,050 per week) and that most of us would get offers to return.

We soon broke up into teams of two for the firm tour. A short, dark-haired woman and I made the rounds with Tom Spence, a first-year associate from the trusts and estates department. We met dozens of attorneys who all asked the same thing. "What area of practice are you interested in?" I never answered the question directly. Instead, I said I was assigned to do corporate work with

Kevin Carome and trusts and estates work with Susan Shapiro.

In March, Ropes & Gray had sent us letters asking us to choose practice areas for the summer. Among the choices were labor, trusts and estates, corporate, real estate, municipal bonds, employee benefits, and health care. I was at a loss, so I called George to hear about his experience the previous summer at O'Melveny & Myers. He wasn't in but later left a long message on my machine.

> Labor law is basically oppressing laborers. Estates and probate work is largely planning the estates of very wealthy individuals in the Boston area. Corporate and business law tends to be helping large corporations take over smaller corporations, and therefore leads to the oligopoly of the wealthy and basically screwing the workers over to make enough money to pay for the loans they have to take on, which lawyers negotiate, incidentally. Corporate work also involves giving middle management and the above what they call "golden parachutes," which tend to be extremely large payments paid to management so that they will not object to and try to bar a takeover attempt.
>
> Real estate law involves helping large corporate developers buy up property at low prices, usually by using the mechanism of the state to rake in huge tax write-offs. Municipal-bond work involves floating bond issues which are bought by wealthy individuals in the United States and produce tax-free benefits for the wealthy individuals at high marginal tax rates . . . Employee benefits—figuring the best way to pay employees without incurring tax liabilities for either party so that they can compensate their employees at a lower wage scale and therefore save money for the corporation, which, needless to say, accrues to the high management's benefit in that they can pay themselves higher wages.
>
> I think they're all equally enjoyable, you fascist pig. Bye-bye.

I had put down trusts and estates because it was reputed to have the best hours. (How else could Louis Auchincloss churn out all those novels?) Later, one T&E lawyer justified his job—making sure wealthy people can keep their huge sums of money in the family—by stressing the lawyer as humanitarian, making life easier for people at a time when they have just lost a spouse or a loved one.

The other question, invariably, was: Where do you go to law school? My partner was from Northwestern. She then experienced subtle condescension from all the Harvard associates and partners: "Oh, Northwestern." (Brightening) "That's an excellent law school."

Tom was very interested in the history of Ropes & Gray, pointing out pictures of the founders, John Codman Ropes, and John Chipman Gray, Jr., who wrote the most dreadful treatise on the Rule against Perpetuities, which has confused property law students for generations. We walked past Eleanor Acheson's office. "That's Dean's granddaughter," Tom whispered. The tour ended in the library, which was very, very nice—Oriental rugs and luxurious chairs—a place for deep reflection on profound legal questions.

After an introductory lunch, they flooded us with papers and procedures. They handed us W-4s, calculators, Dictaphones, and a key (to what, I would never find out). They also gave us two books: a face book listing all the attorneys and their alma maters and a bound 215-page history of Ropes & Gray, a pompous volume whose bias toward Harvard was obvious when it made references to, simply, "the Law School," as if there were no other.

I was exhausted by mid-afternoon, when we completed orientation. I was told to call Ed Joyce and Susan Shapiro to get my first T&E assignment. I was to write a memo on the legal standing of the will of a deceased woman which made reference to a second will, that of her husband, which had been subsequently revoked. I left at six, thoroughly confused.

Day 2. All I remember is the Lunch. That's the common rap on law firm jobs: summer associates don't remember the work they do, only the lunches. Maybe that's the plan. The lunch was at Maison Robert, a pricey restaurant Rebecca and I had been to once on some special occasion in college. Tom Spence (my tour guide) came, as well as my two supervising attorneys. The assemblage was intentionally well balanced: first-year associate, mid-level associate, partner.

There was an awkwardness to the group that made it nonthreatening. Susan was a nonconformist who had come to R&G in the years when women didn't do such things, which made you feel she wasn't looking for Right Answers to her questions. Kevin was quiet and thoughtful and wore what used to be called Earth shoes. Tom, with his bow tie, was the only one who fit the proper Ropes & Gray stereotype; but he was a first-year peon and wasn't powerful enough to intimidate me. Susan asked me why I wanted to be a lawyer. I talked about wanting to shape public policy, etc. Tom said he had been very interested in politics but had almost entirely lost interest. (What was he interested in? Trusts and estates?) Susan asked why I'd come to Ropes & Gray. "For the prestige" didn't sound good, and being a basically truthful person, I fumbled for an answer. All I could muster was: "It's not a union-busting firm . . . is it?" When I sensed I was on the ropes, my interview-dodging skills snapped back into place and I instinctively found myself asking Tom, Kevin, and Susan about *pro bono.* Kevin and Tom didn't seem to do any at all and mumbled about wanting to. Susan said she did some Bar Association stuff.

It began to rain. Our lunch was approaching two and a half hours. I asked perhaps the most clichéd of law student questions: "What's the structure of the firm?" Susan said it was based on the Harvard Corporation, which is to say that power is concentrated in a small, self-perpetuating board called the Policy Committee. When we returned from lunch, I felt like taking a nap. On my desk was a memo asking whether I wanted filet mignon or poached salmon at the firm outing.

As the first weeks passed, I found the work uninteresting but not particularly "bad guy." The estates research generally involved which wealthy party would get the money. Kevin had me do some research for J. Bildner, a yuppie grocery store which eventually filed for bankruptcy. No foreclosures of penniless widows, but, in all, rather uninspiring work. Kevin, I noticed, had a practice of crossing days off his calendar as they passed. I began to do the same. But for him, the end was not in ten weeks; it was partnership, perhaps, or retirement, or eternity.

I shared my frustration at the monotonous, uninspiring work with another summer associate on the subway home one night. I told Danny, a Yalie, that I didn't like applying other people's rules; I wanted to be involved in writing the rules. That's why I wanted to work on a Senate staff: to help make policy. Danny laughed and said it would be some time before we would be in a position to make policy. Fair enough, but I felt his attitude was at the heart of the problem. The feeling of impotence creates indifference: why work myself to death under unpleasant conditions on a government salary when one person cannot make much of a difference anyway? I should have quoted him Tocqueville on the importance of lawyers in American society.

The tedium of the work was broken only by the Lunch Challenge. There was a competition, of sorts, to see who could get invited to the most free lunches. I was the champion. (At last I was a legal star!) There was the weekly Associates Lunch at the Veritas Room at the Harvard Club. The monthly Probate Lunch at the Downtown Club. The Venture Capital Lunch. The Health Care Lunch. The Labor Lunch. My heartfelt interest in each of these areas was timed to their lunch meetings. But even this grew tiresome, for in order for the lunches to be tax deductible, "business" had to be discussed. (At one probate lunch, an associate posed a particularly complex legal question. "How much money is involved?" someone asked. $40,000 was the answer. "Don't research it," two partners said at the same time, both of them laughing.)

Monday, June 6, was full of unwelcome excitement. At 11:00 I went to return a Blue Sky Reporter to a corporate associate, Megan Chambers. Megan was a master of Blue Sky Laws, the state corporation laws designed to protect investors from fraudulent sale of stock—speculative schemes having "no more basis than so many feet of blue sky." For fun, Megan competed with another Blue Sky attorney in memorizing section references. As I approached the elevator, I noticed the glass door to the elevator lobby was closed. A man with a walkie-talkie let me through and closed the door behind me. The receptionist looked nervous. A young black man walked down the stairs from the twenty-sixth floor and she grew tense. He walked past and she yelled to someone upstairs, "Who was that black kid in shorts?"

Another lawyer who had been waiting for the elevator with me looked down at the ground. To be sure, R&G had three black attorneys out of 234, but that was said to be related to "standards." The secretary's form of racism was more embarrassing. The lawyer introduced himself as Chris Klem. I asked him what was going on and he said a group of people were on the twenty-sixth floor protesting Harvard's investment in South Africa. They had taken over Thomas O'Donnell's office. (O'Donnell was a senior partner, member of Harvard's Board of Overseers, and co-chair of Harvard's committee considering whether the university should divest.)

At the weekly summer associate lunch, all the talk was of the protesters. Rob Shapiro made some jokes about starting a counter chant and almost everyone laughed. When I returned to my office, I·had a stern Office Memorandum sitting on my desk: "A small group has gathered in Mr. O'Donnell's office to demonstrate against apartheid. We would appreciate all personnel staying away from that area of the firm."

At 4:45, I went on a walk. I could see about ten or fifteen individuals milling about, filling the air with their cigarette smoke. They were much older than I expected, few college kids. Almost all were white. From the back, I could see Archie Epps, the Harvard Dean of Students who had dealt with Harvard protesters for years. It was, once again, the black dean negotiating with a group of white protesters about apartheid. The anti-apartheid rally had brought more blacks to Ropes & Gray than I'd ever seen before—that is, the forces brought in to deal with the group of white radicals, from Epps down to the security guards, were almost all black.

After ten hours, the eighteen protesters were arrested for trespassing and were carted away in a police bus. That night, pictures of the chanting protesters—"Hey, hey, ho, ho, there's blood on your portfolio"—were all over the evening news. The activists charged that Ropes & Gray's representation of corporations that did business in South Africa created a conflict of interest for O'Donnell. Channel 7's Rehema Ellis interviewed Bruce Mark, of the Apartheid Divestment Coalition, saying, "I think it shows the true colors of Ropes & Gray. They clearly don't have any concern for what's going on in South Africa." The camera cut to a sweating, bespectacled, buttoned-down Tom O'Donnell saying, "They insisted on remaining in the office, and we finally felt we had no alternative but to have them removed." He sounded eminently reasonable, no Bull Connor with fire hoses, but the sweat was a little too reminiscent of Nixon.

But on Channel 5, the Ropes & Gray incident was tied to stories about a general strike in South Africa and to Robert Kennedy. As the demonstrators had been occupying the offices in Boston, there had been a mass of remembrance and rededication for Kennedy in Arlington, Virginia. Channel 5 showed clips from the service, and then Natalie Jacobsen made the painful transition: "Robert Kennedy was ahead of his time in many ways. Even some twenty-two years ago, he was an outspoken opponent of apartheid, a bitter struggle that continues even now in South Africa." Channel 5 briefly ran the South Africa general-strike story, then told of the Ropes & Gray protest, with pictures of a phalanx of police on motorcycles in front of Ropes. This was more like Bull Connor, with Robert Kennedy and black South Africans on the other side. "Harvard has roughly $200 million invested in companies that do business in South Africa," it was noted. Of course, that's why Joy had worn an armband at graduation in 1978. That's why, freshman year, I had protested in front of the Harvard Faculty Club. That's why Elizabeth Whitman participated in a sit-in outside Bok's office. Freshman year, I had discovered that I was not really at ease with the hard-core drug-consuming left that was the backbone of these protests. But never did I think I would see myself working for the opposite side.

The next evening, at the cocktail party for summer associates, the protest was still on everyone's mind. A partner, Paul F. Perkins, Jr. (Harvard College '45, HLS '48), nostalgically remembered the takeovers at Harvard in the late 1960s, when he had worked with Archibald Cox to thwart student demonstrations. I said I had taken a course with Cox as a freshman, that he was a hero of mine from Watergate. Perkins came back about how smart Cox was in outfoxing student demonstrators. We were on entirely different wavelengths, both of us admiring Archibald Cox, but for very different reasons.

On Friday, I attended the weekly Partners' Lunch at the Meridien. I sat with what turned out to be the Policy Committee: Thomas O'Donnell, Francis H. Burr (who ran Harvard's 350th Anniversary Celebration Commission), Truman Casner, and a few others. Casner began asking about the Harvard graduation ceremonies, held the day before. O'Donnell and Burr, both of whom had sat on the dais, said they had some problems with "Derek's speech."

To my mind, the speech, which I read, had been brilliant. "At one commencement after another, speakers point to such problems [as crime and poverty] and exhort students to address them with vigor and dedication," Bok declared. "I will not repeat this message. On the contrary, I would like to question its sincerity, or at least its seriousness." Then he turned inward. "Let us consider our own Harvard students. In our law school, the percentage of graduates going into public interest and legal aid has dropped to less than 2 percent while the percentage of graduates entering government service has drifted downward from 4 percent or more ten years ago to slightly more than 2 percent today. Almost all of our remaining law school graduates go into private law firms, either immediately or after a year of clerking for a judge."

Bok, though, went beyond the statistics to ask why. He looked at the obvious answer first. "Much of the explanation, I fear, has to do with compensation." He explained that, in the last fifteen years, the gap between the starting salary of a Wall Street firm and the Justice Department had grown from $3,000 to $40,000, with a few top law firms now paying as much as $85,000 starting salaries. But Bok looked deeper to the nation's commitment to national service; he compared the days of John Kennedy, when "public service was the exciting career for college students across the nation," to the last twelve years, in which politicians competed in berating government. Bok ended by quoting "our distinguished alumnus Franklin Roosevelt," who had told Harvard to train its students "to be citizens in that high Athenian sense," which compels them "to live a life unceasingly aware that its civic significance is its most abiding." This was not the first time Bok had deplored the rush to corporate law. In the early 1980s, he had blasted the legal profession for taking the nation's best and brightest students and diverting their talents to "pursuits that often add little to the growth of the economy, the pursuit of culture, or the enhancement of the human spirit."

Now, at lunch, O'Donnell fastened on to the $85,000 starting salary figure Bok had cited, saying that it wasn't accurate. Burr pointed out that Bok was not completely correct when he said Lee Iacocca made $16 million last year: much of that was in stock options, not cash. Perfectly true, I thought, but could these men's minds have been so narrowed by the law as to miss the larger picture? To recognize that even if the starting salary was $50,000 and Iacocca's salary $1 million, it still might be obscene? I didn't

say anything, of course, being the direct beneficiary of this particular obscenity, and not wanting to damage my chances of an offer.

Instead, I turned to the attorney sitting next to me, Bill Mc-
Carthy, and asked him about the tightened security that had gone
into effect again that morning. "So, do you know if we're expecting
more protesters?"

He said he didn't know but was annoyed by the inconvenience.
I wasn't particularly bothered—the security was no different from
that at the U.S. Attorney's Office or the LDF. But then I realized
there was more at stake here. The absence of security is important
to a firm's notion that it's not involved in politics, only pure law.
(Politics inspires anger and passion; law does not.) Security guards
at 225 Franklin Street were a stunning concession to the crits' belief
that all law is political.

McCarthy said he had been away Monday and had missed the
South Africa protest, but that the television commemorations of
R.F.K.'s life brought back memories of his days at Harvard Law
in the late 1960s and early 1970s, when the hard-core left was in
ascendancy. He said his law school roommate was from Berkeley
and told him, "Let's go check out the protests. It's a great place to
pick up women." I smiled awkwardly. O'Donnell and Burr loved
it.

The same day that Bok gave his commencement address, George
Bush was giving a speech to the Texas Republican Convention
deriding Michael Dukakis's "Harvard Yard Boutique" foreign policy, while also blasting liberal elitism and hypocrisy. "Bush Paints
Rival as Elitist with 'Harvard Yard' View," *The New York Times*
wrote. Never mind that Bush, the Yalie, was showing just a little
hypocrisy himself in attacking Harvard elitism. In his use of the
Harvard Yard Boutique metaphor, Bush had managed to encap-
sulate the central problem of the Democratic Party: the dominance
of liberal elitists—out of touch with the everyday concerns of working Americans—who espoused lofty ideals like civil liberties and
integration while exempting themselves from the consequences.
Bush realized that the problem with American liberalism was the
problem with Harvard: the deeds never seemed to match the lofty,
high-minded level of the words. The press picked up on Bush's
critique and concluded that while Bush represented a financial elite,
Dukakis represented an intellectual elite. But the whole point about

Harvard Law School was that the sharp distinction between financial and intellectual elite was false, the line was blurred. The intellectually elite students at HLS were dead set on becoming the financial elites of tomorrow. Liberal intellectuals wanted to be rich, too, and no one said there was anything wrong with that. To be a liberal was easy: you could act one way and all that anyone really expected was that you continue to mouth the right words.

As the summer at Ropes & Gray progressed, there were more lunches and outings. There was the Labor Law Lunch, where the firm's lawyers discussed the ways to counter various worker claims, including how to combat an age discrimination case and how to open a new position in a hospital without getting union approval. There was the firm outing, on June 15, held at the Essex Club— a day filled with golf and tennis and filet mignon and speeches. Someone said the South Africa protesters should have been given water but not allowed to use the restrooms. Conservative humor.

There was the Corporate Lunch at the Meridien—attended by a hundred men and a handful of women—where I learned that women at Ropes do trusts and estates and health care but not corporate law. There was the outing to see Mats Wilander and André Agassi play at the Longwood Tennis Club, where I spent much of the evening talking with a summer associate's boyfriend about leftist deconstructionist theory. There was the summer associates night at Fenway, where an R&G attorney sat with a stack of twenty-dollar bills to cover whatever food or drink people desired. And there was the annual Lobster and Clambake at Dave Donaldson's enormous house on Weston Road in the fancy suburb of Lincoln, with the subtext: Come to R&G and this could all be yours.

Amid it all, I did end up doing a little bit of work. Lawyer-client privilege prevents me from getting too specific (as does the desire not to put the reader to sleep), but suffice it to say that I spent time trying to help the New England Patriots avoid paying John Hannah damages for allegedly making him play when they knew it would cripple him. I helped a number of wealthy individuals make sure that their money would stay in their families or, in one case, that the money would go to that most worthy charity, Harvard's ultra-elite Porcellian Club. And I worked on one *"pro bono"* project to revise the Massachusetts Corporate Law to make it more favorable to corporations. When I suggested that we recommend that workers be represented on boards of directors, the idea was not taken to kindly.

It was against this background of tedium and boredom and purposelessness that, on June 27, Rebecca gave birth to little Cynthia Ann Kahlenberg. I took a week off work, and when I returned I would spend my days wanting to be home with my two beauties. While I was writing meaningless memos, Cindy began learning how to smile, to hold her head up, to roll over, and to become adjusted to this world.

During the rest of the summer, there were more lunches and dinners. Ed Hanify spoke to summer associates about the history of the firm and the committee presently updating the firm's history book. (Hanify, I was told, had defended Ted Kennedy at Chappaquiddick; now, that would have been interesting to hear about. But instead, my eyes glazed at the recitation of the R&G history.) The following day, there was a special Exit lunch at the Meridien, at which we were supposed to say what we liked and disliked about the summer program. But with our offers not yet clinched, the discussion was, of course, rather one-sided. The offer—indelicately nicknamed "The Big O" by summer associates—was an obsession for many, especially those who didn't go to name schools. I'd always assumed I'd get an offer, until a friend told me that one of the few students rejected the previous summer was an arrogant summer associate from Harvard.

August 3 was the dreaded Steve Perlman lunch. For two weeks, Perlman, a partner in the firm, had been taking out groups of summer associates to talk about the future—making partner, the firm's organization—which seemed presumptuous to me, since we hadn't even received offers to be associates. Perlman loved talking about the firm and, in particular, money. He said not to worry about the fact that at R&G it took nine years to make partner; he boasted that he had made more as an associate than lawyers in other firms made as partner. And so it went.

That evening, Susan Shapiro had Rebecca, Cindy, and me—along with a first-year T&E associate—over to her huge house on Essex Road in Chestnut Hill. It was one of those no-trade-off houses: convenient location with lots of land in a safe, established neighborhood. As the maid cooked dinner for us, I asked the first-year associate what the difference was between being a summer associate and being a real associate. "You have to work," he said. We all laughed.

As the summer came to a close, I realized that a part of me would miss Ropes & Gray. Many of the lawyers, especially the younger associates like Kevin, were sensitive, interesting, and kind. The money was nice, as was my large office on the twenty-fifth floor with a great view of Boston Harbor. I had grown to like the free cab rides when I stayed late, and the night typing pool, which allowed me to put in a marked-up memo at night and have a cleanly typed copy the next morning. The work itself generally seemed ideologically neutral. "You can't see people as wearing white hats and black hats," Rob Shapiro told me at my Exit Interview. "If all these people—the vast majority of practicing lawyers—are doing something wrong, that's quite an indictment of our system."

By the end of the summer, I had come to believe that most high-priced attorneys did not wear white hats or black hats: they wore no hats at all. They just came to work every day to do jobs that were of little social importance. They had no "cause" to get excited about—which is why lunches and money became paramount.

PART III

Three L

11

Bore You to Death

The bearded man, dressed in a lavender shirt and blue seersucker jacket, was sitting Indian style on top of a desk in the front of the room. "This course is designed to have no practical value," he said.

Welcome to Third Year.

The old adage about law school is that first year they scare you to death, second year they work you to death, and third year they bore you to death. Indeed, since the inception of formal legal education, various thoughtful people have suggested abolishing the third year entirely. Because that blessed day had not arrived and I was determined to get my money's worth, I stacked my schedule with five courses: Labor Law and Antitrust were important populist arrows for my legal quiver; Government Lawyer described what I might become; a Kennedy School course on press treatment of the (ongoing) 1988 presidential campaign sounded interesting; and before I left law school, I simply had to take a course with the man with the lavender shirt and blue seersucker jacket who prided himself on teaching impractical courses—Duncan Kennedy.

Kennedy, the self-proclaimed "radical," affects the life of every Harvard Law student, whether they take his course or not. From day one, you hear about "Dunc's" antics and outlandish ideas: his proposal to admit students with minimum qualifications to Harvard Law School by lottery; his plan to pay law professors, secretaries, and janitors identical salaries. And so, Dunc's course in Legal History, which will win you no job and advance no one's career, has grown each year, as the devoted and the curious come together to watch him in action.

"This is a lecture course, so you don't have to do the reading," Kennedy told us the first day of class. We laughed. Kennedy wasn't one to sugar-coat. "The phrase 'theoretical, abstract bullshit' will often run through your mind as I lecture," he warned.

Kennedy divided American legal history into three periods: rise (pre-classical), apogee (classical), and fall (realist). The pre-classical period ran from the American Revolution to about 1850; the classical period, when everything fit neatly and made sense, ran from 1850 to 1935; and the realist period, since 1935, attacked classicism as oversimplified and began a period of disintegration. "This course could be called a Death of Law course," he said triumphantly—as triumphantly as Christopher Langdell had proclaimed the classical period in his own era. Aware that his three-part division of history was itself an oversimplification, Kennedy deadpanned that if an 1830 opinion looks classical, it's labeled a "precursor," and if a classical opinion appears "too late," it's termed a "remnant."

As with all good CLS courses, Kennedy assigned Karl Marx's "Essay on the Jewish Question" for the first class. Kennedy explained Marx's theory, expanding on the well-known dictum that religion is the opiate of the masses. Religion allows people to be "grubby" with property was Kennedy's translation. You have a right to withhold food from your neighbor—to deny subsistence to others—if you own the property. The rationale is that civil society is neatly divided between property rights (the right to be selfish) and religious rights (which push people toward altruism once a week). The benevolent impulses are put on the state, but the state is restrained from redistributing too much wealth.

This was all very fine and good, but I wondered why Kennedy didn't update Marx's dichotomy and point out how many Harvard Law students use it, in a modern form, for their own purposes. HLS graduates pronounce their politically correct positions just as loudly as people used to advertise their religious devotion. You could be a greedy corporate lawyer by day because your liberal, political side made it okay. The good impulses were channeled into your politics, but the demands of your job (time and need for respect) restrained the impulse. The hypocrisy built into the old system survived with or without religion.

By the end of September, Kennedy had begun his march through history. He was especially fascinated by the American Revolution. "It was something big," he said, as opposed to the ongoing presidential race between George Bush and Michael Dukakis, "which does not make any difference." The Revolutionary era decided great questions, Dunc said in an animated voice, like what to do with the glebe lands of the previously established Church of Virginia. In *Turpin v. Lockett* (1804), the court upheld a legislative decision to sell the lands of the Church and give the proceeds to the poor. "Those were the days," Dunc joked.

He was at his most provocative, however, one afternoon in mid-October when alumni flooded his class to catch a glimpse of the infamous Marxist. He took a jab at alums who were hoping he would say something outrageous by arguing that practicing lawyers earn their salaries every day, proving the CLS theory: that the law has gaps, conflicts, and ambiguities. If the law were settled and clear, he said, lawyers wouldn't have anything to argue. I wondered, as I watched the alumni watching Dunc, whether my fiftieth-anniversary class would remember Dunc and his movement. Would this period in legal history be known as the Critical Legal Studies period? Kennedy seemed confident, pointing out that the Realists really made inroads only at Columbia Law in their day and were a smaller group than CLS.

But as Kennedy babbled on about "legitimation," "hegemony," and "mystification," one often wondered what the hell he was talking about. During a break one afternoon, I heard a student complain that he hadn't understood a word Kennedy had said. "How can you evaluate what he's saying?" he asked. Maybe that was part of the point. Kennedy realized that he was getting less and less lucid. ("This is really fuzzy, dangerous-of-sliding-into-bullshit stuff," he said one class.) But the self-awareness never brought forth subsequent clarity.

To try to understand Kennedy better, I purchased his "little red book," *Legal Education and the Reproduction of Hierarchy: A Polemic Against the System*. It was stacked near the checkout counter at the Harvard Book Store law annex, and as I picked up a copy, I asked the clerk how popular it was.

She said it sold well. "We keep it up front—it's an impulse item."

The book was more concrete and readable than any of Kennedy's other essays, which is perhaps why it is the one most widely cited. Putting into practice the CLS credo to "fight illegitimate hierarchy wherever you are," Kennedy's book focused on legal education, arguing that law schools contributed to illegitimate hierarchy in the bar and in society as a whole. Kennedy's admonition to students was "Resist!"

At the outset, Kennedy set himself in opposition to the traditional liberal idea "associated with Brandeis" of the law as being "socially constructive"—an idea that I held dear. Kennedy's view was more radical—that "law is a tool of established interests." Still, as I read on, I found myself agreeing with a great deal of what Kennedy had to say. I fully concurred with his general thesis: that "law schools are intensely political places." Kennedy argued that the faculty tried to obscure the political nature of law—by distinguishing between law and policy—in a number of ways. Within a given subject area, such as contracts, cases were divided into those that presented "the law," on the one hand, and the "cutting edge" cases, which raised "policy issues," on the other. By implication, policy issues were not present in the first, larger, set of cases. The distinction, Kennedy said, "between the unproblematic legal case and the policy oriented case is a mere artifact." Likewise, the overall law school curriculum reinforced the law/policy distinction. First-year courses—Contracts, Torts, Property, Criminal Law, and Civil Procedure—were hard law. Second- and third-year courses, having to do with the New Deal regulatory state, involved policy. The implication, again, was that the laissez-faire rules of property, contract, and tort law stem from "legal reasoning, rather than from politics and economics."

Kennedy's book also talked about the way first-year law professors sapped their students of common sense, to say nothing of common decency. When a case is presented in which the law allows a coal company to swindle an Appalachian farm family, the point of class is to show that "your initial reaction of outrage is naïve, non-legal . . . There are good reasons for the awful result, when you take a legal and logical view, as opposed to a knee-jerk passionate view, and if you can't muster those reasons, maybe you aren't cut out to be a lawyer."

The heart of Kennedy's essay was that legal education reproduced hierarchy in the bar in three ways: by analogy, by legitimating the status quo, and by structuring law graduates hierarchically. First, because legal education was internally structured like the bar—law schools were ranked, just like law firms—the former reinforced the latter by analogy. And the hierarchical relationship between professors and students (professorial use of the Socratic method and failure to provide detailed feedback indicated a general disrespect) modeled the relationship between partners and associates. Second, legal education legitimized the status quo by trying to depoliticize law; by saying that legal reasoning was different from policy analysis, professors taught that legal reasoning was not really open to question. Finally, because the "best" (richest) law schools got the "best" professors and the "best" students, the inequality among law schools was accentuated, making the bar's hierarchy among firms seem natural.

Beyond all this, there were other links between law schools and the legal bar which Kennedy's book made me see for the first time. For example, there was a connection between the erosion of student self-esteem and the flow of graduates into large law firms. "Law school . . . teaches students that they are weak, lazy, incompetent and insecure. And it also teaches them that . . . large institutions will take care of them almost no matter what." Likewise, the fact that law schools teach doctrine rather than legal skills makes an apprenticeship with someone who can afford to provide it, generally law firms, the most enticing option upon graduation. (Government jobs can provide good trial experience, but many students shy away from their "sink or swim" method of training.)

And, reading Kennedy's book, I came to realize that his ideas had been misrepresented by some of his opponents. For one thing, Kennedy was not waiting for some grand revolution. Even if a "band of revolutionaries" took over, he said, they would be incapable of changing much of the "hateful stuff." In fact, he wrote, a full-scale revolution might degenerate "into revolutionary dictatorship." His ideas, he said, had "nothing to do with preparations for a violent mass uprising or a coup d'état." Likewise, Kennedy had his disagreements with Karl Marx: "There is no 'logic' to monopoly capitalism," Kennedy wrote; and later: "In the modern structure of hierarchy, the proletariat has ceased to exist . . . Welfare mothers, illegal immigrants and urban squatters simply are not a revolutionary class." Nor was Kennedy a complete nihilist. "What is needed is to . . . criticize [law] without utterly rejecting it," he said. *The New Republic*, in particular, had unfairly ridiculed Kennedy for advocating minor professional risk-taking, "because 'all over the world, workers and peasants and political activists have risked and lost their lives.' " In Kennedy's next sentence, he explicitly states, "There is a gulf between these two kinds of action, and I have no desire to minimize it."

Still, some of Kennedy's ideas did seem outlandish. He proposed randomly assigning professors and students to different law schools; he also would pay lawyers, law professors, secretaries, and janitors the same salary, as mentioned, rotating everyone periodically. And, fundamentally, I disagreed with Kennedy that all the hierarchy he described was necessarily "illegitimate." Dunc admitted that some hierarchical order—e.g., parental power over children—was legitimate, but his antipathy for hierarchy put him in opposition to traditional notions of meritocracy. Now, I had my own problems with meritocracy and hierarchy—namely that meritocracy doesn't exist, because rich people start out ahead of the game, and that the amount of inequality isn't justified by the social need for it. But Kennedy said even if those objections were addressed, even if meritocracy accurately reflected merit and the amount of inequality maximized the efficiency of labor, he'd still be opposed to it. Hierarchy, he wrote, "is something to be hated even as we enjoy its benefits."

Likewise, Kennedy never really answered—in class or in his book—the criticism that the crits tear everything down without proposing anything in its place. They did put forth superficially concrete proposals (lottery admission to law school, etc.), but their proposals were largely designed to make people think and to "reveal the hidden ideological presuppositions of institutional life" rather than to be adopted.

In class, Kennedy's response was that CLS never intended to scorch the earth; it wanted, rather, to unravel the sweater, so that law could be used to achieve the correct outcome. But rather than flesh out what he meant by this, Kennedy jokingly analyzed his own position. "Notice the domestic metaphors," he said, paying homage to the feminist complaint about the use of male-dominated sports metaphors in legal education. (Kennedy also likened the American Revolution to a pasta machine.) In his book, all Kennedy could muster was "Even though we have to make it up as we go along, it is something to know what one is against."

But what really disappointed me about Duncan Kennedy was his inability to inspire; indeed, his penchant to ridicule that which was inspiring. In his last lecture of the year, while other professors were doing their best to portray the law as an elevating force, Dunc belittled one of the great liberal justices, Felix Frankfurter, and the generation of Harvard lawyers he encouraged to join in Franklin Roosevelt's New Deal, with the cynical phrase, "Frankfurter and his hot dogs."

Not only did he forfeit idealism, Kennedy also forswore an appeal to *noblesse oblige*. The corollary of his basic argument—that hierarchy was bad, that to be a Harvard Law student didn't mean beans (a lottery would work better than the admissions system that allowed you in)—was that the Harvard Law student had no special obligation. The problem was, if you destroy elitism, you destroy its benevolent fruit.

Dunc's pervasive cynicism appeared, at first, to be a good defense against charges of hypocrisy. He couldn't be accused—as the liberals could—of saying the law was noble while being ignoble himself. But in the end, it became clear to me that Duncan Kennedy didn't live by the standards he set for himself either. Dunc said he was a radical, and "the radical is the person who *wants to go further*, right now, practically, to dismantle existing structures of hierarchy that look evil." But the semester I had him, he didn't do it.

Dunc said that there was a much greater need for "constant, detailed feedback" from professors; but Legal History had, like all other courses, a single exam. He said that students needed clinical training; indeed, he required it in his utopian proposal, because if the law schools didn't provide it, corporate law firms would fill the vacuum; and yet, Kennedy bragged that our Legal History course had "no practical value." Dunc complained that the richest schools got the best professors, thus accentuating inequality; but Kennedy qualified as "the best" by all the familiar meritocratic criteria and had not spread the wealth by going to Northeastern.

But worst of all, I thought the manner in which Kennedy presented his ideas was a massive contradiction of his avowed hatred of hierarchy. Because much of his work was incomprehensible, affected, abstract, and theoretical, it was put outside the reach of most people, most Harvard Law students, and even some Harvard Law faculty. To Kennedy's credit, it is tough to translate complex ideas into laymen's language. (Archibald Cox used to say he liked to teach constitutional law to undergraduates because it was more of a challenge.) But there were some basic things Kennedy could have done to broaden his readership. He could have skipped the pretentious analogies to art and music. (In class, when he began analogizing classical legal thought to Brahms, he tripped himself up and was buried by students who knew better.) He and the crits could have dropped some of their references to semiotics, the French deconstructionism of philosopher Jacques Derrida, and the Frankfurt school of German neo-Marxists. And Kennedy should never have employed that horribly elitist phrase "false consciousness," which implies that all those who disagree with you are stupid.

In the end, the critical techniques Kennedy employed to show the gaps and internal contradictions in today's legal doctrine could be redirected at him. But the gap between Kennedy's ideas and his actions does not make the theory wrong and the practice right. Time will tell whether Duncan Kennedy and the movement he leads turn out to be a mere impulse item or something much more.

On the occasions when Duncan Kennedy sank further into abstraction, I would turn to my customary reading, the *Harvard Law Record*, which happened to be distributed on the days Legal History met. In early November, the top news was the upcoming student referendum on a Fairness Amendment to the Law School Council Constitution. The amendment, backed by conservatives, forbade ideological discrimination in the naming of student government committee members. (Discriminations based on gender, race, sexual orientation, or ethnicity were already banned.) Conservatives, primarily members of the Federalist Society, complained that they had been excluded from a student dean-selection committee and said they needed the constitutional amendment to protect them against further abuse by the liberal majority at HLS. (In April 1988, Dean James Vorenberg had announced his decision to resign effective June 1989, and the search was in full swing.)

I was incredulous. While conservatives were clearly a minority at HLS (a *Record* random survey that week found Dukakis defeating

Bush 73–23 among HLS students), it was inconceivable to compare an ideological minority circumstance with the status of women and racial minorities, who had an entire history of racism and sexism to overcome. As I read the *Record* article, I realized that the Federalists had employed an old conservative trick: frame an issue in terms of abstract theory (fairness) and ignore the concrete social reality (that America's real victims have been blacks and women, not white male conservatives). For years, judicial opinions had mystified the underlying conflicts they addressed by referring to the parties as "plaintiff" and "defendant" rather than, say, "the impoverished tenant" and "the wealthy landlord." By dehumanizing the parties, abstracting them into the realm of legal theory, judges could help diffuse whatever humane sympathies students instinctively held for the underdog. Concrete reality was almost always on the side of the left (which is why Kennedy's forfeiture of that fertile ground for the netherworld of abstraction was so puzzling).

On November 7, I voted against the so-called Fairness Amendment. It was soundly defeated, but the issue didn't die. During the debate over the amendment, Federalist Society president Robert Schwartz, a conservative backer of the proposal, received a note from Luke Houghton stating, "I think you and your *untermenschen* are full of it." *Untermenschen* was Hitler's term to describe Jews and other non-Aryan groups, and Schwartz, who was Jewish, understandably took offense. At first, it appeared that Houghton had slipped into the type of anti-Semitism that had driven a number of Jews into the neoconservative camp. But Houghton later said he did not know the history of the word. He had read it "in a manuscript some days before and, not speaking German, roughly translated it as 'undermen,' " he explained. "In the context of what I read, it was used in the sense of 'underling.' " Thus, if not anti-Semitic, Houghton was, instead, guilty of the left's penchant to be pretentious.

Postscript: Second semester, Derek Bok appointed Robert Clark to replace Jim Vorenberg as dean. Everyone was astounded. Clark was to the right what Kennedy was to the left: its leading and most vocal advocate. All the articles leading up to the choice had speculated that Bok would choose someone who could heal the ideological divisions within the faculty. Instead, Bok picked the one figure who represented all that the left despised. Clark championed the fight against Dalton and successfully appealed the faculty decision to grant David Trubek tenure; he taught corporate law, had practiced at Ropes & Gray, and had thought about becoming a priest. He was, more often than any other professor, the subject of lampoon in Houghton's weekly cartoon. When *Time* did a story about CLS at Harvard, they ran three pictures: " 'Crit' Kennedy" on the left, Dean Vorenberg in the middle, and "Foe Clark" on the right. And now Bok had chosen the Foe to run Harvard Law School. The liberals and the crits on the faculty were outraged. Jerry Frug said, "This was the worst possible choice Bok could have made." David Kennedy said, "Bok could not have picked a dean who was more likely to exacerbate divisions in the faculty." And Morton Horwitz commented, "It is a disaster for the law school."

In one fell swoop, Bok completely destroyed all the Federalist Society talk about conservatives being a minority at Harvard Law School, on a par with the blacks and Hispanics. Sure, the vocal students were often left of center, as were many of the professors. But when push came to shove, the people that really mattered weren't the students on the dean-selection committee. The people to whom Bok wanted to send a clear message were not the students or the faculty or the *Boston Globe* but the alumni, who, after all, financed the place. Poor Jim Vorenberg had been a little soft; after contributions had fallen and a conservative had left the faculty, Vorenberg had had to write 28,000 alumni and say that no, the crits weren't taking over Harvard Law. Derek Bok wasn't about to make that mistake again. The large headline in *The New York Times*—TRADITIONALIST IS NAMED AS HARVARD LAW DEAN—was reassuring news to the large firms on Wall Street and Park Avenue. The students could wail and the faculty could grumble but, in the end, Derek Bok knew who his real constituents were.

The postscript to the postscript is that when Robert C. Clark became dean of Harvard Law in 1989, one of his first acts was to shut down Ron Fox's public-interest office. Another was to deliver a widely quoted speech telling students that practicing law for a large corporate firm was not "selling out," as if HLS graduates needed any further encouragement to pursue that option. Gifts to Harvard Law School increased 64 percent.

———

Labor Law, taught by Paul Weiler, was in many ways everything Duncan Kennedy's Legal History was not. Weiler, a quiet, mild-mannered liberal, taught a basic course in a real area of law without revolutionary expectations—all of which meant Weiler caught the ire of Kennedy's followers in the class. When Weiler began laying out the history of the labor movement in America, the hard left attacked, asking why he didn't spend more time discussing the radical Knights of Labor. Weiler disposed of them (the students) neatly, quoting the great Samuel Gompers, who had said that the American Federation of Labor (AFL) was more interested in improving the conditions of the workers here and now than in hastening the advent of a utopian society. Also, in contrast to Kennedy, Weiler was careful to note the important contribution of Harvard graduates and professors who'd done concrete work on labor law. Louis Brandeis wrote much of the 1914 Clayton Act Section 6 exemption for labor from antitrust law; Felix Frankfurter wrote the Norris–La Guardia Act in the 1920s; and Paul Freund, as a young HLS grad, helped develop the Wagner Act. I found it all inspiring.

Indeed, I found the subject matter of the course uniquely exciting. It dealt with what I saw as the central conflict in America—class—rather than the clash of interests between one amoral corporation and another. And the subject had an immediacy to it, as Harvard was then attempting to block the formation of a union for the university's 3,400 clerical and technical workers.

The union drive, the latest round of which had begun in 1987, drew national attention for two reasons. First, it represented a new effort by unions to attract female members. Eighty-three percent of the clerical and technical workers were women, according to *Ms.* magazine. (Many of Harvard's male-dominated trades were already organized.) The effort, therefore, stressed issues of particular concern to women, like affordable child care, as well as the more traditional concern about wages. One employee said Harvard's on-site day-care center would cost 75 percent of her salary for her nine-month-old son. Second, this organizing effort involved Harvard, which naturally drew a certain amount of national attention. Union organizers capitalized on Harvard's name, with slogans like "We can't eat prestige." The average salary—$19,000, according to the union—was inevitably discussed in the context of Harvard's enormous wealth.

But what I found most interesting was the role of Harvard president and former labor-law professor Derek Bok. Bok was, according to *The New York Times*, "a man who had made his academic reputation defending the right of collective bargaining." His 1970 book, *Labor and the American Community*, laid out strong arguments about the importance of unions to workers and the poor. But now, as university president, he vigorously opposed unionization and, in a letter to employees, warned: "Unions have typically resisted efforts to reward superior achievement with greater compensation or to allow supervisors and employees to vary the way they work in response to their special needs and capabilities."

Bok and Harvard had narrowly beaten union drives in 1977 and 1981. Harvard's lawyers then went to court to widen the bargaining unit in an effort to make unionization harder. And when, in May of 1988, the workers voted narrowly to join the union, Bok appealed the vote, arguing that union organizers had violated NLRB rules. Union proponents called the move sour grapes. Said one, "I think it's a big corporation that's never lost anything before reacting badly." In late October, Weiler told us that an administrative-law judge, after lengthy hearings, had rejected all twelve of Harvard's objections. Weiler didn't talk about Derek Bok's role. (A union organizer said, "Derek Bok has one foot in one world and one foot in another world, and he's being torn apart.") But Weiler's approach to the practical application of labor law theory was very different from his boss's. In December, on the last day of class, Weiler told us he was going down to Williamsburg that Thursday to speak at a workshop for the AFL–CIO on labor reform which had been organized, he hastened to add, before the Dukakis–Bush election. The class laughed. Maybe Weiler was tilting at windmills, but at least he was consistent.

The Labor Law exam contained a question in a form I had never seen. Instead of asking me to play the typical role of an associate at a law firm, the exam began, "You are the legislative assistant to a newly elected Senator who has just been appointed to the Senate Labor and Human Resources Committee." I smiled to myself.

My third class was Government Lawyer, with the equally earnest Nick Littlefield, a tall man with frizzy hair, thick glasses, and a bubbling enthusiasm. I had seen Littlefield at various public forums, including Scott Turow's speech, when Littlefield introduced Turow as a former student.

The first day of class, Littlefield outlined the various functions of a government lawyer and spoke of his own involvement in government: he had been, among other things, an assistant U.S. attorney in the Southern District of New York and an attorney at the Middlesex County (MA) D.A.'s office. Littlefield mumbled that he was currently doing criminal defense work. My friend George leaned over and told me Littlefield was at Foley, Hoag, a distinguished Boston firm.

Littlefield then launched into a discussion of how powerful government lawyers are. It was this rather uncomplicated theme that he would pound away at, class after class, as if the only thing that could lure us away from the lucrative salaries of the private sector was the power of the public sector. Littlefield seemed to get excited as he spoke about power, his sleeves rolled up, his voice rising. He had the same look in his eyes that Giuliani's lawyers had had. The investigation stage of a prosecution is key, he said, because a solid investigation can make a prosecution a "slam dunk of a case." No feminine metaphors for this macho prosecutor.

But the following week, when Littlefield argued that the government lawyer's goal was not just to win cases but to do justice, the class began to regard him as soft. Fundamentally, one student said, all lawyers want to win their cases.

"What if the opposing lawyer gives his client bad advice?" Littlefield asked earnestly.

"That's not my job" was the response.

This discussion seemed to arouse a number of dormant hard-ass white males who chose this class because they were interested in putting some people behind bars. In class discussion, the conservatives would argue for prosecution in a given case and add comments like "Have fun in jail," with a Clint Eastwood flourish. In the coming weeks, the class would increasingly come to resemble the *Morton Downey Show*. Littlefield tried to get the class excited by illustrating the power of young government attorneys with the entrepreneurial work of young SEC lawyers who went after foreign corruption of U.S. companies in the 1970s. No one in class seemed to care; in some foreign cultures, one student argued, you have to give bribes to get ahead.

By mid-October, the conservatives, who, for once, seemed to

represent a sizable chunk of the class, were openly grumbling about Littlefield's flabby liberalism. He got as little respect as government lawyers do. At one point, when the class took a ten-minute break, a student set the clock ahead. It was embarrassing when Littlefield figured it out. Even worse was that he looked at George and me as if we had done it.

As the weeks wore on, Littlefield relied more and more heavily on guest speakers. One week, he brought in Professor Robert Blakely of Notre Dame, a man who, he said, has "one of those great government careers." After graduating from law school, Blakely held a number of positions, including ones with the McClellan Committee, R.F.K.'s Department of Justice, and the congressional subcommittee which drafted the nation's major racketeering statute known as RICO. Blakely spent most of the class defending RICO against attacks from the civil libertarians present. He parried them well and ended by telling us that one person can make a difference, that one of us could do something comparable to writing RICO. The speech, which won me over, would have been a hit anywhere else. But all Blakely got was a bunch of cynical stares.

My fourth course was a Kennedy School class taught by Gary Orren on the press and the 1988 presidential election. Orren announced the first day that he would require an extensive research paper from each of us and that the best student pieces might be included in a book. Because the class was oversubscribed, he asked each of us to write a short essay—on an aspect of media coverage of the 1988 campaign—which he would use as the basis for choosing class members.

I wrote about the media's widespread use of the term "Reagan Democrats." I argued that the expression, used to describe white working-class Democrats who voted for Reagan, was deceptive and misleading. It implied that that group of voters was swayed by one man's charm and that it would be easy to win back. In fact, students of American politics knew that Reagan Democrats were nothing new; before Reagan, they were Nixon Democrats, and before that, Wallace Democrats. I cited the relevant statistics illustrating that blue-collar defection began in 1968 and had been a major weakness for Democrats ever since. The problem was much older, deeper, and more complicated than Ronald Reagan's smile. The division had its roots in race; for at least twenty years, the Republicans had shrewdly exploited the racial animosity between lower-middle-income whites and blacks and Hispanics to dismantle the New Deal coalition. As I worked on my essay, I couldn't believe it was for a course for which I would receive law school credit. I realized that politics and public policy were my passion, not law. And when I was accepted into Orren's class, I began to wonder more and more whether I would have been better off joining Rebecca at the Kennedy School.

The tone of the place was so very different from HLS's. For one thing, the professors were more approachable. Professor Orren told us to call him Gary, and Rebecca's Kennedy School professors were known to invite their students over for parties. For another, the K-School courses were designed to take on the great social and political problems of our time, involving issues such as health care, foreign relations, and poverty. The Kennedy School's purpose was so much more grand than that of the law school. I had gone to law school because lawyers have, traditionally, played an important public role in American society. The majority of the signers of the Constitution were lawyers, as were more than half our Presidents. Today, more than half the U.S. Senate is schooled in law. As Tocqueville observed, lawyers are "a somewhat privileged intellectual class" in America, who "serve as arbiters between citizens." When I was applying to law school and asked Dick Neustadt for a recommendation, he sighed and said that most of his undergraduate students went to law school. As one of the Kennedy School's architects, Neustadt was disappointed that more of the brightest were not attracted to the master's in Public Administration or Public Policy.

But if my experience is any measure, I think Neustadt will, in the long run, win that battle. As the Kennedy School grows older and more established, its prestige will begin to match that of the law school. Students who are truly interested in tackling some of society's most important problems will increasingly gravitate toward the Kennedy School and see law as a more narrow field akin to accounting. Not that the Kennedy School doesn't have its own problems. The school's emphasis on mechanics and management

over vision is a perennial concern. And the pressure to sell out to
the private sector, though not as intense as in law school, reaches
one-third of the Kennedy School, as McKinsey and other consulting
firms look to Kennedy School graduates for recruitment. But there
is a vibrancy at the K-School absent in the law school, an excitement
that stems from a general sense that people are there because they
want to be, not because they feel they should be.

I delved into my research project, comparing the press treatment
of George Bush and Richard Gephardt, with a verve unknown to
me since college. The thing I found most fascinating about the 1988
presidential campaign was that the George Bush of Andover, Yale,
and Skull & Bones was able to portray himself as a pork-rind-eating
populist and label his opponent a Harvard elitist. I thought the
press was disgraceful in letting Bush get away with it. At the same
time, I noticed that the media was ruthless in its coverage of the
one genuine populist in the field, Missouri congressman Dick Gephardt. The media labeled him all but a fraud, making front-page
news out of the accusation that he darkened his eyebrows.

My examination of press coverage by the news weeklies and the
television networks confirmed my hunch. Even though Bush's cul-
tural populism (emphasizing the flag and the ACLU) had much less
substance to it than Gephardt's economic populism (centering
around economic nationalism), it was Gephardt who was called a
phony, while Bush was given a fairly free ride. Why was there
differential treatment? After sorting out a number of possibilities,
I argued that the press had become an elite which was highly
uncomfortable with Gephardt's economic populism. George Bush
could rant and rave about symbolic social issues, but the press
thought there was little chance that a Yalie would really implement
the Archie Bunker wish list.

Along the way, I had a wonderful time interviewing a number
of political journalists whose careers I had followed for some time.
I talked to *Washington Post* columnist Mark Shields, whom I found
delightful, and Ellen Hume of *The Wall Street Journal*, whom I did
not. Hendrik Hertzberg, a speechwriter for Carter and editor for
The New Republic, met me at his cubbyhole on 53 Church Street
near the Kennedy School. I had to sit in the hallway because you
couldn't fit two chairs in his office. Hertzberg was as intelligent,
articulate, and funny as his articles, although there was something

truly bizarre in finding that a man at the top of his profession was working in such cramped, dark, dreary surroundings.

My fifth and final course first semester of third year was Antitrust with Stephen Breyer. I signed up for the class in part because my populist philosophy said that the concentration of wealth and power is inherently bad and in part because Breyer was a practitioner of the law, not a woolly-headed theoretician. He had tried antitrust cases, had served as Ted Kennedy's aide on the Senate Judiciary Committee, and was now a federal judge on the First Circuit Court of Appeals.

But the class did not live up to either of my expectations. Antitrust law, it turned out, now had little to do with the idea that concentration was dangerous in itself and was more concerned with the efficiency of markets than with fairness. And Breyer, the practitioner, turned out to be the most eccentric and academic of all my professors, Dunc notwithstanding. He made highly intellectual jokes about antitrust theory which almost always went over most of our heads.

As my disenchantment grew, I began scheduling all my fly-out interviews on the days when Antitrust met. On the occasions I did attend Breyer's class, I would rush home afterward on my bike and enter an entirely different world. My daughter, Cindy, was six months old and represented all that the law school crowd was not: she was innocent, where it was cynical; youthful and fresh, where it was dried and old before its time. At law school, there was the continual chattering of the same old teeth, whereas at home, each tooth was new, painfully earned, but original. When Rebecca brought Cindy to the law school to pick me up, my fellow law students would gasp at her with wonder and say they couldn't even begin to contemplate having a baby. I relished my role as proud papa.

In the third year, as in the second, Harvard Law had a three-week winter term in which students took one intensive course, which met daily. I chose Alan Morrison's Litigation Workshop.

Morrison, a short, bearded man with thinning hair, began his class by saying he hoped it would be different from other HLS classes. In other classes, he said, you're taught "on the one hand . . . on the other." Life doesn't work that way, he claimed, and it was his aim to help us reach a bottom line, to teach us "judgment."

I was intrigued by Morrison's background. In a reversal of the more predictable pattern, he had left law school apparently expecting to be a traditional corporate attorney (he went to the New York firm of Cleary, Gottlieb, Steen & Hamilton for two years). It was later that he went on to the U.S. Attorney's Office for the Southern District and then on to the Public Citizen Litigation Group, founded in the early 1970s in association with Ralph Nader's public-interest movement. In 1986, Morrison's reported salary was just over $40,000 a year. "I'm giving up some things, but I don't consider them as important as the things I'm getting," he told *The National Law Journal.* "I really think I'm making a contribution to the public good." As director of the premier public-interest law group in the country, Morrison had argued ten cases before the Supreme Court. In recent years, he had won victories striking down the legislative veto in the historic Supreme Court decision *INS v. Chadha*, and had temporarily dismantled the Gramm-Rudman deficit-reduction law in the Supreme Court case of *Bowsher v. Synar*.

Morrison had a zealot's drive to win, which shaped his course. The seminar was meant to teach us techniques for each stage of litigation, and the cases he drew upon for illustration were ones in which he himself had been involved. "You have to know the drug company's arguments," he said, discussing the first day's case, "because they'll hire the best high-priced lawyers." In real life, the company had hired Covington & Burling. Morrison joked, "They're certainly high-priced lawyers."

Each student was given a different case and asked to prepare a document representing a different phase of litigation. On January 19, the class discussion centered on my case, which involved the conditions under which class-action suits could be brought in state court. My assignment was to write an *amicus* (friend of the court) brief. This was of great interest to the other students, since *amicus* briefs are generally written only for important appellate cases. Several students asked successive questions about *amicus* briefs. I began to daydream until I remembered I was on the hot seat!

My task was to argue that it was valid to try a national class-action suit (with plaintiffs from several different states) in an Illinois state court. Federal court was unavailable because the case did not raise a federal question and each claim did not satisfy the federal $10,000 minimum requirement. Defendants of the suit argued that plaintiffs would have to try fifty separate class actions in fifty separate states, because to apply Illinois law to New Jersey or Pennsylvania plaintiffs violated the principle that a court must have "personal jurisdiction" over the case.

In the real case, Arthur Miller, representing the defendants, had argued that an Illinois court lacked personal jurisdiction over nonresident plaintiffs in a class-action suit because granting jurisdiction would violate the sovereignty of other state courts. Miller said personal jurisdiction doctrine was based on federalism and "turf." In my brief, I spent a great deal of time arguing that nonresident plaintiffs in a class action deserved only "due process"—protection of individual liberty; territorial, or federalism, concerns did not enter in.

"You used a cannon to shoot a fly," Morrison said.

I responded that I had spent a lot of time on the question because the territoriality argument was put forth by the nation's leading authority on civil procedure. "I guess I was intimidated by Arthur Miller." The class laughed.

"I wasn't intimidated by Arthur Miller," Morrison shot back in classic Morrison fashion. *The National Law Journal*'s front-page profile of Morrison in 1986 read, "He's Not Humble—But He Gets Results."

Still, as the term wore on, Morrison began to grow on me—the way David Rosenberg had—by sheer dint of dedication. Unlike most professors, Morrison read each of our briefs carefully and offered detailed remarks. He knew the importance of evaluative comments. In discussing *certiorari* petitions, which are used when appealing to the U.S. Supreme Court, Morrison said, "If you don't think the Harvard Law School gives you feedback, the Supreme Court gives you none." Just "cert. denied." At the end of the term, he said he'd help people with job recommendations and advice because he probably knew our work better than most people. He was right. In any event, he told us to look him up when we got to Washington, and I felt he actually meant it. Morrison was an unusual combination: a progressive, a practitioner, and a nice guy; he defied the Dickens stereotype of the reformer who loves humanity but hates humans. And he was a living refutation of all those at the firms who said that in order to be influential you had to spend your life in a firm handling Big Dollar cases, waiting to be tapped by a Democratic President. For all these reasons, Alan Morrison was truly subversive.

12

Out of the Question

. . . just up ahead, from the swell-looking doorway of 44 West Seventy-seventh Street . . . was . . . Andy Heller! No doubt about it whatsoever. He had been in Kramer's class at Columbia Law School—and how superior Kramer had felt when Andy, chubby bright little Andy, had done the usual thing, namely, gone to work Downtown, for Angstrom & Molner. Andy and hundreds like him would spend the next five or ten years humped over their desks checking commas, document citations, and block phrases to zip up and fortify the greed of mortgage brokers, health-and-beauty-aid manufacturers, merger-and-acquisition arbitragers, and re-insurance discounters . . .

Why, then, did Kramer now hold back? Why didn't he march right up and sing out, "Hi, Andy"? He was no more than twenty feet from his old classmate. Instead, he stopped and turned his head toward the front of the building and put his hand to his face, as if he had something in his eye. He was damned if he felt like having Andy Heller—while his doorman held his car door open for him and his driver waited for the signal to depart—he was damned if he felt like having Andy Heller look him in the face and say, "Larry Kramer, how you doing!" and then, "What you doing?" And he would have to say, "Well, I'm an assistant district attorney up in the Bronx." He wouldn't even have to add, "Making $36,600 a year." That was common knowledge. All the while, Andy Heller would be scanning his dirty raincoat, his old gray suit, which was too short in the pants, his Nike sneakers, his A&P shopping bag.

—TOM WOLFE, *The Bonfire of the Vanities*

I read this passage in August of 1988 and replayed it in my mind a hundred times during the third year of law school, as I thought about what kind of lawyer I wanted to be. This was the real thing. No more trial runs. No more summer flings. No more postponing

what most law students go to law school to put off in the first place.
I had to decide (for now at least) what to do with my life.

Law firm practice was out of the question. It was boring. It
required endless hours away from family. It was amoral at best,
immoral at worst. (One friend told me that she came across a law
firm which, in defense of a baby-car-seat manufacturer against a
tort claim, had argued that because the baby, now a quadriplegic,
was black, damages should be reduced since, statistically speaking,
the victim's earning potential was small.)

And then I'd think of Larry Kramer hiding from Andy Heller
and wonder if choosing an unusual path was shortsighted. I would
read a *New York Times* article about the skyrocketing price of houses
in the Washington, D.C., market. I'd look down at Cindy, playing
on her quilt, and want to provide well for her. I was quite genuinely
conflicted—much more so than I expected to be.

Rebecca and I had decided we would move to D.C. after graduation, and when we went on a three-week vacation, I laid out all
the options before me. In the executive branch, I could do something in President Dukakis's Administration, for the Department
of Justice or the Securities and Exchange Commission, perhaps,
assuming the poll numbers held and Dukakis won. In the legislative
branch, I could be a "bright young staffer" to the Judiciary or Labor
Committee, or to an individual member like Senator Gore, Kennedy, Moynihan, or Biden. That's what Walinsky and Greenfield
had done for Robert Kennedy, indeed what R.F.K. himself had
done soon after law school. In the judicial branch, there was still
the possibility of a clerkship, since some judges put off the decision
to hire until third year. I felt ambivalent about pursuing a
clerkship—I wasn't looking forward to more humiliation and I was
more interested in policy than law. (Later, a friend of mine who
was clerking for the Supreme Court told me how frustrating it was
dressing up policy arguments as legal doctrine while the Congress
across the street could debate the pure policy questions without
pretense.) Still, a clerkship was an important credential, and if one
landed in my lap I probably wouldn't turn it down. On the public-
interest front, the best places in Washington were Public Citizen
and the Children's Defense Fund, though neither generally hired
straight out of law school. There were plenty of civil rights and
civil liberties groups, but as my politics evolved from liberalism to

populism, I'd come to think vindicating legal rights, while important, didn't go to the central problem of economic injustice—which was handled in the political arena. I thought about trying to pursue a career in journalism, at places like *The New Republic* or *The Washington Monthly*—but even if I could land such a job, it would take a good deal of courage to jettison law entirely. And finally, of course, there were plenty of law firms in Washington. The best (according to Arthur's sources at the Law Review) were Arnold & Porter, Wilmer, Cutler & Pickering, Williams & Connolly, and Covington & Burling. They'd all rejected me the previous year, so I had to consider the so-called second-tier firms, Steptoe & Johnson, Hogan & Hartson, and the D.C. branch offices of O'Melveny & Myers, Davis Polk, and Paul, Weiss.

Ropes & Gray also had a Washington office, and in early September I received a call at home from one of their attorneys.

"Rick?"

"Yes."

"This is Peter Erichsen calling."

"Oh, hi, Peter, how are you?" (enthusiastically).

"Fine." Pause. A very long pause. Oh no, I thought, I'm getting the ax. It had happened to others.

"I'd like to extend an offer to work full-time at Ropes & Gray."

Cindy smiled at me. I took it as a sign from above that she wanted me to take the money, support her in the way she ought to be supported.

Then I realized she was just responding to her daddy's smile.

I told Peter we were thinking of moving to Washington and that I was interested in the Ropes D.C. branch office.

My interest in firm practice grew, ironically, the more I spoke to people in the public-interest and government community. When I met with Ron Fox, the public-interest coordinator, in late September, I asked him about HLS grads going to Capitol Hill. He said there had been one the previous year and she had had to wait until June to get a job (which, it turned out, was with the Post Office Committee). He reminded me that law firms which interview at Harvard have to keep offers open until April 15 to allow students to pursue public-interest options. But when I spoke with a friend from Senator Proxmire's office, he told me it was virtually impossible to get a senator to commit by April 15 to hire someone who wouldn't start until June. (Another Hill veteran later told me if you are hired April 15, they'll want you to start April 16.)

I also met with Neustadt, who said going to a firm for a few years was the safer, conventional route. He was right: people don't go straight to a Senate staff; they practice law and go over to the Hill at a higher level. And who should know better than Neustadt, the author of *Presidential Power*, how to maneuver in Washington? What was discouraging was that no one said, "Go be a Senate staffer right now." Not Neustadt and the Establishment, not Duncan Kennedy and the anti-Establishment. I told Neustadt that I was tired of jumping through hoops, that law school had been one big, extremely unpleasant stepping-stone and I'd had enough for a while. But I stated the words with more conviction than I really possessed. Harvard Law School gave me an engraved invitation to join the Liberal Establishment, that group of powerful Democrats who move back and forth between the public and private sectors, and it was awfully hard to pass up. Indeed, that invitation was to me far more seductive than the money.

I decided not to decide. I would look at the top D.C. firms, choose one, and hope that a better job would become available before April 15. This strategy had the added advantage of getting me down to Washington a number of times for free, visits in which I would spend part of the day with the firm who'd flown me down and part on the Hill looking for jobs. I felt slightly guilty about this, but as there was a good chance I would end up at one of the firms, I felt justified. I was told I was a prude for having qualms at all. Many students used the free fly-outs for more clearly personal reasons—like seeing family—and then bragged about it.

And so, on October 6 I found myself back in the Sheraton Hotel, clad in a suit, along with all the others, ready for another round. I knocked on the door and Larry Tu of O'Melveny & Myers's Washington office opened the door and invited me in. He offered me drinks and coffee. Here I go again, I thought.

Tu asked me why I was looking at O'Melveny and I told him I was interested in working for a firm in Washington because that seemed the way to get into policy-making positions in government. Tu agreed. He seemed, in fact, to have the same sort of plan in mind, saying he didn't know what he would do if Dukakis won. He said he had assisted O'Melveny partner William T. Coleman,

Jr., Transportation Secretary under President Ford, in Coleman's testimony against Robert Bork. It also turned out that Tu had worked for former Attorney General Ramsey Clark's firm one summer on the basis of the firm's one-page "manifesto." "We will extend our practice to any area of law we find interesting, any cause which is just, any principle we see imperiled, any worthy enterprise needing our skills," the firm had declared. "We will not appear on behalf of any cause which we believe is wrong."

I said that Clark's firm sounded wonderful; Tu laughed and cautioned me that I was talking to an interviewer from O'Melveny, and a corporate lawyer to boot. Tu said he thought his social impact was neutral on the surface (it was one large corporation against another), but in the larger scheme, he was supporting the system, which wasn't neutral.

I told Tu I was worried about having enough time for Rebecca and Cindy. He had a two-month-old son, and his wife was a partner at Kirkland & Ellis. They were on their third live-in nanny. "It's not an ideal situation," he said.

The morning of October 12, I was up at 6:00 a.m. to catch the 7:30 shuttle to D.C. to visit the Ropes & Gray branch office. On the plane, the flight attendant was handing out complimentary copies of *The Wall Street Journal*. A front-page story revealed that Roger Fisher, the progressive HLS professor known for his book on negotiation—whom I had seen at a peace conference freshman year— had been hired by the life-insurance industry to smooth out the differences between investor-owned and mutual companies, to present a unified front against tax changes. On page 4, another liberal hero, Iran-contra investigator Arthur Liman, was now passionately arguing, "I'm not going to be intimidated by any judge for asserting the rights of my client." His client?—chief Drexel junk-bond king, Michael Milken.

As the plane touched down at National Airport, I looked out the window and saw the Capitol dome, which I still found thrilling. I took a subway to the Hill for a series of interviews with staffers. I had started my search at the HLS public-interest office, which kept a file of alumni who were willing to help students find jobs. I would meet with as many people as possible now in the hope that they would call me if they heard of openings later. Hardly any jobs on the Hill are formally advertised, and when they open up, they are quickly filled by word of mouth. A few jobs are advertised by the Democratic Study Group (DSG), which serves as a clearinghouse of sorts, so before my first interview I stopped by the House-side DSG office. There was no one there. I went to the next room, where a DSG official was immersed in a deep discussion with a fellow employee about a personal matter. When he became available, the DSG staffer told me, in a perfect monotone, to fill out an application form and take a typing test. I said I was skipping the typing test because I was not interested in a secretarial position and he gave me a look that said, "Oh, you're one of those."

My first appointment was with David Heymsfeld, counsel to the House Aviation Subcommittee. He ushered me into a cubicle, which was his office. I asked him how he liked his job and he complained about the difficulty of getting things typed, but said his work was highly fulfilling. Here was a fifty-year-old Harvard lawyer without a real office but content with his choices in life. It turned out, someone told me, that Heymsfeld had written most of the nation's aviation legislation. Heymsfeld put me on to Congressman Norm Mineta's (D-CA) administrative assistant (AA), Susanne Elfving, whom I met with at 12:20. The AA is the top person in a congressional office, but she, too, had to share an office—in her case with the congressman! Elfving was extremely pessimistic and said it was very, very difficult to get a job on the Hill.

After a quick lunch, I grabbed a cab to Ropes & Gray, where they'd already given me a job. The office had dark wood, gold elevators, and smiling secretaries. Everyone was very kind. *They wanted me!*

I met with a couple of Harvard grads and was then ushered in to see partner Tom Susman, the resident politico. I had heard about Susman my summer in Boston. He had worked for Ted Kennedy's 1980 presidential campaign, had served on the senator's personal staff, and had run Kennedy's Judiciary Committee. All this made Susman a key element of Ropes's D.C. presence. I asked him what he told people who claimed he'd sold out. Puffing on his cigar, he replied in a Texas drawl, "That's a softball." A nonissue. He did *pro bono* work, and in his view, it was important to spend time in private practice because it sharpened your mind. Next question.

Back in Cambridge, I continued my bifurcated job search. I interviewed with Harry Jones, Jr., of Hogan & Hartson, a black partner who said the *pro bono* program (set up by Judge John Ferren) was one of the best and that there were lots of liberals at the firm. I sent out a stack of about seventy letters to representatives, senators, and congressional committees. I had lunch with a couple of friends who had worked on the Hill before law school and got from them names (which were like gold) of staffers on Capitol Hill. I had brunch with George and his girlfriend, Jessica, neither of whom was looking at firms, which made me feel better about public-interest law.

The next night, Rebecca and I had dinner with another couple, Steve and Jane Boutris. Steve, who had graduated from HLS in June, was at a small firm in Boston called Rich, May, Bilodeau & Flaherty, making $50,000 a year. Steve said he felt good about his work. He said he was involved in facilitating commerce and creating jobs—bringing people together to build shopping malls and to produce electricity. Of course, Steve's point would have been stronger if the function of lawyers was to create rather than to shuffle papers. But the reality is, under current circumstances, lawyers are a necessary ingredient for promoting commerce. Besides, Steve said, since I'd gone to law school, I should at least try to be a real lawyer for a few years before diving into politics. He claimed, as Susman had, that private legal work sharpens you. I found myself agreeing with Steve, just as I had agreed with Heymsfeld when he said public service was more rewarding. I began to feel like Ronald Reagan: I agreed with whomever I talked to last.

Meanwhile, I was continually frustrated in my attempt to pursue public-interest or government law. When the House Legislative Counsel—the office which drafts laws for the House of Representatives—came to Harvard to interview (one of the few public groups that did) I was frozen out of one of the twelve available slots, which had been awarded by lot. During a break in Antitrust class, I attempted to meet the interviewer to see if I could squeeze in an appointment, but was unsuccessful. I later called the Counsel's office to make an appointment in D.C., but they said because I had lost out in the Harvard lottery I had simply missed the boat.

It was quickly becoming clear that law firms provided the most certainty of providing gainful employment. They were the ones who were quick to give callbacks and solid offers of employment. While the firms were receiving me enthusiastically, no one on the Hill was even nibbling.

And so, on October 26, I was up again at 6:00 a.m., preparing to go down to Washington to visit O'Melveny & Myers, the large Los Angeles firm which had a highly political D.C. branch office. Among the lawyers were Warren Christopher, Carter's Deputy Secretary of State, who'd negotiated release of the American hostages in Iran; Tom Donilon, a hot-shot political operative then in the throes of the Dukakis campaign; and, as mentioned, William T. Coleman, Jr., Transportation Secretary under Ford and a distinguished officer with the LDF.

The cab took me to the O'Melveny offices at 555 13th Street, N.W., just a few blocks from the Ropes & Gray office. The building was comparably plush. But what was truly impressive was the firm's glossy brochure, featuring photographs by Ansel Adams. I was handed a card listing the people I was to see—twelve in all! (This would be the source of much small talk with subsequent recruitment coordinators—"Seven interviews? That's nothing. At O'Melveny I had twelve." Ha ha ha.) The D.C. office was small, I was told, so the attorneys wanted to be very sure they didn't get stuck with a jerk.

My first appointment was with a partner who looked over my résumé and said he knew people in Ridgewood, New Jersey, my parents' community. It was a bad sign. People who knew people in Ridgewood were invariably bland Republicans. At 10:30, I met with another attorney who saw Nairobi on my résumé and wanted to talk about her safari. Another bad sign. People who liked to talk about safaris usually knew people in Ridgewood. They loved animals and didn't bother to meet any Kenyans. My 11:00 appointment was an improvement. He headed the *pro bono* effort in the office and did some exciting appellate litigation.

Lunch was wonderful. I went to the Occidental, a cushy Washington restaurant, with John Holum, special counsel to the firm who'd been with George McGovern forever, and Jonathan Moore, a young associate who was straight out of Yale Law and was, therefore, completely in tune with what I was going through. Holum spent the lunch entertaining us with his political stories. He said Gary Hart was really a decent, caring human being, but that whenever Holum would set up dinners with journalists to show Hart's human side, the candidate would blow it by getting into arguments. After Hart dropped out of the race, Holum said he had been summoned to Arkansas along with a few others by the state's governor, Bill Clinton. They expected Clinton to announce he was going to throw his hat in the ring. Instead, Clinton told them he had decided not to run when his daughter asked him, "Would running for President mean you couldn't coach our soccer team?"

I realized midway through lunch that we hadn't spoken a single word about firm practice.

I asked Holum whether he ever received ribbing from his old liberal friends for having sold out.

"No," he replied. "They've all sold out, too." Laughter.

"The one who used to lord it over me was Frank Mankiewicz," Holum said. But even Mankiewicz had become an executive at Gray & Co., now Hill & Knowlton. The talk turned to sailing and Holum's new house in Annapolis, where he went on weekends. Selling out had its advantages.

I walked back to the office with Jonathan. Our backgrounds were similar: he'd gone to Princeton, then abroad on a fellowship, then to law school. He said people actually liked Yale, and made me wish I'd gone there. I wondered whether passing up O'Melveny might not be another mistake.

After lunch, there were more interviews. One associate told me he spent a great deal of time in homeless shelters, asking people about their legal problems, because those concerns are too often overlooked for the sexy big-impact *pro bono* work. In the same breath, he told me about his ongoing litigation in defense of Ford Motor Company against a class-action suit. My 3:00 appointment revolved around not *pro bono* but O'Melveny's profit-sharing plan, which kicked in after a few years' service with the firm. I was somewhat surprised. Money had never been explicitly mentioned in my interviews, even though it was every firm's central selling point. But O'Melveny's profit-sharing program—which brought associate salaries up to the level of New York firms'—came up again and again. As the interviews continued, I, too, broke down my façade; I began saying bluntly that the only reason I would come to O'Melveny was to step into a better government job.

The O'Melveny method was working, and by interview number 10 I was reduced to brutal honesty. The interviewer was a middle-aged woman named Saone Crocker, who happened to be the wife of Chester Crocker, the architect of the Reagan Administration's "constructive engagement" policy toward South Africa. As Reagan's Assistant Secretary of State for Africa, Crocker was seen as the embodiment of evil at the University of Nairobi. But "Darth Vader's" wife turned out to be quite engaging. When I told her I was trying to decide between working on the Hill and a firm, she was the first lawyer to tell me to go to the Hill. She said if I went to a firm first, it would be tough to take a cut in pay, and it might even be harder to get a job, because lawyers coming out of firms are seen as having attitude problems. Crocker also talked about the downside of law practice: the unpredictability of the hours. "You can't have season tickets to the symphony," she said. "You'll never end up going." She said the associates at O'Melveny had voted against a pay increase when Cravath started a round of price wars because they saw the writing on the wall: More pay, more hours. But the firm ignored the referendum and approved the pay raise anyway.

I asked her what kept her there. She smiled and said the work was challenging, but that she reevaluates her situation every six months.

At 4:30, I moved on to another attorney who I was told had worked on the Hill. He was everything I didn't like about politics. He was blow-dried, a bit too smooth, constantly addressing me by name, "Well, Rick . . ." as if he had read in a book that this was effective. As he talked about his trade practice, my eyes glazed over.

At 5:00, I was back to Larry Tu, the lawyer who had interviewed me in Cambridge. In the interim, I had looked Tu up in the *Martindale-Hubbell* catalogue on lawyers. He was a Harvard *summa* undergraduate, *Harvard Law Review*, Rhodes Scholar, clerk to Justice Marshall, and legal advisor in the State Department. I told him I was impressed that none of this had come up in our first meeting. Most people would have worked it all into conversation in the first thirty seconds. Larry and I talked about careers: mine (whether I should go to a Senate staff or a firm) and his (whether to teach or stay where he was). He said that going to a firm first, before a Senate staff, was "the way it is done." I told him he should teach, given that he had the credentials. He was hesitant. He said he hated the Law Review types (which immediately won him points with me), that Law Review articles were pretentious displays of knowledge (to get tenure), and that most professors disdained the practice of law. He actually thought his private practice might hurt him with law schools. He was also worried about the money. He said a friend of his who taught at Yale was making less than his students. I gave him a skeptical glance, which read: "Larry, c'mon, you've lived on less. You worked for Ramsey Clark, clerked for Thurgood Marshall, and did a stint at the State Department. Now you have a wife earning megabucks as a Kirkland & Ellis partner. How much is enough?" He could, of course, have responded to me that, if that was really my view, what the hell was I doing wasting his time interviewing at O'Melveny?

Back in Cambridge the next day, I had my last two first-round law firm interviews: Steptoe & Johnson and Paul, Weiss. The Steptoe attorney started the interview by asking for my transcript. Most lawyers were embarrassed about asking and quickly filed it away. This one studied my grades and asked, point-blank, why they had improved so much. "It's a quite dramatic shift," he said. I told him I enjoyed law school more second year. A more complete answer would have been that grades are somewhat random. My interviewer said he found D.C. practice exciting and bragged that he had just pushed through a $2 million tax loophole for a client. I asked him whether he thought it was right for Congress to hand out tax write-offs to various interests. He said, "If you want to do good, be a doctor."

The Paul, Weiss attorney was Jerome Kurtz, a partner in the D.C. branch office. I asked him my question about whether a liberal could work for a large law firm. "I still struggle with it," he said. "There's never enough time for *pro bono*," he continued, which is why he had taken leave from private practice to serve in the government during the Carter Administration.

"What did you do?"

"I was commissioner of the Internal Revenue Service."

I felt stupid.

As my interviewing in Cambridge came to a close, I realized, again, that I had liked most of the attorneys I'd met. I also realized, though, that the fact that they were nice did not mean they had made the right choice. And they were not necessarily representative of the firms for which they worked. Law firms aren't stupid. They hide away the jerks at recruitment time. So, too, apparently, the white men. Of the nine people I spoke with in Cambridge, only three were white men. Three were black men, two were white women, and one was an Asian man. The blacks I had spoken with were partners from Covington, Hogan, and Wilmer. Of Covington's ninety-three partners, two were black; at Hogan & Hartson, three out of 104; at Wilmer, two out of 74. That is to say, in the three firms, there were seven black partners out of 271. Statistically, in order to see three of the seven, I would have had to go to 116 interviews. But I managed it in three!

November 2. Before going to visit Arnold & Porter, I spent the morning with Harvard Law alums, friends of friends, and other contacts on the Hill: Patrick Mulloy of the Senate Banking Committee; Bari Schwartz, Congressman Howard Berman's legislative director; and Howard Homonoff, of the House Subcommittee on Telecommunications and Finance. None had gone straight from law school to the Hill. Schwartz had done legal services before going to Berman's office, but said that if she had it to do over again she would probably go to a firm for a few years. Homonoff had worked for Wilmer, Cutler & Pickering for seven months before landing a top job on the Telecommunications & Finance Subcommittee. He said his law firm experience gave him a certain cachet and respect on the Hill. I asked him whether the people at Wilmer were upset with him when he left after only seven months. He said no, that they'd given him a big party. From the firm's perspective, he was a good contact on the Hill and they figured he'd come back in a few years anyway. Heavens, no one would stay on the Hill long, given the miserable salaries.

I started to wonder whether the Homonoff model wasn't the right one: Go to a firm. Have them move you down and pay for your bar review. Let them train you. Pick up the credential of having practiced law at a top-flight firm, and then do what you really want to do.

In fact, I was beginning to believe I had no choice but to follow the Homonoff model. In a wild failure of capitalism, I was faring much better with the $70,000 law firm jobs than the $30,000 jobs on the Hill. For one thing, it was somehow much easier to get a permanent job with a firm third year than a summer associate position second year. And, in my case, my grades had improved. I was, of course, the exact same person I had been the previous year, but I was viewed quite differently by the law firms. Firms that had rejected me outright second year—Arnold & Porter, Covington & Burling, and Paul, Weiss—had all invited me back for more interviews this year. My tally was 7–0–2: seven callbacks, no rejections, and, at that point, two unknowns. By contrast, I'd sent out seventy letters for Hill jobs and had received not a single positive response. I'd gotten forty-two form-letter rejections. The rest hadn't even bothered to write. Congressman Mel Levine, on the other hand, wrote twice—in the envelope was a letter to me and also a Mr. Hansen of Chevy Chase. We both must have been strikingly similar candidates, because we received exactly the same rejection letter.

I arrived at Arnold & Porter's offices with high expectations. A&P was the Washington analogue to Paul, Weiss: the city's leading liberal firm. I also liked the fact that they'd rejected me the previous summer on the Groucho Marx theory that I wouldn't want to join a club that would have me as a member.

Once inside, I realized that the members were just people. With my first interviewer, a litigator, I shared my qualms about large-firm private practice. She volunteered that she did litigation for the giant cigarette company Philip Morris, and laughed, "We've all sold out," as if stating it so boldly made the charge sound silly. Another associate shared my concerns. She told me she was a "conscientious objector" and refused to do work for Philip Morris, although she still felt guilty knowing that part of her salary came from them.

A&P was a decidedly impersonal place. None of my interviewers had an easy time finding the next attorney's office and they rarely knew each other. This made for some awkward moments. When Barbara Holden-Smith, a black associate, introduced me to another A&P attorney, he called her "Joni," mistaking her for the recruitment coordinator. But the partner wasn't a sexist; he was rude to me, too. He asked whether I was clerking for a judge. (Third-year students who have clerkships still interview with firms for summer positions before the clerkship starts.) I said no. "Why not?" he pressed. "Because I'm stupid," I felt like saying. The attorney had been at Paul, Weiss before coming to A&P. When I pointed out the obvious pattern, going from the top liberal Democratic firm in New York to its equivalent in Washington, he said yes, the comparison was not lost on him.

I had once heard A&P referred to as "the Harvard of Washington law firms" and now I knew why. It was huge and impersonal and supposedly liberal, and a very, very handy credential. If I decided to go to A&P, I knew I would probably dislike it just as much.

On the shuttle home, I watched a troop of weary travelers filing in, and recognized the familiar face of Susan Estrich, Harvard Law professor turned Dukakis campaign manager. It was six days before the election and she looked exhausted. It struck me that the direction of her flight—D.C. to Boston—was a bad omen. Yet she fought on. She stood there as an example of someone who had used her Harvard Law degree to get involved. After becoming the first woman president of the *Harvard Law Review*, Estrich clerked for Judge J. Skelly Wright and then for John Paul Stevens on the Supreme Court. Instead of going to a firm, she went to work for Ted Kennedy on the Senate Judiciary Committee and served as deputy national issues director in his 1980 presidential bid. From there, she had used her teaching post at Harvard as a base to work as senior policy advisor to the Mondale-Ferraro campaign and manager of Dukakis's effort. She had done the unusual thing—as had other law school graduates, like Jeff Greenfield, who'd worked for R.F.K., John Lindsay, and ABC News, and Michael Kinsley of *The New Republic*. But they were superstars. What about those who'd strayed from the beaten path and ended as failures? Was I cocky enough to think I could succeed?

November 4. I was scheduled to interview with the Justice Department at 11:30. I wasn't sure why I was there. The DOJ briefing a month earlier had been full of people who bragged about being able to argue before the "big courts" at a young age. The emphasis was all on process, with never a word about justice. Maybe that just didn't sell—or, worse, wasn't credible.

But the interviewer today, Michael Boudin, was different. Boudin, who taught antitrust at Harvard, was the son of Leonard Boudin, a New York civil liberties lawyer who had defended the likes of Daniel Ellsberg, Julian Bond, and Benjamin Spock. (Michael Boudin's sister, Kathy, was a member of the militant Weather Underground and was serving a twenty-year term in a New York State prison for armed robbery.) Boudin's wife, Martha Field, was an HLS professor of family and constitutional law. Michael somehow ended up at Covington & Burling, and was currently serving as the deputy assistant attorney general for antitrust in Ronald Reagan's Justice Department.

Boudin ushered me into Ron Fox's office for the interview. How appropriate. I sat in the seat where Fox had encouraged me to do the U.S. Attorney's Office first year, and earlier this year had encouraged me to get a job on the Hill.

Boudin started by asking about Dickens and the Law. A couple of interviewers from firms had noticed the class on my transcript, but with them, it had been a joke, something I needed to explain and justify. Boudin seemed to like the fact that I'd taken it. I said that part of the reason I was looking at firms was an insecurity— that everyone else was doing it. He said he understood, that he had had twenty-some years of insecurity before he moved away from his firm. I told him I was interested in antitrust because of my populist instincts. He said that element of antitrust had been miss-ing in the last eight years; it was really the economic-efficiency arguments that prevailed today and would continue to under a Bush Administration. I told Boudin that my interest in the job depended, in part, on the outcome of the presidential election. This surprised him. He said most people came to Justice to learn litigation skills, rather than for political reasons. At the end, Boudin said he would be interested in having me work for the division. We arranged for me to visit the department and speak with some lawyers the morn-ing of November 15, when I would be in Washington interviewing with Steptoe.

November 8. Election Day, 1988. A lot was riding on the election—for the nation, for Dukakis, for all those Democratic lawyers waiting in the wings in D.C. firms, for Harvard, and for me. In the Government Lawyer class, Nick Littlefield was as gung-ho as ever. "Voting in the morning and reading *Yick Wo* (an anti-discrimination case) at lunch. It doesn't get any better than that," he said to loud, cynical laughter from the class. Littlefield, ever the enthusiast, said the exit polls showed Dukakis doing much better than expected. For a fleeting moment, I thought it might be pos-sible. Dukakis was flying frantically from state to state, making last-minute appearances to boost voter turnout. Maybe he could really pull it off!

I went home and watched Ohio go to Bush, then Michigan. I began watching NBC, because as they were so far behind in their projections, the defeat was less certain there. I grew angry and wondered whether working for the government really made sense. Was it worth all the hassles and the low pay? The American people kept electing the Ronald Reagans and the George Bushes. Dukakis's concession speech argued the opposite: we should stay in public service, he said, and not be disenchanted.

Dukakis's defeat probably had as much to do with Harvard Law School as with Willie Horton or Ronald Reagan or anything else. Dukakis and HLS might have been right or wrong, but they were out of touch. The highly rational, logical, dispassionate thinking pounded into the Harvard Law student came through, most clearly, in Dukakis's response to that famous debate question about what he would do if someone raped his wife, Kitty. He treated the question as if it were a law school hypothetical. His distant, detached response, which would make a Harvard Law professor proud, encapsulated all that people found wanting in Dukakis.

The next day, I flew to Washington for interviews on the Hill, and with Hogan & Hartson. The mood among Democrats on Capitol Hill was bleak following the party's fifth defeat in six presidential elections. My first stop was with Consuela Washington, a powerful staffer on the powerful House Committee on Energy & Commerce. Washington said she had come to the Hill not entirely by choice. From Harvard Law she had gone to a corporate law firm to pay off her loans, but left when the firm told her they did not want a black woman to meet with clients. I was shocked and said so. She just smiled and said, "It happens."

At noon, I met with David Schooler, a friend of Ed Murphy's, who was counsel to the House Energy & Power Subcommittee. He was short, bald, and wore glasses, and was one of the most engaging figures I spoke with on the Hill. He said his job search out of HLS had been a nightmare. He looked and looked for positions on the Hill but ended up having to settle for a volunteer summer internship. He said he felt a little put-out—spending the summer working during the day in a job which didn't pay and wasn't permanent, and going at night to a bar review course which cost a bundle. All his friends and classmates—who were spending their days studying for the bar in a review course paid for by law firms, in preparation for permanent high-paying jobs—thought he was bonkers. But now, he smiled, the tables were turned; they were all miserable (if rich), while he loved his job.

By 2:00, I was over at Hogan & Hartson, where, quite possibly, some of David Schooler's classmates toiled. Harry Jones, Jr., whom I had seen at Harvard, welcomed me. He asked me who else I was seeing this trip and I told him I had come down just for the day because my wife didn't like me to spend nights away. "That will have to change," he chuckled, making clear that Hogan's reputation as being the "humane" firm was a relative term. Trying to make conversation, I told Jones I hoped he wasn't having to spend too much of his time on recruitment. He said the interviews were only the beginning, to be followed by extensive "stroking"—the dinners, the wooing, the groveling. The lawyers oozing, "Oh, but we want you to come to our firm because you're sooo wonderful."

Just as Hogan & Hartson was not as humane as its reputation, so did its commitment to *pro bono* suffer upon closer examination. While Hogan's *pro bono* program is among the best in Washington, the firm was, of course, in the end, a business. Hogan had recently instituted a system of "bonus hours," by which associates who billed extra hours beyond a certain baseline received bonus pay. Two associates told me the system served as a powerful disincentive to do *pro bono* because such work didn't count toward billable hours. Likewise, Hogan's much touted community-service program— started by Judge Ferren as a separate entity dedicated to public-interest work within the firm—was reportedly very selective. One associate told me she had tried (unsuccessfully) to participate for years. Hogan had attracted a flock of Harvard liberals the previous summer, but I now found that they were viewed by some of the associates as quaint idealists. One attorney recounted the times that a liberal classmate of mine had come to her with angst about working for the bad guys. "I'd throw some community-service stuff" her way—she laughed, suggesting she thought our immaturity was touching. I wondered why it was that only the very young and the very old weren't embarrassed to be idealistic.

My last interview was with a Hogan partner who bore an eerie resemblance to me—same eyeglasses, same facial structure—only older. It was dark outside, which made his stunning view of the Washington Monument, now lit up, all the more spectacular. He claimed he liked his practice—defense work for drug companies involved in product liability, and the like—because it was complex, and as we talked about the election, he said he was still waiting for a Democratic administration. I left the interview a little unsettled. There could not have been a more perfect ghost of Christmas Future, warning me away from the Homonoff model.

November 15. I headed for D.C. on an overnight trip to see the

Justice Department, Steptoe & Johnson, and Covington & Burling. At Justice, I made my way through a hallway cluttered with old desks and chairs to Michael Boudin's rather grand and spacious office. (DOJ was even more hierarchical than the firms.) We talked more about the job, which I looked at with reduced interest given George Bush's election. Boudin showed me his desk, which he said R.F.K. had used, and introduced me to Charles Rule, Boudin's younger boss. Boudin called a car, which took us to a nearby building in which much of the antitrust division was housed. I had a number of interviews with antitrust lawyers in the trenches, which bored me no end. The pendulum swung back as I began to wonder whether the traditional model—try to make partner at a top D.C. firm and then move into government at the highest echelon—might make sense after all.

At 2:00, I went over to Steptoe & Johnson for an afternoon of interviews. Unlike the attorneys at most other firms, the Steptoe people made their pitch by running down the competition. A young Steptoe litigation associate told me, "You could line up all the lawyers [at Covington and A&P] and they would all look the same." When I asked a Steptoe partner to compare the D.C. firms I was looking at, he said, "I don't like to bad-mouth other firms, but . . . the reputation is that Covington is full of snobs and Arnold & Porter is a sweatshop." A&P and Covington's stock immediately went up in my book, on the theory that the best are always attacked first.

During one of my interviews, John Nolan, Jr., Steptoe's prize attorney and president of the firm, made an appearance. Nolan said he had read my résumé, noticed my interest in both Robert Kennedy and Kenya, and wanted to stop by. Nolan had been an assistant to R.F.K. and was now on the board of the R.F.K. Memorial, which that very day was giving its annual Human Rights Award to a Nairobi lawyer, Gibson Kamau Kuria. November 15 was Robert Kennedy's birthday.

If I ever went to a firm, I'd want to be like Nolan. He was no longer doing public service full-time, but he remained committed to certain ideals, at least in his spare time. Still, I couldn't get past the fact that here was another Kennedy person spending the vast bulk of his time serving large, established economic interests. His *pro bono* was commendable—most people didn't do any—but was it enough? I didn't really know.

My final appointment was with a mid-level associate, who tried to sell the firm for the diversity of its lawyers, particularly the diversity of schools represented. For some reason, he had prominently displayed on his office wall degrees from Harvard Law School and Oxford. Perhaps it was only amid "diversity" that those degrees would shine.

The next day I set off for interviews at the firm all the others had attacked most, Covington & Burling. Covington, like Ropes & Gray in Boston, had a certain mystique, primarily because Harvard Law professors (many of whom had been there) were always talking about it. The roster of ex-Covington professors included Abe Chayes, Clare Dalton, Roger Fisher, Albert Sacks, and others. The firm was so well known among students that professors would refer to it simply as "Covington." (Thus, Professor Breyer in Antitrust would say things like "It is tough to prove an agreement to fix prices, unless there's an actual letter saying so, which happened to Roger Fisher when he was at Covington." There was no need to explain the reference.)

The firm held its own mystique for me because it was, back in October of 1987, the first law firm with which I had interviewed. Located at 1201 Pennsylvania Avenue, between the White House and the Capitol, it stood, both literally and figuratively, at the crossroads of national power. Among the firm's original nine lawyers was Dean Acheson. As Truman's Secretary of State, Acheson was, of course, one of the "Wise Men" described in Walter Isaacson and Evan Thomas's book of that title, a breed of successful men who served at the highest levels of government following World War II, out of a sense of *noblesse oblige*. In perfect keeping with that tradition of service, Covington's current list of lawyers included James McKay, the special prosecutor appointed to investigate Attorney General Ed Meese in an attempt to uphold the standards of old. The firm was clearly proud of its tradition: its brochure began, "For nearly seventy years, Covington & Burling has maintained a national reputation for two equally important traditions—representation of our clients according to the highest professional standards and dedication to public service."

And yet, the other reality was that Covington's defense of the Establishment could be very pernicious indeed. Among Covington's clients were the Tobacco Institute and various large drug companies which needed defending when their products turned out to have lethal side effects. One line in the brochure read, "At present, we are actively involved with a number of industry associations and individual clients in the many-faceted problems of hazardous waste disposal and pesticide usage." And Covington, like most firms, also practiced "antitrust," which was really pro-trust, and "labor law," which was really management law.

I arrived at the firm at 10:00 and was greeted by the recruitment coordinator, Lorraine Brown. She was older, and more matronly than the recruitment coordinators at the other firms, all of whom were women. Lorraine was less threatening, somehow, than the others—more Barbara Bush than Nancy Reagan.

I spent forty-five unmemorable minutes with a third-year litigation associate before moving on to a towering Italian man named Paul Tagliabue. I'd never heard of Tagliabue, nor was there really any reason I should have. He was then the primary lawyer for the National Football League, but had operated behind the scenes. It wasn't for another seven months that he was appointed NFL Commissioner. We talked not about football but about government. I said I was wrestling between going to a firm and going to the Hill. He was intrigued by this and told me that he had done work in the international security division of the Defense Department during the Kennedy Administration, in the days when the top students were flocking to government. He said there was a certain *esprit de corps* in government then that was lacking today, in part because the starting salary gap between the public and private sectors had since widened dramatically. He said he'd send me a book about Washington government, Will Sparks's *Who Talked to the President Last?* which he later did, with a note which read, "There is indeed something special about government service if it is the right place at the right time."

My 11:30 appointment was with Roderick DeArment, a partner who had been Bob Dole's chief of staff when Dole was majority leader. (He would subsequently serve as Deputy Secretary of Labor under Elizabeth Dole.) DeArment said that if I wanted a career in Washington, it would be best to start out at a firm like Covington, go to the Hill, and then come back. The firm is your base. I agreed, but the problem was that DeArment was a Republican, and Republicans, I am convinced, look at the Hill in a fundamentally different way than Democrats do. At bottom, the essential purpose of Republican senators and representatives is to stop the Democrats from enacting what the Republicans see as harmful legislation. That is, Republicans don't want to "save the world"; they want to save the country from those who would "save the world." Being a lawyer at Covington—and protecting the status quo—was perfectly consistent with working on the Hill. The Democratic worldview is substantially different, and I wasn't sure where Covington fit in, if at all.

With these issues in mind, I had lunch with two Covington associates. When I asked whether a liberal could work for Covington, one of them taunted me, "You represent the seller against the consumer, the polluter against the environmentalist, management against the workers." "But," I said, "aren't there a lot of Democrats at the firm?" "The partners are conservative Republicans and the associates liberal Democrats," he said. After lunch, we toured the firm's weight room, sauna, and bilevel library. Impressive, though less so than Arnold & Porter's squash facility.

Next I met with Jeff Pash, a partner who had dated my sister Joy in college and had gone to Harvard Law School. I poured out my soul to him—told him my qualms about private practice, my desire to work on the Hill at some point. I asked him to compare the firms honestly. He said he wouldn't tear down other firms, but that, when he had asked Tribe and Lloyd Weinreb which D.C. firm he should go to, they had both said Covington. Jeff, who worked with Tagliabue on NFL litigation, had just been made partner and was very, very happy with his practice. He was, at least on the question of which firm, utterly convincing.

When I was finished with Jeff, I went back to Rod DeArment, who had invited me to talk some more. The discussion turned to Congress's new ethics bill, which sought to slow the revolving-door syndrome, in which government employees join the private sector only to lobby their former colleagues. DeArment, who had perfected the revolving-door technique to an art form, said he opposed the ethics proposal because it would deter good people from going into government. Perhaps Covington had changed, I thought to myself. Dean Acheson had become Rod DeArment.

Three days later, I called a friend to get some advice about D.C. firms. I explained to her that I had received offers from Arnold &

Porter, O'Melveny & Myers, and Hogan & Hartson. I had interviewed with Covington and with Steptoe, and was waiting to hear
back. And I had callback interviews scheduled with Paul, Weiss
and Davis Polk, and had been invited to a callback with Williams
& Connolly. (Wilmer, Cutler had given me a rejection and I had
rejected Ropes & Gray.)

The compensation seemed to be equally lavish at each firm.
Arnold & Porter's first-year associate salary was $60,000. In ad-
dition, A&P would pay a $2,500 bar-review stipend, all moving
and travel costs, an additional $2,000 transition stipend, and provide
four weeks' vacation, a free parking spot, use of the firm's squash
court and sauna, and all sorts of health, life, and disability insurance. Hogan & Hartson had a $63,000 base salary, with opportunity
to earn a bonus of up to $7,000 more if you were willing to put in
the extra hours. This package included a $2,500 bar-review stipend
and a $1,500 moving expense reimbursement. (The recruitment
coordinator at another firm scoffed, "How can anyone move on
$1,500?") O'Melveny's starting salary was $60,000, rising to
$65,000 after five months. In addition, the firm provided a $5,000
bar-exam stipend, reimbursement of moving and travel expenses,
a $500 relocation allowance, and payment for a relocation consultant
to assist in finding housing.

My friend said the people she knew at A&P were unhappy, that
you needed a mentor there or you got lost. She liked O'Melveny
a great deal, said the practice was interesting and the people were
wonderful. She advised against the antitrust division of DOJ, arguing that it was a riskier career move. I told her Larry Tribe had
said that Covington was the best D.C. firm. "That may be out-
dated," she responded. You could supposedly get lost, and much
depended on whom you were assigned to. She said Steptoe was
also large and impersonal, and Davis Polk and Paul, Weiss were
too close to their New York headquarters to have independence.
As I talked to her, I realized that maybe someday all those dis-
tinctions would matter to me. But for now, all I really wanted to
know was which firm would provide the best entry to the Hill.

In late November, I finished up my law firm interviews with
two more trips to see the two D.C. branch offices of New York
firms: Davis Polk and Paul, Weiss. When I visited Davis Polk, I
went to lunch at the Old Ebbitt Grill with two young associates,

who explained to me the distinct advantage of living in Washington on a fat New York salary. I met with a handful of other attorneys, but I was most excited about my 4:30 appointment with Richard Moe, the partner in charge of hiring. Moe had been Mondale's top aide and had been, more recently, an advisor to Gephardt's presidential campaign. Moe looked different from what I expected, more Wall Street than political operative. I told him that I really wanted to work on the Hill, but that everyone was telling me the better career move was to go to a firm first. I didn't know how he'd react.

Dick Moe looked me straight in the eye, told me that public service was the highest calling, and said, "If that's your interest, you should go do it." This from the Davis Polk hiring partner! Moe volunteered that he was in private practice to put his kids through college. My final interview was with a corporate partner who shared my public-sector bent and had been involved in the debate preparation for Mondale in 1984. He said that at times he found his work at Davis Polk less than fulfilling. "Making the world safe for Morgan Guaranty," he quipped.

Nine days later, I interviewed with the D.C. office of Paul, Weiss. Jerome Kurtz, whom I'd interviewed with in Cambridge, began by asking me what practice area I was interested in. Since the office did not have a large diversified practice—it was broken down into tax and international trade—I couldn't blurt out my usual agnostic answer, "Litigation." I was interested in Paul, Weiss because it was liberal, top-notch, and paid well. What did I know about the work? I said I didn't know, and worried that he thought I was not serious enough.

I rambled through an afternoon of interviews in which only one episode now remains in my mind: my interview with an attorney who had worked for the Commerce Department for a number of years and gave voice to my worst fear about going into government. "I was lucky to get out," she said, to make the transition to private practice. "There are people there with degrees from Harvard and Yale who can't." That was my nightmare. The best thing going for private practice was the easy escape hatch. If you grew tired of the work, the hours, the people, you could always leave, at least from the top firms I was considering. The reverse was not necessarily true. If you went into government or public interest and found that you hated it, you might get stuck. I had always relied

on the arrogant notion that Harvard Law would exempt me from
that fate. If I wanted to leave government, I could always wave
my Harvard law degree as a passport out. The rules were not
supposed to apply to us. But now I was told that that was naïve.
People from name schools could be and had been trapped.

The immediate decision facing me, however, was not government
vs. private practice but which law firm would I tentatively accept
(at least until April 15). Offers from Covington and Steptoe were
forthcoming, so my choice for the moment was among those two
firms, Hogan & Hartson, Arnold & Porter, and O'Melveny &
Myers. I had not heard from Davis Polk or Paul, Weiss, but I now
ruled them out anyway. The extra money wasn't worth it.

The process of wooing and persuasion hit full swing. Hogan &
Hartson offered to fly me down for dinner so I could meet more
attorneys. Steptoe & Johnson sent me a list detailing the govern-
mental backgrounds of their attorneys. Covington & Burling gave
me the names of young fathers who could address my concerns
about having enough time for family. One of the fathers was Bruce
Kuhlik, a hot-shot litigator who had served in the Solicitor General's
Office and worked 80 percent of the time while he helped raise his
daughter. The whole story had been written up in a front-page
Washington Post piece, which explained that he and his lawyer wife
both worked a four-day week. He was home on Mondays, she on
Fridays. Somehow, I never got through to talk with Kuhlik, but I
did reach another young father at Covington, who said he worked
9:15 to 7:00 each day, billing eight hours a day and traveling five
days a month. The Bruce Kuhlik story written up in the *Post* was
a bit of a sham, he said. "He worked crazy hours." I said I'd really
like to have a lot of time for my family. "You can do that if you
want to be a trusts and estates lawyer in Springfield, Massachusetts," he snapped. That was the bargain cut: obscenely high pay,
horrible hours.

I drew up an elaborate chart listing the pros and cons of each
firm. All paid roughly the same and offered similar benefits. I
narrowed the list down to Arnold & Porter, Covington & Burling,
and O'Melveny & Myers. A&P was supposed to be "Democratic,"
but the hours bothered me and I wasn't sure there was such a thing
as a liberal firm anyway. (Earlier, when a lawyer from Hogan called
to press me on an answer, he told me that if being a family man

was so important, I "should have eliminated Arnold & Porter long ago.") I now agreed and was down to two. O'Melveny was intimate and filled with interesting lawyers. Covington was a larger, leading D.C. firm with more traditional lawyers, a less risky move than a branch office of a Los Angeles firm. In the end, I went with Covington, for the same reason I'd chosen Harvard and Ropes & Gray; which is, not incidentally, the same reason a lot of my classmates chose big, well-known firms: we were all insecure and somewhat scared and found credentials to be comforting. Covington was familiar and it was safe and it was respectable. I told Covington I'd tentatively accept, assuming nothing else came up before April 15.

CHAPTER

13

Qualms Is Good

Leo Frank was a Jewish factory manager who lived and died in Georgia in the early part of this century. He was convicted of murdering a young factory employee and was sentenced to death. The only hitch was that he didn't do it; another man confessed to an Atlanta attorney that he was the actual murderer. The confession, however, was supposed to be kept secret, according to the dictates of lawyer-client privilege. What was the lawyer to do? Surely he could not sit back and let an innocent man hang. But if the attorney revealed the existence of the confession or, more precisely, the identity of the confessor, he would violate the principle that—even if the whole world is against you—the one person you can always trust is your defense attorney. On a more pragmatic level, if the lawyer broke the lawyer-client privilege in this situation, the next time a guilty party thought about confessing to a lawyer, she (the murderer) would keep her mouth shut. In class discussion of the case, one student said he would keep the confession confidential, "but I'd have qualms about it."

"Qualms is good," the professor, Alan Dershowitz, exclaimed.

Qualms were at the heart of the course, Legal Ethics, and Dershowitz reveled in them, which meant that during the second half of third year I had to revel in them, too. I had five courses my final semester—Legal Ethics with Dershowitz, Election Law with Estrich, TV and the First Amendment with Larry Grossman, Copyright Law with Weinreb, and an independent term paper, also with

Dershowitz. But Legal Ethics was always the most eventful, whether or not Dershowitz himself was there.

Dershowitz was an active litigator and personality for whom teaching Harvard Law students was but one of many pursuits. He had two columns, one syndicated, another in *Penthouse*. He wrote books. He ran a kosher deli until it failed. ("When you're losing two dollars a sandwich, you can't make up the loss in volume," he quipped.) He appeared on *Morton Downey*, *Nightline*, *Phil Donahue*, and even had his own show. He defended Claus von Bülow, then wrote a book about the case which, in turn, became a movie, *Reversal of Fortune*. The second week of classes, Boston attorney Harvey Silverglate guest-lectured. Someone asked him, "Where's Professor Dershowitz?" "In Hollywood," Silverglate said. It might have been a joke, but then again it might not.

There was an advantage to all of Dershowitz's extracurricular activities. For a practitioner, legal ethics was not a highly theoretical abstraction but a daily challenge. And his own cases provided fertile ground for ethical discussions because Dershowitz constantly tested the definition of "zealous advocacy." He assigned us his 1982 book, *The Best Defense*, which discussed a number of his cases involving the Jewish Defense League (JDL), Bernard Bergman, *Deep Throat*, and the U.S. Attorney's Office for the Southern District of New York.

Even the cases Dershowitz wasn't alive to argue had his imprimatur. Thus the Leo Frank case from 1915 was introduced to us in the form of a nonfiction play, "A Matter of Death," by Alan Dershowitz. The case clearly tested the outer bounds of the lawyer-client privilege; and I was astounded to hear the willingness of students to stand by the legal principle and let an innocent person die. The attorney who was witness to the confession in real life tried to find a middle ground: he privately gave his "gentleman's word" to the governor that Frank was innocent. The governor commuted the death sentence, but an angry mob, unaware that another man had confessed, hanged Frank on their own. You would think, given the horrific facts of this case, that the class would be ready to condemn adherence to lawyer-client privilege as absurd. Instead, what one heard were "qualms." (I agreed with Dershowitz that qualms were good, but, in this case, not good enough.)

He said that's what he wanted—qualms and questions—not answers. "This is not a class in chapel," he said, but as the class progressed it became clear that Dershowitz usually did have a notion of what was "the right thing to do."

The toughest cases, obviously, were the ones where tactics and ethics conflicted. His standard question was: "What would you do if you knew you wouldn't get caught?" Dershowitz said that ethics and tactics were often at odds, even though judges wouldn't admit it. In *Nix v. Whiteside*, the Supreme Court endorsed a defense attorney's decision to tell his client he would quit if the defendant lied on the witness stand. The Supreme Court said the lawyer had not acted improperly because tactics and ethics didn't conflict— lying was a stupid tactic because the client would get caught and be found guilty of perjury on top of the original crime. But Dershowitz felt the opinion ducked the issue. "Lying works," he said. "I wish it weren't so."

Our second-week class with Silverglate—a well-known defense attorney in Boston—involved what to do when you discover that a star prosecution witness has told your client, "Give me $200,000 or I'll lie against you." My instinct was to inform the authorities, who would presumably dismiss the case. Silverglate said that was the last thing he'd do. Even if the prosecutors were state or local and you informed federal authorities of the extortion, the feds might tip off the prosecution witness. The best thing was to try to get the prosecution witness to repeat his extortionist threat on hidden tape. This anti-Establishment thinking I was learning was deeply ingrained in the psyche of the defense attorney. The authorities were the enemy. (Dershowitz often referred to federal informers as "finks.")

"The job of the defense lawyer," Dershowitz would say, "is usually to keep the truth from getting out." This was obviously tough for some of us to swallow. Here was a man who taught about ethics telling us the truth didn't matter. But Dershowitz had a point. Whether or not your client was guilty, he argued, you had to make sure the state proved its case fairly. "The police often frame guilty people," he explained. And even though the end result may be "right" in a particular case, to allow such government behavior to go unchecked increases the chances that an innocent person will accidentally be set up. The Dershowitz rationale made limited sense. What worried me was that law students would apply the idea—everyone deserves a lawyer—to the civil context as an agnostic cover for defending polluters, price gougers, and all the rest. Very few Harvard Law students would actually end up defending criminals, but the vast majority could twist Dershowitz's arguments to justify defending the interests of just about anyone. (In fact, at the end of one class, Dershowitz asked, "How many people are going to do criminal work?" Only a few raised their hands.)

In late February, Charles Ogletree, a black HLS professor who had headed the D.C. public-defender service, spoke to our class and stressed that very point—one of the toughest things about becoming a defense lawyer, he said, was that few of his HLS classmates got anywhere near the field. Dershowitz agreed and announced that he was not going to teach criminal law the following year as a protest against a decision to move the class to second semester. The best time to get students to do criminal work was the summer after first year, he said, so it was vital to expose students to criminal law in the first semester.

Ogletree told us he had decided to become a defense attorney after watching the Angela Davis trial. Davis was acquitted by an all-white jury, Ogletree said, because defense attorneys had made the system work. But when Ogletree first interviewed for a defense post, he said, he told his interviewer he wouldn't represent drug dealers, who were destroying the black community . . . or murderers . . . or those who used guns . . . or sexual assault suspects . . . or those who had broken into homes. "I wanted to defend shoplifters," he said, grinning. In the end, Ogletree came to terms with his role as a defense attorney and spent several successful years in public defense.

In early March, C. Vernon Mason gave an address at HLS which provided fertile ground for our Ethics class. Mason, the controversial black attorney, had teamed up with Alton H. Maddox, Jr., and advised Tawana Brawley and the victims in the Howard Beach incident not to cooperate with the police. So intent on showing that the system was unjust, these lawyers were apparently willing to counsel silence, even if that made convictions difficult or impossible. Mason and Maddox were, in a sense, the logical, practical extension of CLS theory. Because law was used to suppress the masses, it must be circumvented and twisted. The question was, could they really do this as lawyers and get away with it?

The New York State Attorney General, Robert Abrams, didn't think so. Once the Dutchess County grand jury determined without question that Tawana Brawley's tale—of being abducted and raped by a group of six white men, including an assistant district attorney—was a hoax, Abrams charged Mason and Maddox with violating the disciplinary rules of the Code of Professional Responsibility, which was grounds for disbarment. The attorney general alleged, among other things, that Mason and Maddox had repeatedly and knowingly made false statements of fact. Mason's defense against disbarment could have been that he thought *at the time* his client, Tawana Brawley, was telling the truth. But instead, in his HLS speech, he continued to maintain the truthfulness of Brawley's accusations.

According to a press report, Mason received a standing ovation from his audience of 270 HLS students when he concluded, "I want to repeat to everyone within the sound of my voice that Stephen Pagones, Scott Patterson, and Harry Crist, amongst others, raped, kidnapped, and sodomized Tawana Brawley." Dershowitz challenged Mason before the audience and later told the *Harvard Law Record*, "Falsely accusing an innocent man . . . is a fearful and unacceptable way of practicing law."

One by one, students in class now defended Mason and Maddox, claiming that many of the lawyers' statements were true. One student said it was true that Governor Mario Cuomo's schooling was financed by the Mafia (an allegation made during the Brawley case). Others said that because blacks couldn't get justice in New York City, some of Mason's more outrageous statements might be justified. Dershowitz pleaded for sanity. Didn't Mason and Maddox realize that by promoting the Brawley hoax they injured the credibility of the real black rape victims? At the same time, Dershowitz defended the right of lawyers to make out-of-court statements and said disbarment was inappropriate.

The class moved on to other cases raising ethical questions, like Dershowitz's decision to appeal the conviction of Claus von Bülow, the Rhode Island socialite who was accused of putting his wife, Sunny, into a coma. One student asked Dershowitz why a particular defense witness, David Marriott, had come forward after the first trial was over. "Money, glamour, publicity," he replied.

"But those are all the reasons you had," the student shot back.

The class erupted. Dershowitz just smiled sheepishly and shrugged his shoulders.

As the semester wore on, the class grew increasingly weary of Dershowitz, while my own admiration of him grew. I found his egotism tolerable because he was smart, concerned about fairness, and laden with "qualms." Early in the semester, I asked him to advise me on a special independent paper I wanted to write concerning affirmative action: because class was more central to the American dilemma than race, why not base affirmative action on class considerations?

I sought out Dershowitz specifically because sixteen months earlier I'd seen him speak at a law school forum on affirmative action with Mel King, Avi Nelson, and Charles Fried. The forum was largely a disaster, with Mel King, a former black candidate for mayor, arguing for affirmative action as a kind of reparations, and Avi Nelson, a neoconservative, Boston-based TV commentator, arguing for "equal opportunity," as if our country had no history to come to terms with. At one point, Nelson got into an argument with some black students about which was worse, the Holocaust or slavery. Dershowitz was brilliant. He had, in fact, tried to heal the division between the blacks and Jews in the audience by pointing out that Israel's law of return—giving Jews automatic Israeli citizenship—was meant as a kind of affirmative action, following World War II. Dershowitz had spoken at the forum about basing affirmative action on disadvantage (which was primarily economic), precisely as I thought it should be.

I walked into his office and told him of my interest. "Especially now, after the recent Supreme Court decision, I think class-based affirmative action is more politically salable." The Supreme Court had decided in *City of Richmond v. Croson* that racial set-aside programs were unconstitutional.

"And morally," he said.

"Yes, I should have said that first." What a scheming pragmatist I'd become. My whole interest in class-based affirmative action was moral—the political salability was a bonus.

"And I was wondering whether you'd be willing to advise me."

"Sure," he said, signing the form I handed to him.

It was just as when I had asked Tribe for a judicial clerkship recommendation. In both instances, I expected to be put off. Dershowitz and Tribe were always being accused of shunting students aside in favor of their famous cases, or their books, or their television appearances. But in truth they were both willing to help.

I told Dershowitz I had become extremely interested in class-based affirmative action when I read an article by Bayard Rustin in *The New Republic* suggesting that the second phase of Martin Luther King, Jr.'s crusade was shifting from race to class. "Any preferential approach postulated along racial, ethnic, religious, or sexual lines will only disrupt a multicultural society and lead to a backlash," Rustin wrote. "However, special treatment can be provided to those who have been exploited or denied opportunities if solutions are predicated along class lines, precisely because all religious, ethnic, and racial groups have a depressed class who would benefit." I had arranged to meet with Rustin in late August during the summer after first year, to talk with him more about the idea, but his assistant called to say he'd have to reschedule. The next day Rustin was admitted to Lenox Hill Hospital, and on the twenty-fourth of August he died. Dershowitz said that he knew of Rustin's views and had consulted him once on an article about affirmative action for the *Cardozo Law Review*.

I asked if my paper had to be strictly legal; he said no, the Supreme Court hadn't said much that was intelligent on the subject anyway.

I left energized.

I worked very hard on my paper that semester. The premise, that class mattered more than race, was of great importance to me, and I argued that race-based affirmative action had problems because people knew that the "fit" was wrong. Intuitively, most people knew class differences had more to do with life's unfairness than racial differences. Thus, if you had to choose between helping a wealthy black or a poor white, most people would help the latter. People didn't believe the pure Reaganite laissez-faire slogan, because they knew that the rich had an advantage in life's competition from day one. But people didn't feel the same way about blacks— or if they did concede blacks have a tougher time in America, they'd say that poor people generally have it worse.

From the primacy of class over race flowed any number of criticisms of race-based affirmative action. Because racial discrimination wasn't the *key* handicap, people began to suspect the reason blacks needed affirmative action was that there was something "wrong" with them or their culture. Worse, racially based affirmative action split natural allies, poisoning the relationship between blacks and working-class whites, two groups which needed to work together in the fight for a more fair society. Equality of opportunity had to be redefined, I argued. It could not mean just treating each application (to college, for employment) the same. Merit, I argued, should measure how far someone has come, as much as where they ended up. (And to the extent that blacks— kept down by racial discrimination—were disproportionately poor, they would benefit, disproportionately, from a class-based affirmative action.)

I met with Dershowitz on May 3. He had read my paper and said he liked it. I told him I planned to go to Capitol Hill after graduation and asked him whether ideas like these could go anywhere. Dershowitz smiled and said no, politicians would stay away from them for fear of being labeled racist.

My third class my last semester at HLS was Election Law with Susan Estrich. She was an expert, of course, having just completed her term as Mike Dukakis's campaign manager. "I learned election law the hard way," she said.

The class was designed as a seminar in which students presented individual research papers. The first several classes, however, were devoted to the basics: teaching a bunch of rule-bound students how election law really works. Estrich told us a bit about fund-raising: you get more money if you sit on the Energy Committee than on the Judiciary Committee, because if you don't get money from big oil, you get it from the independents; and giving has little to do with ideology—if a senior law partner asks you to support John Glenn, what are you going to say? And she told us about the loose interpretation of election laws; it's no good to lose while the other guy breaks the rules and then say, on November 9, "Yeah, but we were within the spirit of the law." And yet Estrich, even with all her campaign commitments, still had her heart in the right place. Even as she worked on campaigns for Kennedy and Mondale and

Dukakis, she was still associated with Common Cause, and seemed genuinely concerned about a system where candidates spent all their time chasing big money rather than meeting ordinary people. She was, in short, a street-smart idealist.

On March 14, I met with Estrich in her office to nail down a final paper topic. We tossed around a few ideas, none of which seemed to fit the bill.

Estrich asked, "What interests you?"

I told her populism, and realized that it was the first time a Harvard Law professor had asked me that question. We launched into a long discussion of how the Democratic Party's nomination process was slanted toward liberal elites, who were out of touch with so-called Reagan Democrats—those voters necessary to recapture the White House.

I gave my presentation on April 18. I argued that the Democratic nominating process was skewed to upper-middle-class liberals (who vote disproportionately in primaries) and that this fact hurt Democrats in the general election. I knew that my message would not be popular at Harvard Law. People in our class had done papers on more "fashionable" concerns—Hispanics and women—and to think we should give Archie Bunker a greater voice in the Democratic Party, why that was anathema! But I was not prepared for the fury of the attack. My idea of shifting away from primaries was denounced as undemocratic. And the underlying notion that the Democratic Party needed to be more moderate was seen as selling out. Michelle Steinberg, a very bright woman (who later clerked for the Supreme Court), said that I was a defeatist and that Lloyd Bentsen was no better than George Bush. It was the classic left thinking; there were no shades of gray. I knew the complaint: I had been one of those who, in 1984, when John Glenn was running for the Democratic nomination, had said just what Michelle now said: "He's just as bad as the Republicans." But of course he wasn't. Still, the tone of the class was not nasty. I didn't really know anyone, but they all addressed me as Rick. (Law students usually don't use each other's names.) At the end, I was applauded, as was the custom.

When the class met for the last time, in early May, someone addressed a question to "Professor Estrich." No one had really called her anything up to that point. "Susan's fine," she said. At any other graduate school in the country that would have been natural. At Harvard Law School, it was astounding.

My foray into the informal atmosphere at the K-School first semester had been a success, and so, second semester, I chose as my fourth class TV and the Limits of the First Amendment, taught by Lawrence Grossman, former president of NBC News and president of PBS. I was particularly intrigued by Grossman because his résumé suggested he was another lawyer-turned-journalist. (Grossman attended Harvard Law School after graduating from Columbia College.) It was also my first and only chance to take a course with Rebecca since college. When I attended the first class, I was greeted by a number of K-School students who had been in Gary Orren's seminar. I felt more welcome at the Kennedy School than at the law school!

The course was about controversial TV newsmaking decisions: how to cover terrorism, the private lives of politicians, and sensitive issues involving national security. Grossman had lived through many of the questions, both at NBC and at PBS, where he had helped to create *The MacNeil/Lehrer Newshour*.

The class turned out to be something less than I expected, mostly because many of the students were wedded to particular ideas about the media which had little bearing on reality. One week, Senator Tim Wirth spoke to the class about the Fairness Doctrine, which says that television coverage of major issues should include a fair representation of opposing viewpoints. One student argued that, under the doctrine, time should be given to non-Christians to respond to Christian broadcasting. Wirth looked at him and said, "That's a good point to make . . . in a debating society."

If the class occasionally sounded like a debating society, it came down to earth whenever Grossman intervened. Rebecca and I both liked Grossman a great deal, and in late April, we had lunch with him in the Kennedy School faculty dining room. Grossman asked me about the law school and I said I really didn't care for it. He said that had been his reaction, which is why he'd left without finishing. I joked that he was in good company: Henry James is said to have left Harvard Law School after the second year exclaiming, "Never, nevermore."

At the last class, people brought champagne and cookies. Grossman told us to keep in touch. He handed out business cards and people went scurrying for them as if they were gold.

I did take one hard-core law school class my last semester: Lloyd Weinreb's Copyright course. I worried that my schedule was filled with interesting but "soft" classes—Ethics, Election Law, a paper, and a course about television. Copyright involved real legal doctrine all right. It also reminded me of why I hated law school.

First, there was the Socratic method. By spring semester of third year, you don't really want to worry about being caught unprepared for class. Being embarrassed before one hundred people was always intolerable, but by third year you truly resented it. And yet Weinreb insisted on this system, and early on he sent a seating chart around the class. I knew better and just didn't sign up. But on February 14, I received a typed letter from Weinreb saying I was among several students who needed to sign up or be dropped from the class. First year, Arthur had gotten a letter from Weinreb, too, congratulating him on writing the best Criminal Law exam that year. I had, of course, never received any such letter, and now this threatening note demonstrated just how low I had sunk.

The other thing that bothered me about Copyright was the obsessiveness with details, and worse, the way some students thrived on it. Once, while discussing the federal preemption of state copyright law, a student asked a question and read the statute out loud, fascinated by the words, the puzzle, rather than the underlying policy or the greater significance of the issue at hand—more interested in the "is" than the "ought." On another day, a different student said, "I'm worried about the transitional nexus to the *res judicata* problem." Even Weinreb was overwhelmed. "Wow," he replied, to great laughter.

On April 21, we began talking briefly about patent law. I perked up. My beloved grandfather had been a leading patent attorney in Chicago. In fourth grade, on career day, I had said I wanted to be a patent attorney. I had no idea what they did, but I knew he made big bucks. As Weinreb droned on, I now found patent law to be insufferably boring.

Throughout law school, I had become more and more aware

that, under the veneer of respectability and prestige, all the law profession allowed was some pretty dreary detail. The Kennedy School courses, denigrated as "touchy-feely" by my fellow HLS students, were to my mind exciting and interesting; the patent-law doctrine requiring novelty, functionality, efficacy, and non-obviousness was not. What my grandfather had done was not immoral; indeed, an argument could be made that patent attorneys are essential to make sure that those who invent things get the return they deserve. But to me it was dreadfully dull.

Exams were light my last semester because of all the papers I had to write. Copyright was my last final. People all around me uncorked champagne bottles. I didn't celebrate with my fellow law students. I walked outside Langdell, and there were Rebecca and Cindy, waiting for me. In law school, I had become a husband and a father, and those things were much more important to me than being a student, or even a lawyer.

14

Hill Search Blues

When I tentatively accepted Covington & Burling's job offer on December 4, my work had really just begun. No more free trips to Washington. No more lavish lunches. I had laid the groundwork for getting a job on the Hill, but nothing had yet developed and I had no idea if anything would. All I knew was that I had until April 15—a little more than four months—to scratch and claw for the type of job I might be excited about going to each morning.

I planned to spend much of Christmas break in D.C. looking for jobs on the Hill. In the middle of studying for exams, I found myself once again using the public-interest phone to set up appointments. I made fifteen calls one afternoon and reached only one person, Paul Donovan of Ted Kennedy's staff, who said he could not meet with me. (He's the one who told me if I wanted to be hired by April 15, I'd have to start April 16.)

It became clear that a job on the Hill could mean many things. One staffer told me that, with a law degree, I'd be overqualified to work on the personal staff of a House member. Then a Senate Banking Committee staffer told me the competition was keen for jobs with his committee. Résumés had been flowing in from people earning more than $100,000 at law firms.

My first real break came on December 21. Littlefield had told us the last day of class that he was willing to try to help people get jobs in government. I took him at his word and wrote him a letter telling him I wanted to work on Capitol Hill. On December 21, I phoned Littlefield and he told me, confidentially, that he was about to be appointed head of Ted Kennedy's Senate Committee on Labor and Human Resources and that he might be in a position to help me out. "I'm going to start practicing what I preach," he said. What phenomenal good luck! Kennedy's Labor Committee did all the exciting work involving basic bread-and-butter Democratic issues like minimum wage, child care, and education.

Still, I knew I couldn't count on the Labor position, so after Christmas, Rebecca, Cindy, and I drove down to Washington, where I had scheduled a slew of meetings with Hill staffers. My first stop was the Senate Judiciary Committee's Constitutional Law Subcommittee. I had been trying for some time to meet with the subcommittee's chief counsel, Deborah Leavy, and when I noticed, by chance, her name in the wedding pages, I added "Best wishes" to the form letter I had been sending out. Leavy refused to meet with me, but when an HLS alum on the Hill suggested to her that we meet, the door was suddenly open. Leavy said she had been at Hogan & Hartson (where all the liberals seemed to go) for one and a half years, but had been miserable and was delighted to have landed her Senate job. I came away more convinced that a firm was not for me, but still uncertain whether it provided the necessary entree to top-level Hill jobs. My next appointment, with Susan Coskey of the House Subcommittee on Courts, confirmed that thinking. Coskey (another Hogan alumna) said that, as a career matter, she would never take a legislative assistant's job on a personal staff over a law firm position. (LAs generally advise senators how to vote; committee staff hammer out the details of legislation.) My last stop was the Senate Placement Office. A woman there told me my chances of lining up a June job by April 15 were nil. I rushed home to Cindy and Rebecca. Cindy was sick and so they'd both been cooped up all day in a small room in the College Park Days Inn.

The next morning, I had breakfast with *Washington Post* columnist Mark Shields, whom I was interviewing for my Kennedy School paper on press treatment of Bush and Gephardt in the 1988 presidential campaign. Shields had, for a number of years, been a keen observer of class dynamics in American politics and he was especially critical of the way the press treated Gephardt. We talked about populism and elitism in the press, about Bobby Kennedy and Bill Proxmire (he had worked for both), and it was clear that we were of similar mind.

Shields asked me what I was planning to do after graduation and I explained my situation. He told me to send him a copy of my thesis and a résumé. He would try to help out. It was the kind of encouragement I had craved from HLS professors, and here was someone who barely knew me, not to mention a big-name columnist, willing to do more than almost anyone at the law school.

I spent the rest of the day talking with four more staffers, who gave me yet more names to pursue. In the late afternoon, as I waited in front of the Supreme Court for Rebecca to pick me up, I read over an article which a Hill aide had given me from *The Washington Post*'s "Outlook" section. The article, by Phyllis Theroux, was entitled "Money v. Morals: A Tough Case. If a Lawyer Keeps His Conscience, Can He Also Keep His Job?" The staffer who gave me the article said he thought it was about me. "I know a man, in his mid-20's, who recently came to Washington to interview at various law firms," the piece began. "Virtually every single firm with which he interviewed enthusiastically offered him a job. Finally, he accepted a position in what many people think is the best law firm in the city. I don't think he will stay." The pay would be excellent and would allow him to live in a very nice home, she wrote, but "he will leave because the same combination of intelligence and insight that made him so attractive to the law firm that hired him will tell him to do it . . . He will begin to feel poorly used by the wealthy patrons who are paying for his services." In the end, she wrote that "being paid to represent less than the entire truth can be spiritually damaging to the practitioner." She predicted that the twenty-five-year-old lawyer, with a wife and two kids, would, after a period of time, leave the law firm. "Then again," she concluded, "he is an unusually intelligent person and being a lawyer, he may proceed to formulate an argument defending a decision to remain."

I looked up from the page and saw a young man, dressed in a suit, accompanied by a pretty woman. I stared at him because I was convinced he was one of the one hundred or so young attorneys I'd interviewed with in the past few months.

"You look lost," he said.

"No," I mumbled. But maybe he was right.

In late January, I gave Nick Littlefield a follow-up call. He said he was very interested in meeting with me, that my exam in his Government Lawyer class had been "spectacular." He said he'd given me an A, if he remembered correctly. He put me on hold to look it up. I was convinced it was someone else's exam, but he said it was mine. We arranged to meet at Littlefield's Foley, Hoag office at 6:00 p.m. on January 30.

I was flying high. I told a friend about Littlefield's decision to be staff director of the Labor Committee and my hope to tag along. My friend asked whether Littlefield had failed to make partner at Foley. It was one of those cutting remarks I'd hear every so often about public service. People would ask whether working on the Hill "is something you want to do long term?" Or, "Where does that lead to?" All were fair questions from well-intentioned people who, unwittingly, were eating away at my desire to do the unusual.

On the thirtieth, Littlefield sat me down in his office and said he might have two or three openings for which he had four or five people in mind. He said there was one particular job open involving communications. I expressed my interest and added that I had written for newspapers in college, had earned a degree in journalism during my year in Africa, and had, in fact, been torn between pursuing law or journalism.

Littlefield said it was important to be open to new positions, new challenges. He said Dean Vorenberg had been his mentor and told him to take opportunities and chances when they came along. In the last Government Lawyer lecture, he had urged students to be daring and advised us to "zigzag" between opportunities in the public and private sectors. That is what Littlefield himself had done. He told me he started out at Hughes, Hubbard & Reed, a large Wall Street law firm, but left after six months to work on a campaign to end the Vietnam War. He ran one of activist Allard Lowenstein's campaigns for Congress (and later married Lowenstein's former wife) and subsequently served as prosecutor. Littlefield was now a high-priced defense attorney at Foley, a position he'd held for eight years. There was something appealing and exciting about his career path, but I wondered about its lack of coherence. He had advised us to zigzag rather than go the straight corporate route, but why hadn't he even raised the possibility that we might be interested in a straight career on behalf of the public?

We got to talking about the law school and why so many people went straight to firms. I said it was mostly the prestige, but added that many students were from working-class families and that the idea of making more money at twenty-five than their fathers ever did had to be seductive to them and, in many ways, irresistible. He said that was great, the American dream, to do better than the previous generation. I came back sharply, too sharply, saying that the diversion of some of the best and brightest into corporate law firms was a tragic waste, that too many of us were just "prostituting" ourselves. I said that law firm practice was intellectually challenging, but in the same way as a crossword puzzle, with no greater social importance.

As I left, I wondered what the hell had I done? Here was a guy who might be able to land me a great job with Ted Kennedy and I had just told him, in essence, that for the past eight years he had been, at best, wasting his time and, at worst, committing a moral crime. More to the point, I had overstated my own beliefs. I didn't believe that making money was evil, and besides, each individual's motivation for going to a firm was different and often complicated. Who was I to judge individual cases? I considered writing Littlefield a letter of apology, saying I had oversimplified matters.

But as I sat down to write the letter, I couldn't get out of my mind the figure of Al Lowenstein. Lowenstein's name rekindled all sorts of memories for me. Although I never knew Al Lowenstein and had not even heard of him the day he was shot in March of 1980, I did remember reading about him later and crying about his death. For my birthday in 1983, Rebecca gave me a book entitled *Lowenstein: Acts of Courage and Belief.* I had written a review of it for the *Harvard Political Review.*

The book was a collection of essays by and about Lowenstein, a lawyer who spent his life trying to right wrongs, in South Africa, in Mississippi, in Vietnam—everywhere where people were hurting. "He was," as Ted Kennedy said in a speech commemorating Lowenstein's life, "a gifted lawyer who could have made himself rich: instead, he lived modestly, often it seemed from month to month, giving of himself to make this a better land." It would have been unimaginable for Lowenstein to spend eight years at Foley defending white-collar criminals, people whose culpability is not generally tempered by a ghetto upbringing without hope. Lowenstein would not have perpetuated the maldistribution of legal talent described so vividly by Dershowitz: "It's as if all the medical doctors in America were performing elective cosmetic surgery while the emergency wards of our hospitals had no doctors." Was that something to be celebrated, just because the plastic surgeons were upwardly mobile? The fact that some of the country's brightest students would work for the wealthiest clients was a truism, taken for granted. But was it acceptable?

I had come to understand that particular individuals might need a corporate law job for their own valid reasons. For all I knew, Littlefield was at Foley to build a nest egg to pay college tuition for Lowenstein's kids. Who could fault him for that? But I could still hate the system which played on people's weaknesses, and I could still deplore the fact that it sucked in a lot of young idealistic law graduates, many of whom did not, in fact, need the money. I decided against writing Nick the letter.

Thinking about Lowenstein got me all charged up. When the Kennedy School offered a seminar on "How to Get a Job on Capitol Hill," I was there, along with about thirty K-Schoolers. (I didn't recognize any other law students.) The message was dismal. Tony Coelho's former press secretary told us looking for a job on the Hill was like being an out-of-work actor. You had to wait on tables. A lawyer in the K-School mid-career program told us about a person who'd gone to Princeton and to Cambridge University and was a doorman waiting for a Senate job. Some students reacted in anger, saying it was offensive to be told that, after investing thousands of dollars in a Kennedy School degree, they'd still have to play by all the rules. Spring break, we were told, was a good time to start looking.

I cranked out twenty-seven more letters and decided it was time to pull out the big guns from college. I called Marty Peretz and explained my situation, including my job offer from Covington. "They're very good," he said, but he was glad to sit down and talk. I went to his house and we came up with a list of nineteen senators and fifteen congressmen Peretz knew for whom I was interested in working. He asked who I was getting to write for me from law school and I said no one. Lewis and Tribe had written when I applied for judicial clerkships, but they didn't know me well. I also met with Neustadt, who said he would write to Kennedy as well as Al Gore, who was a former student. Neustadt had suggested I get Phil Heymann and Stephen Breyer to help me, but again, I had to admit I just didn't know them.

On March 23, I received a call from Congressman Sander Levin of Michigan. He said Mark Shields had given him my paper comparing press coverage of Gephardt and Bush and had mentioned that I was looking for a job on the Hill. Levin said he was looking for a new press secretary, someone to do substantive writing, but also the lighter schmoozing required of House press secretaries, who, unlike their counterparts in the Senate, had to call the press rather than vice versa. I was flattered by the call, and even though I had second thoughts about abandoning my legal training entirely, I set up an appointment to see Levin the following week when I would be in D.C.

Spring is far and away Washington's best season. The cherry blossoms are in bloom and the mall is bustling with activity. But there was little time to enjoy it when we visited, March 28 to April 3. The week began and ended in Nick Littlefield's office in 428 Dirksen Senate Office Building. I was nervous, and wondered whether I'd be meeting with Nick's boss, Ted Kennedy. I imagined Kennedy, puffing on his cigar, asking me about my thesis on his brother's campaign, saying he hoped I would come aboard.

I waited for about half an hour until Littlefield, looking tired and run down, ushered me into his office. It was a large office, bigger than the one at Foley. SERVE in large letters ran across a wall. His tone was optimistic. He showed me a desk where I would sit. He showed me the Labor Committee's hearing room, where Robert Kennedy had worked. He said I'd get a little more than $30,000, a parking spot, and access to the senator.

As he showed me around, Nick introduced me to a staffer and said, "When looking for a communications director, it's better to get someone with brains than tired press connections, right?" The staffer gave him a wary look that said, "Don't give us one of those boy wonders who doesn't know squat about the Hill." I knew my inexperience would hurt me and realized that Dukakis's association with Harvard—and HLS in particular—made my law degree a mixed blessing on the Hill. (Harvard Law School now symbolized out-of-touch liberal nerd.) Nick told me to come back the next day to meet some of the other staffers.

The next morning, I had a 9:00 appointment with Senator Jeff Bingaman's administrative assistant. Marty Peretz's thirty-four letters opened the doors of a good many AAs, part of whose job it was to schmooze with friends of important people. Bingaman's AA asked me what my interests were. I told him primarily domestic issues having to do with fairness and social justice. He told me the senator had an opening on his subcommittee dealing with the way government amasses census data and other information. It wasn't for me.

At 10:30, I went over to the House side to meet with two attorneys about a position on the Courts subcommittee. They asked me what my interests were and I feigned an interest in copyright, because that's all I could remember about their work. One, it turned out, was leaving, creating one of two vacancies on the subcommittee staff. He had decided to go to work for a pharmaceutical company, because he had two kids and needed to make some money. They told me that the committee positions were highly sought after and that I was competing with fourth-year associates from Covington and Wilmer, Cutler. I laughed and said that all my classmates were headed to those firms. The other staffer said, yes, that had been true for her law school classmates, too, "especially the other members of the Law Review." (Ah, the Law Review was always with you. She had graduated from law school fourteen years earlier and she still felt a need to talk about it.)

At 12:30, I met with Sean Foley, Congressman Sander Levin's legislative director. He was a law student attending Georgetown at night and about to leave Levin to clerk for Judge Ruth Bader Ginsburg on the D.C. Circuit. It was a bit awkward. This guy had a better job than I would have and he hadn't finished law school yet. I wondered whether I had gone off the deep end. Being a press secretary had nothing to do with law whatsoever. Had I just wasted three years of my life and a lot of money? Was law school a big mistake? Would a legal career be a bigger one?

With my mind swirling, I heard Sean ask me to do a test memo to make sure I could handle the job.

At 2:00, I met with Goody Marshall, son of the Supreme Court Justice and counsel to Senator Kennedy's Judiciary Immigration Subcommittee. We went down to the cafeteria to get some iced tea. He knew everyone there and gave me lots of names I should call. He seemed like a nice guy and he'd had a great career: he'd started at a law firm but had then gone to Al Gore, and then to Ted Kennedy. He told me not to take the Levin job; I should go to Covington. It wasn't what I wanted to hear.

My last appointment of the day was with Montana Senator Max Baucus's AA. He told me that although he didn't have an opening for me, he admired me for bypassing a firm. Most people who came to the Hill from firms didn't do so out of public-spiritedness, he said. They took a temporary paycut, to be sure, but if it was "amortized" over time, the connections gained on the Hill could make for a more financially profitable career in the long run.

March 30. I had arranged to see Littlefield in the morning, but when I arrived at 10:20, he wasn't there. I was sent off to see Paul Donovan, Kennedy's personal staff press secretary, whom Rebecca knew when they both worked for Senator John Kerry's Boston staff. Littlefield hadn't told Paul I was being considered for the Labor Committee press job. Paul was even more surprised when he asked about my public relations experience and I told him I had none. After my meeting, I came back to Littlefield's office and waited for an hour and a half (beating the record of the House Ways & Means Committee staff director, Kenneth Bowler, who had made me wait fifty-five minutes on an earlier visit). When we finally sat down, Littlefield said that in order for him to feel comfortable having a law grad do communications, he'd like me to do a draft memo from Senator Kennedy to the other Democratic members of the Labor Committee on how we should try to sell the Democratic agenda. The request was perfectly reasonable, but because the firms required nothing more than filling out a computer sheet, I found the notion of being tested vaguely annoying.

In the afternoon, I went out to Covington to see Jeff Pash. He had written me a letter saying the firm's "interest in you remains as strong as ever," and I wanted to touch base with him while I was in town. When I arrived at the firm, he saw me immediately.

We chatted at length about the decision I faced, and now that the deadline was fast approaching, I asked about Covington's labor practice. He said he'd put me in touch with a labor partner. As I left, I told him about my interviewing on the Hill and said how much nicer he and the others at the firms were. Jeff said that reflected the difference between a seller's and a buyer's market. Perhaps.

At 4:00, I returned to Littlefield's office to discuss Democratic strategy. After forty-five minutes, he sat me down to discuss ideas for the memo. The theme was: "Let's Make America Powerful Again." It was a variation on Nick's favorite motif from his Government Lawyer class: the only way to get people to do the right thing is to feed on their obsession with power. (Why do we want a higher minimum wage? Not because it's fair, or right, but because it will solve the coming labor shortage, so America can be powerful again.) He explained he needed me to do this memo to make him comfortable hiring someone without experience.

I pointed out that he, too, could have been accused of inexperience and had done a fine job on the Hill nevertheless. "But I've been spinning . . ." he began—I thought he was going to have a moment of self-doubt and say that he'd been spinning his wheels —"and selling all my life. That's what litigators do."

The next morning, I had breakfast with Mark Shields at our hotel restaurant. What a class act he was, going out of his way to make the stranger in town feel welcome. Shields said I shouldn't take a straight press job. What would make me unique, unlike dozens of other press secretaries, would be a position which utilized my legal skills. That would be the job worth taking, he said. I put a lot of stock into what Shields advised. He was one of the few to encourage me to pursue the Hill rather than a law firm. Shields had himself started his career on Capitol Hill working for Senator Bill Proxmire. He'd worked on a bunch of campaigns, including Robert Kennedy's and Ed Muskie's—all of which eventually led to a column in the *Post*. Others had made the transition from Hill staffer to pundit: George Will, Chris Matthews, Jeff Greenfield. It was an idea I dreamed about, though I knew it was highly improbable. Shields had said take the risk and go to the Hill. But the further step of abandoning the law entirely was, he said, something I needed to be careful about.

I spent the morning watching Cindy while Rebecca interviewed with the federal Commerce Department. Rebecca had received a Presidential Management Internship (PMI), a two-year honors program for graduates of public-policy schools who wanted to enter the federal government. Once you had the PMI funding, you could then sell yourself to various departments as free labor. Rebecca was also looking at a management internship position with Prince Georges County in Maryland. The county was going through economic and ethnic transition, and the D.C. crime and drug problem had overflowed into the areas of the county adjacent to the District. In P.G. County, "inside the Beltway" had a far different meaning than it did for those on Capitol Hill. It meant crime and drugs and poverty and homelessness, problems which made a position with the county an attractive challenge for someone interested in addressing social problems.

I had a number of interviews lined up for the afternoon. Pat Schroeder's AA told me not to worry about making use of my law degree. He had graduated from law school but had never practiced and things had worked out quite well for him. Senator John Glenn's legislative director, whom I had known in Proxmire's office, gave me the opposite advice. He said I should stay away from press positions, partly because the fit was not right and partly because they were dead-end jobs with no mobility. Glenn had just hired someone with twenty-five years' experience as press secretary; how could I compete with him—and why would I want to? My 5:00 meeting with Senator Frank Lautenberg's aide was horribly depressing. He told me my best bet was a legislative correspondent position. LCs, who are a rank below legislative assistants, answer constituent mail. Most LCs are straight out of college. The meeting was almost as disheartening as the one I'd had with an AA on the House side who said I might have to take as little as $16,000–$18,000 in salary.

Over the weekend, I intended to rest a little and have dinner with Rebecca's cousins, but instead I was busy working on my two essays and continuing to interview. At 4:00 on Saturday, I met with Congressman Levin's AA at the hotel. She was friendly, promised a salary of $30,000–$35,000, and said she would consider an expanded role for me as press secretary/counsel, along the lines Shields had suggested. On Sunday, Congressman Levin himself stopped by the hotel for a visit. In preparation for the meeting, I reread his biography in *The Almanac of American Politics*. He was University of Chicago '52, Columbia (master's) '54, and HLS '57. He had run for governor in Michigan in 1970 and 1974, and lost in close races both times. He had worked in the Carter Administration as the population control executive at the Agency for International Development (AID) and now had a safe seat in Congress, representing the Detroit suburbs. He was a hard worker, had co-sponsored work-fare legislation with Pat Moynihan and served on the powerful House Ways & Means Committee. Congressman Levin and I talked about all sorts of things and he said he liked me but wasn't sure the fit was right for the job. In fact, he told me his daughter was interested in public policy and he had advised her to try working in a law firm first!

Monday morning, I was back on the Hill, talking with Congresswoman Nita Lowey's AA and with people in Representative Barney Frank's office. At 10:30, I met with David McCloud, AA to Senator Charles Robb. McCloud was a big man with a deep Southern accent and graying hair, a more imposing figure than the AAs on the House side had been. He sat me down in his large office and asked how he could help me. I handed him my résumé and told him I had an offer from Covington & Burling but preferred to work on the Hill. He looked interested and called in the legislative director, Kerry Walsh Skelly, who had graduated from Harvard Law School in 1985. We complained about Harvard and the outspoken liberals who had all marched off together to Wall Street. I told them I was also looking at the Labor Committee and McCloud asked me how much they were willing to pay. I said between $30,000 and $35,000. He glanced at Kerry, said the office had an opening, and that they might like me to see the senator.

Yeah.

I had lunch with three lawyers from the Senate Banking Committee. They said they were interested in me because I appeared committed to public service, unlike most of their applicants, who saw Hill work as a career investment. I asked whether Senator Donald Riegle, the committee chairman, was a populist reformer like Proxmire, the former chair. They said, no, he was generally committed to the status quo. I wondered whether it made sense to go to the committee. As I departed, one of the attorneys took me aside and said I had a real shot at the position, if it was what I wanted.

I took the underground subway over to the House side of the Capitol to meet one last time with Congressman Levin and his top staff. I sat with them as they read the essay they'd asked me to do concerning what press strategy Congressman Levin should pursue. They said they'd give me a call. All this for a job everyone said I shouldn't take.

I finished writing my draft memo for Senator Kennedy to the Democratic members of the Senate Labor Committee and rushed over to drop it off at Littlefield's office. "Our nation faces a triple threat," it began, "an imminent labor shortage which threatens our economic preeminence; a growing class of unemployable people which poisons our dream of equal opportunity; and an Administration utterly ill-prepared to grapple with these problems . . . What is required is an innovative strategy to muster political support throughout the country—to tap the desire to be both fair and excellent once again." The memo went on to describe a plan to provide incentives for the disadvantaged to work (higher minimum wage, minimum health and child care), to provide education for those mistakenly thought "uneducable," and a rekindling of public-spiritedness.

Nick wasn't in. His secretary told me Kerry had called from Senator Robb's office. We were late for our flight, which had non-refundable tickets, so I didn't call her until we were at the airport. She said Senator Robb had had some spare time to meet with me. I had been too busy copying Littlefield's essay over! We agreed to set something up on my next visit.

Back in Cambridge, I took some time to rank my potential options. The Senate Labor Committee was first, because it was Ted Kennedy's and dealt with the right issues. It was press, but communications director suggested a broader strategic role. It was also a committee staff, which was a better career move than a personal staff; and a Hill veteran told me that my knowing the committee staff director personally would "save you a year"—I'd have access, get my views aired, etc. Next in my ranking was Senator Robb, because he was both a star in the Democratic Party and—according to *The Almanac of American Politics*—a "national figure," which meant he might run for President or be tapped as Vice President one day. Robb was not a populist, but his background as a patriotic Marine gave him credibility with working Americans that many Democrats lacked. Next was Senator Carl Levin, who was probably closer to me ideologically than Robb, but was up for a tough re-election and might not survive. Then came his brother, Congressman Levin, with whom I was extremely impressed but who was a somewhat junior congressman, one of 435, rather than one of 100. At the bottom, I couldn't decide between Senate Banking and Covington. People kept telling me that both jobs were the best career moves, but I wasn't really interested in the careers for which they would prepare me.

On April 7, I received a call from Littlefield. He told me he liked my draft memo and that he was completely sold on me. The problem was timing. He just wasn't ready to make a decision to hire before April 15, so it wouldn't work out.

For the first time, I realized that I might really go to a corporate law firm, just like everyone else. I'd been cocky and always assumed something more to my liking would come through. The law firms taught you that you were golden, and I'd begun to believe it. But what if no offer came by April 15? What would I do? Would I turn Covington down and hope a Hill job would open up for me when Rebecca and I moved to Washington?

People I talked to, even the liberals, told me to take Covington: let them relocate my family, pay for my Bar review, give me the summer off, help me to qualify for a mortgage. Telling Covington no—even though I had no other job—had a romantic and noble ring to it. But I had a wife who was going into public service and a daughter to support. I began to think Covington wouldn't be so bad after all. In fact, I had received an interesting call a few days earlier from an engaging Covington labor partner whom Jeff Pash had hooked me up with—a man who had worked for the Peace Corps in Kenya and had done a stint at the Massachusetts Anti-discrimination Commission. He seemed like a great guy. And the money would be nice. The night after I spoke with Littlefield, I took Rebecca to the Boston Ballet at the Wang Center for her birthday and saw, from afar, a Ropes & Gray partner who could no doubt afford to go every week.

I scheduled one last trip to the Hill for April 14, the day before I had to give Covington an answer. I flew down the night before, at my own expense. My first interview was with the Senate Banking Committee. I talked with several staff members, all of them attorneys, about the committee's work. They kept discussing the all-nighter they had had to pull (the way lawyers are wont) for the major S&L bill that reformed the Federal Savings & Loan Insurance Corporation (FSLIC). I asked when they wanted me to start. Their answer? The day after my exams ended. I thought they were joking, but it wasn't entirely clear.

In the late morning, I was scheduled to interview with Senator Charles S. Robb. Though a freshman, Robb brought with him his reputation as the highly successful Governor of Virginia from 1982 to 1986. Robb was so popular in his home state that when it was rumored that he planned to run for the Senate in 1988, the incumbent senator, Republican Paul Trible, announced he would not seek reelection. (Robb trounced his Republican opponent in the general election with 71 percent of the vote.) A former Marine who had served in combat in Vietnam, Robb was married to Lyndon Johnson's older daughter, Lynda, and was said to have aspirations for his father-in-law's job. Following the 1984 presidential election, Robb and fellow Southern Democrats founded the Democratic Leadership Council (DLC), which sought to bring the Democratic Party back into the mainstream.

I went to room 493 in the Russell Senate Office Building and announced to the receptionist that I was there to see the senator. She buzzed someone in the back office and then asked, a few minutes later, "Are you sure your appointment is with the senator and not a staffer?"

I said I was sure, but began to worry. Had I come all the way down here on a mistaken impression?

A minute later, Kerry came out to get me and ushered me into the senator's office. Robb was tall and strong and well-tailored. His voice was deep and his presence senatorial.

He began by asking why I wanted to work on the Hill. I said I felt as though I wanted to contribute something; I'd been lucky enough to get a good education and wanted to use it for public purposes, to make life a little more fair for people. Then I launched into a speech about why I didn't want to be at a law firm, representing what I saw in many cases to be the "wrong" side.

Strike one. It turned out Senator Robb and Kerry both had spent the two years before coming to the Senate at the old-line Richmond firm Hunton & Williams, doing exactly the sort of thing I was questioning. But the senator was understanding; he said private practice didn't hold the allure for him that public service did, and he joked that he wasn't sure why the firm had paid him so much to do so little.

Then he asked why I wanted to work in his office specifically. I talked about the fact that he was seen as a strong Democrat, someone who had the credibility and toughness of a Robert Kennedy, qualities which were essential for Democrats to succeed nationally.

Senator Robb smiled, and said that while he played tennis with the Kennedys and was on good terms, I shouldn't get his wife started on the topic of Bobby.

Strike two. What a buffoon I was! Robert Kennedy, the archenemy of Senator Robb's father-in-law, was the last person I should have cited in conversation.

Somehow I managed to avoid a strike three during the rest of the interview, and the senator told me he'd like to have me join his staff. I'd be a legislative assistant for a number of issues Kerry had temporarily been handling, providing background and advice on how he should vote in those areas. I'm not exactly sure why I was chosen for the job with Senator Robb, but the two of us did seem to connect when we talked about the importance and nobility of public service. We still believed that it was important for the fortunate to give back to society, that much was expected of those to whom much was given—talk which many people found frightfully elitist and most of my colleagues at HLS had ceased to find credible.

There was no event to which you could point as the foundation of the cynicism. Most of the HLS class of '89 didn't remember Vietnam and hardly remembered Watergate. We didn't experience the deaths—on national television—of Kennedy and King and another Kennedy. The cynicism was not earned, it was *taught*, by Presidents of both parties and by our faculty. Lord knows we were willing students—willing to believe in cynicism—because it was convenient. If it became the accepted norm that idealistic law students inevitably sell out, each individual who does so is let off the hook. When there's not much you can do about it, why not just cash in as big as you can?

As we left the senator's office, I told Kerry I had an interview scheduled with Senator Levin's office, so I couldn't officially accept. We agreed to talk about salary after the Levin meeting.

I walked down the hall to Carl Levin's office and met with the AA. We talked about the opening the office had for a speechwriter. He said I would have to travel some, since Levin would be campaigning a great deal in Michigan to retain his Senate seat. When I told him I was leaning toward accepting an offer from Senator Robb, he said I should be cautious. Robb was a freshman senator, just learning his way around. I might end up getting lost. Sure, I thought to myself, but Chuck Robb was a national figure. And while most so-called national figures eventually fade away, no one was saying Carl Levin might one day be at the center of national power.

For a moment, just a moment, I felt a little guilty. I knew what my liberal friends at Harvard would say about choosing Robb over Levin: it was selling out just as surely as going to Covington & Burling, selling out not for affluence but for influence (which was, after all, Faust's bargain). Robb, like Bentsen, was just as bad as the Republicans, they'd say. But then again, that's exactly what I hated about the Harvard liberals. They were so pure that they'd never taint themselves with governance. No one would ever argue that power should be an end in itself, but, my God, if the Democrats never moved in Chuck Robb's direction, they'd never have a chance to implement any of the initiatives about which the liberals cared so deeply.

I walked back to Robb's office and talked with Kerry about salary. She offered me $35,000, which, she said, was "somewhat negotiable." I'd just given my speech to Kerry and the senator about how contributing was more important to me than the money. I didn't negotiate and took the $35,000. And then I turned down my other offers.

I was staying in Washington with a friend from Proxmire's office, and when I went to his house to get my baggage, I explained to his roommate how I had resolved my dilemma between the Hill and the firm. I told her that with Robb I would earn about half of what I would have gotten at Covington and waited for her to tell me how virtuous I was. Instead, she looked at me as if I was a whining yuppie on *thirtysomething*. She was right, of course. Sure,

I'd stuck with certain principles. But working for a senator wasn't like participating in the ongoing Chinese student demonstrations where idealism could cost you your life. It wasn't as if I were doing anonymous legal-services work in the ghetto while swimming in debt. And my decision was tempered by the fact that I had come extremely close—within one day—to toiling for the richest of the rich. In the end, I went to work for Senator Robb for a variety of reasons, including my interest in politics, my interest in not working all the time, as well as loftier motivations. But even that—following one's interests—was something of a triumph at HLS.

My going to work for Robb was decidedly not the traditionally "right" career move. Turning down Covington and going to a personal staff, not even a committee staff, went against all the rules. And because the senator wanted me to start in June, I couldn't realistically take the bar exam. Many people—especially young lawyers and law students—told me that skipping the bar was hip. "That's great," they'd say, even though they would never dream of doing it themselves. My mother-in-law, on the other hand, disagreed with my decision and let me know her position on numerous occasions. All in all, by taking the Robb offer, I was caught in the middle: too Establishment for the left and a bit too unconventional for everyone else.

Rebecca, Cindy, and I moved down to Washington in early June. We spent graduation day, which fell on my birthday, in Annapolis, Maryland, riding on a boat, walking around the town, showing Cindy the water. Graduation day at Harvard Law is always a day for elevated rhetoric. I still believed in the stuff that's always said about Harvard graduates having an obligation to go out and tackle the toughest problems, but I didn't want to hear it in the shadow of Langdell Hall with a bunch of people who no longer believed. One hundred and thirty students had crowded into Ron Fox's public-interest meeting the first month of first year. Among those in that group who reported a career decision (not clerking), more than 70 percent went to big firms. Nancy Marsh, who had worked for Nader's Ohio Public Interest Research Group, was going to Boston's Goulston & Storrs. Lucy Anderson, who had been with the Greenville, South Carolina, public defender, now chose Wilmer, Cutler & Pickering. Bruce Chung, whose passion was environmental law, was going to Cravath; Rachel Levin, who had worked for Democratic Senator Alan Cranston, was headed to O'Melveny & Myers; and Adam Levine, who had been in the Peace Corps in Cameroon, was now headed to Hale and Dorr. The list went on: a UNESCO worker was going to Cleary, Gottlieb, and a student involved with Amnesty International had chosen Baker & Botts. A legal-aid worker was going to Covington, while one who had done work with Common Cause was going to Jones, Day. Lisa Chen, the California radical with the shaved head who had done work with Nader's CALPIRG, was headed to Debevoise & Plimpton. A small group kept the faith. Luke Houghton, for example, went to California Rural Legal Assistance. A few of us went into public service—my friend George went to the Treasury Department and his girlfriend, Jessica, to the Department of Justice. But the three of us constituted precisely half the class's representation in the federal government. About 380 students from our class went to large corporate firms, while most of the rest clerked (a forerunner to firm practice for the vast majority).

We—the class of '89—didn't believe the graduation rhetoric, primarily because we were taught, directly and indirectly, not to believe it. Among the faculty, the right thought corporate law was good; the hard left said that the whole legal system was fruitless; and the liberals, while mouthing the right words, had really given up trying. My liberal professors gave rousing speeches once a semester, generally the last day of class, but we weren't stupid. We saw that few of them offered to take the time to help us pursue non-corporate alternatives. Indeed, many of the liberals actually spent their extracurricular hours working for the types of interests liberals normally opposed—for Pennzoil and Michael Milken and Leona Helmsley. Derek Bok was the master of inconsistency. His speeches were wonderful, and he'd really begin to inspire, until you remembered he was the socially conscious president who blocked Harvard's divestment from South Africa, the labor lawyer who fought tooth and nail the formation of the Harvard clerical union, the proponent of public interest who appointed a law school dean who immediately abolished the public-interest office. The Harvard faculty's inability to inspire us was a tremendous failure of leadership. Their success in infecting us with their cynicism was a tremendous disservice.

Epilogue

"What precisely is your point, Mr. Kahlenberg?" I can hear some law school professor asking. "If we followed your advice and every graduate of law school went off to 'save the world,' wouldn't the wheels of commerce quickly grind to a halt?"

Well, no. For one thing, there is absolutely no chance of that ever happening. My faith in Wall Street's ability to continue to lure law graduates with astronomical salaries is unshakable. Furthermore, there is a great deal of evidence that Wall Street would be better off if it didn't have so many lawyers. The United States has twenty-seven times as many lawyers per capita as Japan; and some economists argue that Japan's success has a great deal to do with that very statistic.

My point is not that every law graduate should go into public-interest law or public service. Students who are philosophically conservative, those who believe that corporate America generally does the right thing, ought to follow their instincts and work diligently to preserve the status quo. My point is not even that the liberals who practice corporate law are somehow deficient. My larger point is that since each of us struggles daily with good and bad impulses, we might want to restructure our social institutions in order to make it a little easier to be good. This could be done for law students, who face a stark career choice, but also for doctors, who go to medical school to serve the poor and end up doing otherwise; writers, who want to elevate the human spirit and instead write advertisements to sell unnecessary products; scientists, who set out to expand the universe of knowledge and end up researching how to make stretchier panty hose.

To start with, our nation's leaders, most importantly the President of the United States, could reassert genuine moral leadership. It's extremely difficult to communicate idealism without sounding sappy and tired and insincere. Somehow, J.F.K. pulled it off, inspiring large numbers of young people to enter public-service careers. No President has since. Most haven't even tried. At a Kennedy School forum during my last week at Harvard Law, Richard Neustadt said he took it for granted that public service was noble, growing up under Roosevelt, and Ellen Hume said the same was true under Kennedy. "Can you imagine coming of age during the Reagan years?" Neustadt asked. Most of my law school class was born too late for Kennedy—many of us, in fact, had been born in 1963, the beginning of the end. Who knows what would happen if we somehow elected another President who asked us to give of our very best?

An inspired President could fashion a domestic peace corps, aimed at professionals: doctors who would otherwise go to the fancy private hospitals; lawyers who would otherwise go to Cravath; writers who would otherwise go to Madison Avenue. The corps, if properly structured, could remove the impediments to public service—the low status, the problem of educational debt, the poor timing of recruitment, the lack of training opportunity.

The corps could be elite. Graduates just starting out seek, even more than money, credentials and status and prestige. If the program was highly selective and given high visibility, the best would come, as they do for clerkships, for attitudes about prestige are more malleable than money. But money would also have to be part of the package. Harvard's Low Income Protection Plan (LIPP), which forgives student loans for those who take low-paying public-interest jobs, could serve as the model for a national program of loan forgiveness, so graduates of schools without Harvard-sized endowments could participate. Recruitment for the corps could be timed to the recruitment seasons of the private sector, in order to eliminate some of the anxiety and fear associated with pursuing a nontraditional career. Finally, the program could recruit high-profile doctors and lawyers to serve, part-time, as mentors. Students would receive excellent training—better, in fact, than at the firms or big hospitals—because they would have the chance for responsibility earlier on.

Critics may say the program would fail because it goes against the grain of capitalism. The best law students will always gravitate toward the top-dollar jobs, it could be argued, just as the highest-quality commodities fetch the highest price. But the more profound truth about certain professions—law, medicine, the arts—is that they attract people who are interested in more than just earning a living.

Law, in particular, is supposed to be about justice. Many are drawn to law because it presents, in Louis Brandeis's words, "special opportunities for usefulness to your fellow-men." These prospective students realize that one side (corporate America) is forever marshaling the best legal talent in an attempt to buy justice, and they come to law school wanting to correct the imbalance. But then, somewhere along the line, they lose two things. First, they lose their innocence, when they realize that a lot of lawyers are just after the bucks, after all. Then, the external becomes internal, and they lose some of their own idealism, accepting that they, too, may not be as good as they thought they were.

That phenomenon is unnatural. The human condition does not require that smart people, when they reach a certain age, must jettison their convictions (even as they mouth those abandoned beliefs with even greater vigor). It is odd that the pursuit of a corporate career, which was once seen as objectionable, becomes acceptable; indeed, that *not* pursuing that career becomes "dangerous." But setting aside all the highfalutin talk about "moral obligation," "convictions," and "doing what's right," it is truly startling that students with some of the best academic records in the country—the brightest futures open to them—will, in large numbers, pursue careers which many of them do not even consider interesting.

And yet every year it happens. A number of students come wanting to be Atticus Finch and leave as Arnie Becker. You can blame the individuals for breaking their personal contracts—the agreements they had with themselves that they were pursuing law not for the money but to do good. You can blame the institution, the Harvard Law School, for breaking its implicit contract, proclaimed on the walls of its buildings, that law is about justice, and then fostering an atmosphere where it is hard not to be a hypocrite. But no matter who is ultimately responsible, the sad truth is that every time an idealistic law student turns into a hardened attorney for the wealthy and powerful, she brings closer to the breaking point another agreement—the social contract—and that is simply unacceptable.

Afterword

Today, ten years after graduating from Harvard Law School, and seven years after the initial publication of *Broken Contract*, I'm now a corporate lawyer at Covington & Burling, pulling in $455,000 a year.

Just kidding. At the time the book was published, it was clear that some of my harshest critics thought I'd eventually wise up, dispense with youthful idealism, and join a big private firm. One particularly acerbic reviewer speculated that after the passage of time, "this book will probably embarrass him" and that had I waited to write the book "with 10 years of perspective" it would have turned out very differently.

On the contrary, ten years out, I'm embarrassed that I came as close as I did to joining a large corporate law firm. That work, and that lifestyle, would have been an enormous mistake for me; and the fact that I seriously considered that option confirms for me, in retrospect, how powerful the law school environment can be in tearing people from their moorings.

To pick up where the story left off: I spent the four years following graduation working for Senator Chuck Robb (D–VA). That was a rough period for Robb, who was linked in the press to a former Miss Virginia not his wife, at a time (the early 1990s) when it was not yet allowable for moderate Southern former governors who would be president to be so associated. But as Robb struggled under that glare, he maintained a focus on work, and I watched with admiration as he took tough stands, in favor of raising the gasoline tax to help prevent another Gulf War, and in favor of gays in the military because it was the right thing to do.

For the most part, I loved being a legislative assistant to a U.S. senator. I was constantly learning about a variety of issues — energy, the environment, campaign finance, crime, and civil rights — and it was fun to work for a moderate freshman because he hadn't staked out positions on all the issues and was open to argument from all sides. When Bill Clinton was elected president, I also had a hand in helping Senator Robb make recommendations on filling federal judgeships and U.S. Attorney openings in Virginia.

Of course, there was no mistaking the senator and staff: my long memos in opposition to Clarence Thomas's nomination didn't have the desired effect. But the whole point of my job was to meet with interest groups, read reports, listen to the debate on amendments, and then make recommendations on how the senator should vote on important issues. Our "client" was, in part, the Virginia citizenry, for one always had to factor in public opinion; but, ultimately, the client was the public interest, which is the best sort of client to have.

I enjoyed myself immensely, but even on Capitol Hill — among the public service crowd — there was a general assumption that the lawyers, after a stint on the Hill, would go to law firms to lobby for special interests. Most of the lobbyists I met with were former Democratic staffers, members of Congress, or members of Democratic administrations arguing for narrower civil rights legislation or other interests that could not be described as progressive. Within the first few months, a lawyer from Hunton & Williams told me it was important that I not stay "too long" on the Hill, by which he meant more than two years. Of my own colleagues on Senator Robb's legislative staff, good people all, one eventually left to lobby for the American Medical Association, one for a major liquor producer, and another for broadcasting interests. Having resisted once, I easily could resist a second time. Besides, publishing *Broken Contract* didn't exactly endear me to Washington law firms, so the temptation was mostly theoretical anyway.

Part of the original attraction to the staff position with Senator Robb was the opportunity to stay a generalist, and to put off specializing. But over time, it became clear to me that my own particular passion was for the debate over civil rights, and equal opportunity, more than global warming or nuclear energy. I began to toy with the idea of writing a book about affirmative action. Building on Robert Kennedy's insight that economic class was the ultimate inequity, I wanted to argue that affirmative action preferences should be open to disadvantaged people of all races, an idea I'd briefly outlined in *Broken Contract*, and which a number of readers had picked up on.

I met with Stephen Joel Trachtenberg, the president of George Washington University, who had written me after reading *Broken Contract*. I asked him about research fellowships, and he smiled and said that if G.W. was going to pay me to write a book, they'd like to get something out of me — like teaching. Trachtenberg set me up with the dean of the law school, who happened to have an opening for a visiting professorship, which he offered to me.

Ironically, publishing a book about how miserable I'd been in law school, and what a wretched place it was, helped land me a return visit. Still, as Scott Turow had noted, teaching law is not a bad choice for people like me who don't want to practice. Teaching would give me a post from which to write my book. And G.W. happened to need someone to teach constitutional law — my favorite subject. Moreover, teaching would give me an opportunity to try to do things differently — to create a more humane classroom environment for students. As a professor, I relied on classroom volunteers, rather than intimidation. I gave a midterm exam to help provide students with better feedback during the semester. And I gave an eight-hour take-home exam, to take some of the pressure off the typical three-hour allotment.

G.W. students had never seen anything like this before, and in the end-of-the-year course evaluations, they expressed mostly positive reactions about my effort to "shake things up," as one student put it. The midterm exam was a big hit. "Keep the midterm. I loved it. It made me review in October," one student wrote. Students generally liked the take-home exam, though a few worried that classmates might cheat. But the reliance on volunteers was met with decidedly mixed reviews. As a student, I had taken Duncan Kennedy's view that the Socratic method was "deeply corrupting" since it gave professors "a license to inflict pain." But at G.W., students had grown accustomed to it. "Go to the Socratic mode," one student urged. "At least we will read for class." Another said the reliance on volunteers made it "altogether too easy to sit back and listen." Others applauded my approach, noting the absence of an "intimidating or demeaning" atmosphere. Then again, it was unlikely that the course would be intimidating to students in any event, since it was a matter of public record that the professor had thrown up before his tax class.

Teaching was difficult, and if I were to write *Broken Contract* over again, I would go easier on two of my first year professors, Martha Minow and Clare Dalton. On the other hand, as a professor I did spend a lot of time in my office talking with students, discussing the struggles they were going through in law school — and I stand by my criticism of Harvard professors for not being more caring. (Shortly after the book came out, I was heartened to receive a letter from Anthony Lewis, my first amendment instructor, gracefully acknowledging: "You are right. I should have met with you instead of discussing the paper on the telephone. No doubt I was busy, just returned from abroad. But still, you are right.")

In talking with G.W. students, I found many of them to be as alienated as Harvard students, some even more so because academic rank could mean the difference between getting a job and not getting one. Although I'd come to G.W. to write, I found these informal counseling sessions highly rewarding. But, in the end, my visiting position was not made permanent, in part, I was told, because I seemed more interested in policy than in the law.

Trachtenberg helped set me up for another semester at the G.W. public policy school, where I taught a seminar on affirmative action and worked on the book, but as the semester drew to an end, I needed to figure out what to do next. I was six years out of law school. My friends were well into their associate positions, developing skills, moving up the ladder. Rebecca and I now had three daughters to support. I was ready for some stability and security.

Having made the jump from legislative aid to writer/policy analyst, I began to look at think tanks and political journals. Unfortunately, the former generally wanted Ph.D.'s and the latter daily journalism experience. I met with the populist political commentator Kevin Phillips, who told me that my decision to criticize established interests — Harvard Law School, affirmative action policies — would further complicate matters. In my case, the risk was softened because

Rebecca and I could always fall back on family for help, but I did begin to wonder about whether I'd taken the right path.

In time, I landed a position as a fellow at a progressive think tank, the Center for National Policy, which was founded by Edmund Muskie, Madeleine Albright, and others in the early 1980s. I was taken on temporarily, and was told I would need to raise my own money for a project. While this "soft money" arrangement is fairly typical of think tanks, for me it just brought back bad memories of student-funded fellowships.

Then, luck turned my way. Affirmative action became a very hot issue, and I found myself writing for publications that hadn't previously been within my reach: the *Washington Post*, the *New Republic*, the *New York Times*, even legal publications, like the *California Law Review*. People were listening to my ideas. The White House asked to see an advance copy of the manuscript of my book, *The Remedy*. Just as the book was published, funding came through for me to write a third book, on education, for the Twentieth Century Fund. I was busy promoting *The Remedy* on television and radio, discussing affirmative action with Katie Couric, and debating my former law professors, Chris Edley and Susan Estrich. The risks had paid off and life was good.

Then, one rainy afternoon in the summer of 1996, our middle daughter, Jessica, then five years old, was in a freak accident in a department store bathroom and fractured her skull. In the ambulance to Washington's Children's Hospital, she literally bled through her ears and she spent much of that night vomiting blood she had swallowed. For five days and nights, she cried and moaned for hours on end, as the doctors examined and watched her. Her hearing was impaired, her vision blurred, her eyes crossed. We waited for the doctors to determine if there was any brain damage. Slowly, over time, she began to improve. Today, sweet Jessica appears to be fine, a vibrant third grader playing sports and doing well in school. We had dodged a bullet.

But the incident made my big writing splash seem awfully insignificant, and I now try to be a little less obsessed with my work — a problem for all professionals, whether or not they keep track of billable hours. For though I love my work, I love my family more. As a writer and think tank fellow, I've been able to spend much of my time working from home. Many days I'm able to have lunch with

Rebecca, also a writer. I try to make more time for the kids — little Cindy, who is now about to start middle school; Jessica, who will soon start fourth grade; and our youngest, Caroline, about to start second.

Last year, I joined on as a fellow at the Twentieth Century Fund (renamed the Century Foundation to avoid its own Y2K problem) which supports progressive public policy research. I spend my time finishing my education book, writing articles and book reviews, giving speeches, and working on projects that address issues I care about: civil rights, education, and equal opportunity. My new book extends the "class before race" theme of *The Remedy* to the field of school desegregation, and argues that every American child should be able to choose to attend a predominantly middle class public school.

Last month, Harvard Law School issued the ten-year report on the class of '89. Most of my classmates — about 70 percent — are still in private practice, working for big firms, corporations, consulting firms, or banks. Roughly 15 percent are in government, 10 percent in academia, and 5 percent in public interest jobs. Some who had begun in corporate law soured on the hours and the work. One classmate, a lawyer with the California Attorney General's office, wrote a very brief essay, which read, in its entirety: "I get to work about 9:30. I leave by 5:30. I'm very happy."

As I read through the report, though, it became clear that many of us had become them — the corporate lawyers who crudely measured success in dollars. One classmate bragged about representing "Fortune 500 companies." Another boasted that his roster of clients included Coca Cola and Sprint, and about the size of his deals (his "$1.85 billion acquisition.")

My friend Arthur Le Palm is now a partner of Ken Starr's in Kirkland & Ellis's Washington branch office. George Alexander is at a private consulting firm. Luke Houghton is still doing environmental justice work at the California Rural Legal Assistance Foundation.

Of course, Harvard Law School itself has chugged along in the last ten years. Some developments were predictable, like Alan Dershowitz's decision to represent O. J. Simpson. (Where were his "qualms"?) Some were wholly unpredictable, like the elevation of my idiosyncratic antitrust professor, Stephen Breyer, to the U.S. Supreme Court. Harvard Law continued to make headlines for nastiness and cruelty. In the spring of 1992, members of the *Harvard Law Review*, in its annual spring spoof issue known as the "Revue," mocked the writings of a feminist law professor, Mary Joe Frug, who had been brutally murdered exactly one year before. The issue, which identified Frug as "Rigor-Mortis Professor of Law," touched off much soul-searching about whether the institution was anti-women. Larry Tribe seriously considered resigning, and asked, "What's the point of teaching? I'm sharpening their knives to stab innocent victims." While the Frug parody was particularly horrific, it's interesting that Tribe apparently had never asked, more generally: what was the point of training liberal students to become defenders of society's most powerful interests?

For a time, Harvard appeared to become more public interest friendly. After Dean Robert Clark fired part-time public interest advisor Ron Fox, there was an uproar, and Clark was forced to hire a new full-time advisor. But letters from Harvard Law School students tell me not much has changed. When I spoke recently at an event on affirmative action sponsored by Asian Harvard Law students, the halls were filled with the large signs from a familiar host of sponsors: Baker & McKenzie; Goodman, Procter & Hoar; Hale & Dorr; Milbank, Tweed — and, of course, Ropes & Gray.

Nationally, Skadden, Arps's admirable effort to establish public interest fellowships was not followed by similar moves from other firms. And two terms of a Democratic president appear to have done little to change the zeitgeist. In 1992, I thought that perhaps the election of a Yale Law School graduate, who had devoted his life to public service, and had spoken during the campaign, Kennedy-like, about a domestic peace corps, would recharge public interest at the nation's law schools.

But Clinton turned out to be Carter II on appointments, filling top positions, for the most part, with a new generation of Lloyd Cutlers. (Cutler himself briefly reappeared as White House counsel.) In a cabinet dominated by lawyers, it was lawyers of a particular type who were well represented, lawyers from firms like O'Melveny & Myers and Steptoe & Johnson. (Some 77 percent of the original cabinet members were millionaires.) Playing off Clinton's pledge for a new compact with the American people, Leon Wieseltier of the *New Republic* dubbed the new administration, "Covenant & Burling." The First Lady, she of the Rose law firm, wasn't in a position to push public-interest lawyers; nor was First Friend Vernon Jordan, of Akin, Gump. In 1998, the Alliance for Justice found that of sixty-five Clinton judges confirmed by the Senate that year, only one had ever had a full time public-interest job other than public defender. The one exception, the Alliance dryly noted, was a judge who had worked for the New York Public Interest Research Group "for a single year in the 1970s." By contrast, nearly half of the judges confirmed were millionaires.

Of course, there are all sorts of ways to try to promote justice short of a presidential appointment. From the Harvard class of 1989, there are lawyers toiling away for low pay at places like Oregon Legal Services, the Disabilities Law Project in Pittsburgh, and the Knoxville Legal Aid Society—noble exceptions swimming against the tide. I have chosen to try to make a contribution through writing about public policy. Like the public-interest lawyers, I haven't succeeded in keeping my options open. But I feel good about what I do and look forward to going to work. At night, I look forward to going home. And it's hard to ask for much more than that.

Richard D. Kahlenberg
Washington, D.C.
June 1, 1999